Pennies from Heaven

Explore the relatively new field of financial astrology as nine well-known astrologers share their wisdom and good fortune with you.

Respected astrologer Joan McEvers gives a brief overview of the subject and delineates the charts of such famous businessmen as billionaire John Paul Getty and automotive giant Walter Chrysler.

Learn about the various types of analysis and how astrology fine-tunes these methods. Stations of each planet as it turns direct or goes retrograde influence the market. Specific planets and aspects as well as planetary sign changes affect trend lines of the price of commodities. New tools such as the 360° dial and the graphic ephemeris can help you spot impending market changes.

An entire chapter has been allotted to the famous Gann Technique where time equals price and the 45° angle signifies change.

Covered cycles include the Lunar Cycle, the Mars/Vesta Cycle, the 4½-Year Martian Cycle, the Kondratieff Wave, the 500-Year Civilization Cycle used by Nostradamus and the Elliott Wave. The David Williams Solar Ingress Method of tallying aspect numerical equivalencies is explained and expanded.

With this book you can interpret corporation charts, understanding the best astrological factors, the time to incorporate and the significance of pre-natal eclipses.

The Moon and Saturn as well as the 4th and 10th Houses reveal much about your success in the real estate profession.

Charts of the New York Stock Exchange, the United States, and major market crashes are analyzed, along with progressions and transits, showing the important influence of Neptune.

Finally, theories of the future of the world economy are presented with cultural and economic trends equated to planetary alignment to the Sun.

Use the sound financial advice this book offers with its added astrological insights to make your fortune.

Joan McEvers

Author of *12 Times 12*, and co-author with Marion D.
March of the highly acclaimed teaching series *The Only Way
to . . . Learn Astrology*, as well as *Astrology: Old Theme, New
Thoughts*, Joan McEvers is a practicing astrologer in Coeur
d'Alene, Idaho.

Born and raised in Chicago where she majored in art
and worked as a model and illustrator for an art studio, she
moved to the Los Angeles area in 1948 and continued her
professional career in the sales field. This is where she met
her husband Dean and raised her four children.

Joan started her serious study of astrology in 1965,
studying on her own until 1969, when she took classes with
Ruth Hale Oliver. Joan has achieved an international reputation as a teacher and lecturer, speaking for many groups
in the U.S. and Canada. A professional member of AFA and
an AFAN coordinator, she has had articles published in
several national astrological magazines.

In 1975, Joan and Marion founded Aquarius Workshops, Inc., with Joan as President. She also helped establish its quarterly publication *Aspects* which is widely recognized for the wealth of astrological information in each issue.

Her latest individual effort is *12 Times 12*, which came out in a revised and updated version in 1984. In this book, each of the 144 possible Sun/Ascendant combinations is discussed in detail. Every description includes information about personality, appearance, health, likely vocational areas, interest and attitudes. Also in 1984, the latest March/McEvers book *Astrology: Old Theme, New Thoughts* was published. This is a collection of concepts, ideas and lectures on various avenues of astrology and is being well received by the public.

Volume IV of *The Only Way* series is finally in the bookstores. It is titled *The Only Way to . . . Learn About Tomorrow* and it deals with all kinds of progressions and forecasting. Joan also has a two-hour video, *Simplified Horary Astrology*. When she isn't busy teaching, lecturing, writing or counseling clients, Joan keeps occupied with quilting and playing bridge.

"Financial Astrology is one of the fastest-growing fields in the world of market analysis today. Ten years ago very little was known about the subject, and far less was even accepted. Today one can see traders on the floor of the Chicago Board of Trade and the Chicago Mercantile Exchange carrying copies of *A Trader's Astrological Almanac* by Jeanne Long.

"Astrology in the marketplace has come a long way in a short time. However, it is still barely in its infancy. The public admittance of its worth by Wall Street is still taboo. Many excellent market technicians who use astrology in their forecasts are still reluctant to acknowledge it publicly for fear of dismissal. Some even use pseudonyms to conceal their true identity and avoid reprisal from the public relations aspects of their firms. It is indeed a shame that something that so many find to be of such value has not yet broken the barrier of public prejudice and ignorance.

"*Financial Astrology for the 1990s* may be a step in the right direction to correcting this unfortunate situation. It does an excellent job of presenting very useful and valuable ideas on the correlation of astrology to the economy and the marketplace. Some of the articles are written by traders, investors and advisors, like Jeanne Long, Carol Mull and Bill Meridian, who have paid their dues in the marketplace. Their insights are truly exceptional to those involved in the stock or commodity markets. Other chapters on real estate and planning one's own business activities via astrological principles are also very good.

"I would think that for one who is looking for an excellent introduction to the field of Financial Astrology, this book is an excellent place to start. By the time one finishes reading it, several tools of great value should be in place."

—**Raymond A. Merriman**
Editor of The Merriman Market Analyst Report
and author of *The Gold Book: Geocosmic Correlations To*
Gold Price Cycles

THE NEW WORLD ASTROLOGY SERIES

This series is designed to give all people who are interested and involved in astrology the latest information on a variety of subjects. Llewellyn has given much thought to the prevailing trends and to the topics that would be most important to our readers.

Future books will include such topics as financial astrology, locational astrology, electional and mundane astrology, astrology and past lives, and many other subjects of interest to a wide range of people. This project has evolved because of the lack of information on these subjects and because we wanted to offer our readers the viewpoints of the best experts in each field in one volume.

This first book, edited by leading astrologer Joan McEvers, is just the beginning. We anticipate publishing approximately six books per year on varying topics and updating previous editions when new material becomes available. This is the first in a series like this and we know that it will fill a gap in your astrological library. We look only for the best writers and article topics when planning the new books and appreciate any feedback from our readers on subjects you would like to see covered.

Llewellyn's New World Astrology Series will be a welcome addition to the novice, student and professional alike. It will provide introductory as well as advanced information on all of the topics listed above—and more.

Enjoy, and feel free to write to Llewellyn with your suggestions or comments.

Other Books in This Series

Spiritual, Metaphysical & New Trends in Modern Astrology
Planets: The Astrological Tools

Forthcoming Books

The Houses: Power Places of the Horoscope
The Astrology of the Macrocosm:
    New Directions in Mundane Astrology
Counseling
Relationships

Llewellyn's New World Astrology Series

FINANCIAL ASTROLOGY FOR THE 1990s

Edited by
Joan McEvers

1989
Llewellyn Publications
St. Paul, Minnesota 55164-0383, U.S.A.

International Standard Book Number: 0-87542-382-5
Library of Congress Catalog Number: 89-12139

First Edition, 1989
First Printing, 1989

Library of Congress Cataloging-in-Publication Data

Financial astrology for the 1990s / edited by Joan McEvers.
    p. cm. — (Llewellyn's new world astrology series)
    Bibliography: p.
    ISBN 0-87542-382-5 : $12.95
    1. Astrology and speculation. I. McEvers, Joan. II. Series.
BF1729.S6F55 1989   89-12139
133.5'83326—dc20   CIP

Cover Design: Terry Buske

Produced by Llewellyn Publications
Typography and Art property of Chester-Kent, Inc.

Published by
LLEWELLYN PUBLICATIONS
A Division of Chester-Kent, Inc.
P.O. Box 64383
St. Paul, MN 55164-0383, U.S.A.

Printed in the United States of America

Table of Contents

INTRODUCTION

When the topic of financial astrology was selected to be explored, I was a bit apprehensive about whether I could objectively edit a book on a subject I knew very little about. One of my children, when he heard the title, laughed and said, "Mom, the only thing you know about money is how to make it and how to spend it." I couldn't argue with him. But while reading, editing and proofing the material presented here, I have learned a tremendous amount about the stock market, the commodities market, real estate, corporations, the world economy and much, much more. I hope you, the reader, will also profit from this information.

In this, the third book in Llewellyn Publications' New World Series, the writers address methods of using astrology to learn about, understand and prosper in the financial market. The material gathered here is truly thought provoking and enlightening.

Financial Astrology

What is financial astrology all about? It has to do with the making of money and the investing of money. Everyone strives for health, wealth and happiness, and often wealth is the easiest to attain. For most of us, money equates to security. In these turbulent times, it is important for astrologers to address practical factors and the application of a person's financial potential in addition to dispensing spiritual and metaphysical advice. This book can be an effective guide for the astrological counselor who seeks to give his or her client practical and useful financial counseling.

Webster's New International Dictionary gives the following definitiions which are applicable to our subject:

Money: Anything customarily used as a medium of exchange and measure of value . . . anything having a conventional use . . . often called *a money of account* and may be any arbitrary amount of property or wealth of any kind . . . .

Investment: The investing of money or capital in some species of property for income or profit; the sum invested or the property purchased.

Finance: The science and practice of raising and expending public revenue; the management of monetary affairs, especially those involving large sums or investment funds.

Speculation: Act of speculating as by engaging in business out of the ordinary, or by dealing with a view to making a profit from conjectural fluctuations in the price rather than from earnings of the ordinary profit of trade, or by entering into a business venture involving unusual risks for a chance of unusually large gain or profits.

Obviously, from the definitions given in *Webster's*, it takes special knowledge and aptitude to be an investor. You may well wonder how astrology can be used to anticipate successful investments. Using astrology as a forecasting tool is a common practice, and the writers presented in this book have honed this ability to a fine edge in the financial world.

Since time immemorial there have been methods and systems for speculating in the various world money markets. Popular magazines offer investment newsletters from so-called successful financial entrepreneurs such as Howard Ruff, Richard Young, Marty Zweig, Mark Skousen and

Adrian Day, just to name a few of the current crop. Joe Granville, who rose in meteoric style a few years ago, made quite a name for himself by predicting with about 60% accuracy the trends of the U.S. stock market, but then lost most of his following when his later predictions failed to manifest.

Astrologer Evangeline Adams successfully counseled J. P. Morgan on his investments, and we all know what a financial wizard he was. He stated that "Millionaires don't hire astrologers; billionaires do." Wise advice from a proven moneymaker.

Financial astrologers who add astrological information to their regular input have an edge in such forecasting because they are familiar with the client's natal chart and thus know whether the person has potential for making money in real estate, mutual funds, the stock market or whatever area may interest him or her. Perhaps if some of the reigning financial gurus had such pertinent, personal information, they might be even more successful in their predictions. Most of them, however, predict general trends rather than specifics, and many have their own favorite spheres of interest, such as money markets, commodities or mutual funds.

Some of the writers in this book are quite specific in certain investment areas; others add segments on the history of the American Stock Exchange and its astrological picture or examine how planetary stations affect the stock market; some discuss how to follow trend lines in commodities trading, how to predict the economy, how to predict the Dow, or how to follow cycles using the Gann techniques. All of these suggestions are based on cycles in astrological timing.

Every stockbroker worth his salt knows that some investors are uncommonly lucky no matter what they invest in. Being familiar with the extraordinary luck of this investor, the broker can use his or her investments as a bellwether in the market.

Your luck and money factors are usually quite visible in your horoscope and often relate to the planets Jupiter, Saturn and Venus as well as the 2nd, 5th and 8th Houses. Having the rulers of those houses or planets in them making strong aspects to each other can be indicative of good luck in speculation or investing. The Sun or chart ruler in similar positions is also quite fortunate. In reference to aspects, note I did not say in "flowing" aspect, although that is always promising. I have found that squares, conjunctions and oppositions, however, can work just as positively as trines and sextiles.

Saturn in the 2nd or 8th House can be indicative of a person who is willing to work hard and who succeeds by sheer application of energy and talent. Neptune in the 5th House often shows the speculator—one who is always willing to take a chance or gamble. Saturn in the 5th, on the other hand, signifies the cautious speculator. Venus in the 2nd or the 8th House generally signals one who is fortunate in most money matters.

Who Should Invest

As you read this book, remember that it is important that your personal horoscope shows that you can be a successful investor. If you have no interest in paying close attention to the market and corresponding astrological indications, if you do not want to spend time tracking the commodities' highs and lows, if you would rather spend than invest, all the excellent tips presented here will be of no valid use to you. In other words, if your chart indicates a lack of concentration, a cavalier attitude toward finances, a lack of challenging aspects to the money planets (Venus, Jupiter and Saturn) as well as to the financial houses (the 2nd, 5th, 8th and 11th), then the information given may not intrigue you. Investing and making money takes persistence, constant vigilance and hard work. Even if your horoscope indicates that you can be a winner or a successful investor, you must be willing to do your part.

If you have a great interest in money, investing or speculation, it is necessary to check your chart to see what field in this area is best for you. Is it real estate? Do you have strong links between the 2nd, 5th and 8th Houses to your 4th House, which represents property? Or would you do better with corporate investments because you have powerful aspects from the money planets to the 10th and 11th Houses? Precious metals may be great investments for you if the Sun and 5th House (gold) or the Moon and 4th House (silver) are the most prominent in your chart. Dealing in foreign currencies may be your métier if Jupiter, the 8th and 9th Houses and Sagittarius are highlighted.

Astrologer Barbara Watters once said that it was her experience that the best time to buy gold was when Pluto reaches 8 degrees declination because the metal would never go lower in price. The last time Pluto was at this declination was from March through August of 1979, and it will be there again from October 1996 to early October 1997. It may be wise to watch and see if this tip from a successful financial astrologer works or to investigate to see if it has worked in the past. She also suggested buying silver when Saturn was in Cancer, gold when it was in Leo, and wheat as it moved into Virgo.

Horoscopes of Successful Investors

Following are some charts of well-known successful investors. Much can be learned about speculation and investment from a careful study of these horoscopes. These investors earned their money in various areas, and their success may help inspire you.

Walter Annenberg became financially prosperous in

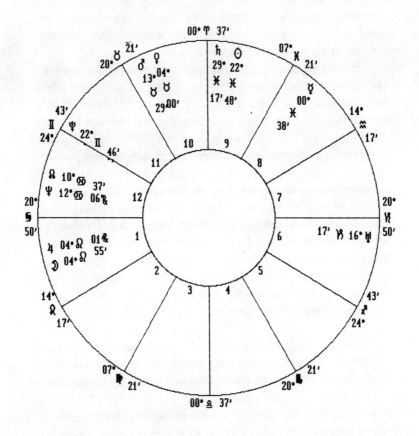

Walter Annenberg
March 13, 1908   12:30 PM CST
43N02   87W55
Milwaukee, Wisconsin
Source: Michel Gauquelin

Natal Chart 1 — Koch Houses

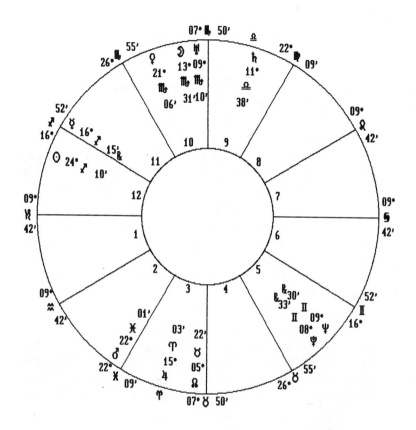

John Paul Getty
December 15, 1892   8:43 AM LMT
44N39   93W16
Minneapolis, Minnesota
Source: *Church of Light*, "Helen Allen," AFA 7/63

Natal Chart 2 — Koch Houses

the publishing business. One of his most successful ventures was *TV Guide* magazine. In his chart (1), the Sun, ruler of his 2nd House of earned income, is in the 9th House of publishing conjunct Saturn, which we find prominently placed in the charts of hard-driving business people. Jupiter, one of the planets of luck (also connected with publishing), rises and exactly squares Venus, a money planet. Mercury, the planet linked with communication, sextiles Venus from the 8th (a money house).

In the chart (2) of J. Paul Getty, who made a fortune in the oil industry, Neptune (the ruler of oil) is in his 5th House of speculation conjunct Pluto, the ruler of his 10th House of business. Saturn, the business planet, trines this conjunction, suggesting an easy flow in his speculative ventures. Venus (luck and money) is in his 10th House and trines Mars in the 2nd House. Obviously Getty was lucky where investments and finance were concerned, but anyone familiar with his life story knows that luck did not guarantee personal happiness.

Conrad Hilton, the hotel magnate, has a fascinating chart (3) for making money with Saturn, the ruler of the 2nd House, in the 8th House square the Moon in the 5th House of investment. The Moon trines his 1st House Sun, which squares Mars, ruler of the 5th elevated in the 10th House of business and achievement. Hilton was involved in his father's many businesses as a young man; he dabbled in politics as a state legislator; and when his attempts to purchase an interest in a small Texas bank failed, he invested in a hotel. The rest is history.

According to Rex Bills' *The Rulership Book: A Directory of Astrological Correspondences*, (Macoy Pub.) hotels are ruled by the Moon and the 4th House. Neptune, ruler of Hilton's 4th House, is in the 6th House of work conjunct Pluto, the natural ruler of the 8th House of financial backing. It opposes the money planet Jupiter, ruler of his Ascendant. Jupiter in

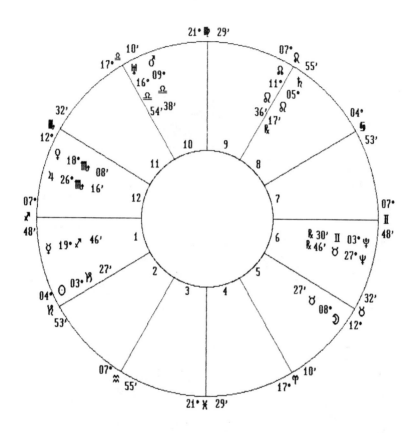

Conrad Hilton
December 25, 1887   5:20 AM MST
35N04   106W31
San Antonio, New Mexico
Source: Autobiography *Be My Guest*

Natal Chart 3 — Koch Houses

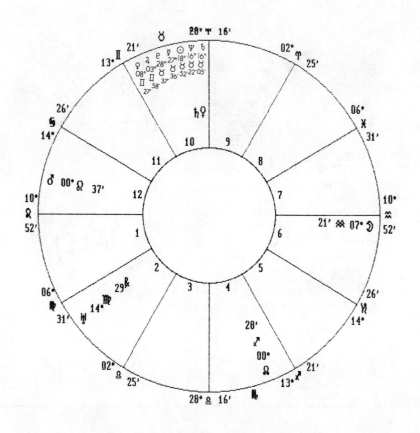

Henry J. Kaiser
May 9, 1882   10:34 AM LMT
42N54   74W35
Canajoharie, New York
Source: *Church of Light*, "Today's Horoscope," 6/58

Natal Chart 4 — Koch Houses

the 12th House has earned the astrological aphorism: an angel on the shoulder. Hilton was extremely successful in the hotel business, rarely making poor moves or bad choices, thus verifying Jupiter in the 12th as being lucky or fortunate. The Moon in the 5th House suggests that investments relating to the Moon would prove successful.

Chart 4 is that of industrialist Henry J. Kaiser who left school at age 13 to work in a dry goods store (Venus in the 10th House rules dry goods). Seguing from photography (Neptune in the 10th) to the hardware business (Aries on the Midheaven) to road-building (Mercury and Saturn elevated) and finally to the construction business, he built Boulder Dam, finishing two years ahead of schedule. Then he was involved with the building of the Oakland Bay Bridge and the Grand Coulee and Bonneville Dams.

At the start of World War II, he established a chain of seven shipyards where 1460 ships were built, most of them cargo vessels to transport war supplies. When he encountered a steel shortage, he constructed the West Coast's first steel plant, then built a magnesium plant to supply needs for that metal. Most of his services to the war effort were provided without profit. Uranus in the 2nd House often indicates unusual expenditure of wealth. In Kaiser's case, it trines Saturn, the Sun and Neptune and illustrates his founding of Kaiser Permanente Foundation, a pioneer nonprofit health-maintenance organization. He was also involved in the manufacture of the aborted Kaiser-Frazer automobile, one of his few failures. His Kaiser aluminum facility is one of the largest aluminum processing organizations in the world. He was the first industrialist to receive the Murray-Green Award from the AFL-CIO Executive Council for outstanding service to the labor movement. All these accomplishments are very fitting for a man with such a powerful chart.

Kaiser's chart with seven planets in the 10th House almost guarantees a measure of business achievement and success. The power of the stellium was used in the most productive way possible, and he probably could have achieved outstanding success in almost any field. Jupiter, ruler of the speculative 5th House conjunct Venus, co-ruler of the 10th, promises good luck in both business and investment or speculative endeavors.

With Pisces on the Midheaven (5), you might suspect that Merv Griffin would find success in the entertainment industry. But what suggests his phenomenal financial achievement? Neptune, ruler of his Midheaven, is in the 2nd House of earned income, caught up in a Yod with Jupiter in the 7th House and the MC, which indicates the potential to change career direction. It was when he moved from band singer to TV performer and talk show host that he started his upward financial march. Pluto, ruler of the 5th House, is conjunct his Sun in the 1st House, often signaling a need to wield power. Most of his financial strength came through shrewd investments. The strong eastern orientation of his chart suggests a self-made, self-motivated person, which his biographical information supports. The Sun/Pluto opposition to the Moon/Jupiter characterizes moodiness, and he admits to this. But this opposition also adds to his business acumen with the Sun ruling the 2nd House and Pluto the 5th House. Saturn in the 4th House of real estate trining the Sun/Pluto indicates the ability to make a profit on investments of this type, and he just recently took on Donald Trump in a deal for Resorts International and bested him. He is now launched into the hotel business.

The chart of Walter Chrysler (6) illustrates his success as a business leader in the automotive field. With the Sun, ruler of the financial 2nd House, in the 10th House trine Uranus in the 1st House, he was able to make his mark as president of Chrysler Corporation. Starting as a machinist (Mars ruling the MC), he had both a love of automobiles and a streak of genius. Willing to take a large cut in salary, he

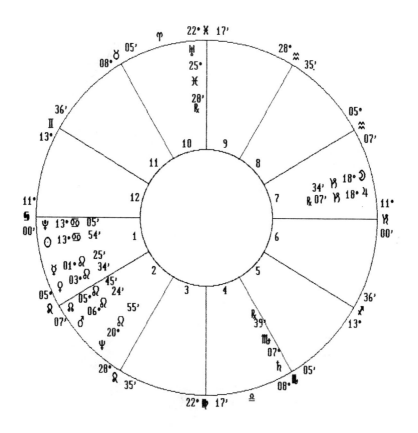

Merv Griffin
July 6, 1925   4:45 AM PST
37N34   122W19
San Mateo, California
Source: *Contemporary Sidereal Horoscopes*

Natal Chart 5 — Koch Houses

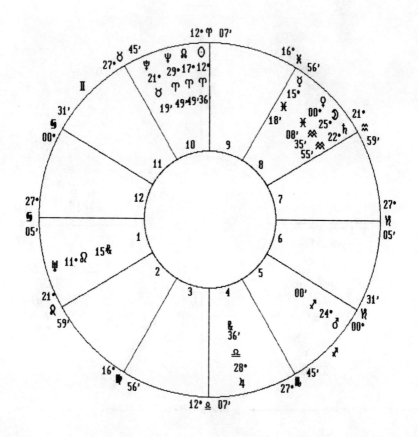

Walter Chrysler
April 2, 1875   12:02 PM LMT
39N12   96W18
Wamego, Kansas
Source: *Sabian Symbols*, 206

Natal Chart 6 — Koch Houses

went to work for General Motors as a kind of executive troubleshooter and was responsible for the modernization of Buick's operations, introducing efficiencies all along the line. His Ascendant ruler, the Moon, conjunct Saturn in Aquarius in the 8th House suggests the ability to economize in unique and unusual ways.

He later took over the reorganization of the Willys-Overland Company, did a similar task for Maxwell Motor Company, and set about producing a new and innovative (Uranus rising) line of Chrysler cars, featuring four-wheel hydraulic brakes and a high-compression engine along with other engineering improvements. The next year the company became the Chrysler Corporation. With the ruler of his MC (Mars) in the 5th House, is it any wonder he was an inventive entrepreneur who made his fortune with automotive ingenuity? Mars trine Neptune is often inspirational. Pluto on an angle (Chrysler, Griffin, Kaiser) seems to be quite evident in the charts of powerful businessmen. In Annenberg's chart, it squares his Sun/Saturn; Pluto conjuncts Getty's Neptune, ruler of oil; Hilton has Pluto opposing his Ascendant. Apparently Pluto is well named. Pluto in Greek mythology was the god of wealth, and its rulership of the 8th House is fitting. In this small sample of plutocrats' charts, it is gratifying to find Pluto so strongly placed.

What This Book is All About

Our contributors to this book are all well-known financial astrologers with vast experience in the field. They were willing to share their knowledge and research with our readers, and we are sure that you will find their insights and expertise very informative as you seek investment guidance in the next decade. The opinions expressed by the authors of this anthology are not necessarily those of the editor or publisher.

Jeanne Long explicitly details the ups and downs of the

commodities market and explains how to draw trend lines and track the correct times to move into and out of this fluctuating, but fascinating, area of trading. You share the benefit of her research as to which planets relate to each commodity. Her techniques include the use of both heliocentric and geocentric placements and insights into combining astrological periods with technical analysis for greater profits and development of your own trading system.

In "An Investor's Guide to Financial Astrology," **Mary B. Downing** tells us that true market-oriented astrology is in its infancy. Using charts of American Can Company and Newmont Mining, she explores the most efficient way to track a corporation chart using the graphic ephemeris, harmonics and helio placements as well as older tried and true astrological methods.

W. D. Gann was a legendary investor who, starting with a $300 investment, parlayed it into a large fortune using his "mathematical" system for trading futures. **Judy Johns** discusses his techniques as she tells his life story. She describes his system of timing and relates it to astrological cycles.

Bill Meridian outlines how periods of planetary retrogradation affect the U.S. stock market through the Dow Jones Industrial Averages, finding that changes in equity prices occur around the time of planetary stations. He explains what to expect from each planet and which trading areas will be affected as it turns retrograde, goes direct and transits the degree on which it turned retrograde.

Describing how Saturn is the designated ruler of real estate (land), **Georgia Stathis** analyzes the effect of planetary and nodal cycles on the real estate market and specific planets that have a bearing on different areas of this market. The significance of rulerships, transits and the investigation of the horoscope for potential success in buying, selling and marketing real estate is also covered. In addition, Georgia has contributed a section on delineating corporate charts, using examples of successful companies and explaining how to choose astrological timing for business success.

Pat Esclavon Hardy interprets the American Stock Exchange chart, providing us with a history of the stock market and examining key years by progression and transits. She presents progressed charts of the crashes of 1929 and 1987 and tells what to expect from the market in the future. She also examines the U.S. chart and points out what was occurring in it at these critical times in our history. Pat uses the 7 Sagittarius rising chart for the United States.

Michael Munkasey offers "A Primer on Market Forecasting," which is an excellent overall introduction to forecasting methods, emphasizing the role of astrology. Non-technical, it characterizes where financial astrology should fit into the realm of economics and market theory. He likens playing the markets to gambling.

According to **Robert Cole**, the economy is predictable, and he offers his daily econograph which shows minute-by-minute aspects between all planets. He explains how to use this to take best advantage of timing market purchases and sales. Some of his future ideas are quite utopian, but nonetheless intriguing.

Blending almost 30 factors in predicting the Dow Jones Industrial Averages is right up Virgo **Carol Mull**'s alley. She discusses the cycles and sub-cycles which affect the U.S. stock market and feels the most reliable are McWhirter's Moon Node cycle, the 28-day Moon cycle, and the four-year cycle that is an overlap of the Kitchin, Mars/Vesta and Mars/Jupiter cycles.

With knowledgeable understanding of your own astrological potential and judicious application of the material presented in this book, you may find yourself following the path blazed by J. P. Morgan and his cohorts.

Michael Munkasey

Michael Munkasey has educational degrees in Engineering and Management and has been studying the markets since early high school. His work experience is in the field of information science, but market forecasting remains a central commitment.

Michael discovered the importance of understanding the role that astrology can play in forecasting market cycles in 1969 and has worked hard at improving forecasting methods ever since. He has been a member of the Board of Directors of the National Council for Geocosmic Research since 1974 and served as their Director of Research from 1985 through 1987. He holds professional astrological certifications from every major astrological organization in this hemisphere. He is currently trying to improve his versions of various market forecasting tools.

A PRIMER ON MARKET FORECASTING

Many people look upon market investing as an effortless way to make money. Investing involves little physical exertion, and the competition occurs between people who, for the most part, are unseen and therefore not able to criticize the investor for any foolish decisions. The investor sees the results of his or her decisions quickly and can also control how these decisions are made, so the personal satisfaction received when investments succeed is direct, financially rewarding, and generally pleasant. However, when losses occur or bad investments are made, as will happen, it is also easy to hide these losses from others and to continue wearing the facade of success as your daily life goes on.

Playing the markets is a form of gambling. There is a potent element of game playing involved, and certain personality types are strongly attracted to the ease with which gains can be made, the joys and thrills associated with risk taking, and the lack of physical exertion. Investing in the markets can be done by almost anyone who is willing to take risks. It carries a high degree of thrill and reward feedback, is potentially lucrative, and makes for a very good occupation! Investing offers you many psychological rewards.

Investors need forecasts and thus require an understanding of forecasting methods. The purpose of this chapter is to very briefly review the many different forecasting methods people can and do use for selecting trading instruments. While the markets offer head to head competition, there are several underlying methods of analysis which, when used properly, improve your chances for making successful trades. This chapter presents some of the primary forecasting methods and strategies available, but does not recommend one method over another because, quite frankly, they all have their place and use. What you will find here is an objective look at these different investment strategies from a fresh perspective as well as comments which may help you judge how to use these approaches. References of recommended books are included at the end of the chapter.

The Nature of the Marketplace

A marketplace provides a means for people to trade or exchange goods. In today's world we have marketplaces where your ability to exchange money for instruments (stocks, bonds, commodities, futures, options, etc.) is greatly simplified because rules are standardized and able middlemen can effect such transactions very quickly. There are trading days when over 200,000,000 such individual exchanges (of say, 100 shares of a certain stock) can occur worldwide. This volume shows a strong and active interest in the various trading techniques. When you invest, many questions can arise, such as: how much of your money should you invest, when should you invest it, how should you allocate your money among your investments, and what returns on your money can you expect?

At any particular moment, the marketplace is the sum of the expectations of *all* the people involved in it. This is a very important point to understand because until you are actually participating in the marketplace you are merely an observer, and your role as an observer is very different from your role as a trader. An observer watches and can remain emotionally detached from the trading activities, whereas a trader is involved by adding his or her emotional desires to those of the other market participants. Thus, it is easier to observe than it is to participate, and the moment you change your role from observer to participant, the nature of the marketplace changes not only for you but for everyone else involved therein. It is absolutely *fundamental* that you clearly understand this **principle of emotional involvement** and the effect that your participation has on both you and the markets.

I will not discuss the responsibility you have to yourself and your dependents for proper and sound money management. Devise and set your investment goals, use sound money management techniques, and understand your investment procedures. If you choose to ignore money management, then you do not need any investment strategy other than to make other people wealthy with your money.

You have a responsibility to collect information on the nature of your investment vehicle(s), to judge how these fit against your money management plans, to analyze this information properly and to define and set your own investment goals. Typical instruments you can select today are: stocks, commodities, mutual funds, bonds, options, notes, futures, certificates of deposit, savings accounts, etc. There are many different ways to invest whatever resources you desire. You can select to invest for a long time or for a short time. But whatever you choose, the concept of **timing** in the purchase and selection of this instrument is first and foremost. It is this concept of timing that is at the center of the various types of forecasting methods to be discussed here. For the purpose of this chapter, I will discuss transactions as if shares of stock are being sold or bought, but the principles discussed apply equally well for other forms of investments.

MARKET ANALYSIS

There are four ways to analyze the best time or ways to invest your resources—*fundamental analysis, technical analysis, cyclical analysis,* and *guessing.* All four play a part in almost every form of investment, but any of the four can be used in any combination without affecting the other methods. Some people use one form exclusively, while others use the various forms in combination with each other.

Fundamental analysis relies on the proper analysis of marketplace fundamentals, or economic data. The assumption which lies behind fundamental analysis is that the marketplace is ultimately a perfect place where eventually the vehicle with the best overall intrinsic value will also be selected by others for investment purposes. As people purchase this instrument *long*, it shall rise in price. The reverse also applies, and fundamental analysis allows you to determine if a price is excessive and if the instrument should be disposed of or sold short. *The primary purpose of fundamental analysis is to select instruments which have a very sound economic basis.*

To do fundamental analysis, you must have access to accurate economic data. This data can come from a variety of places, such as government or business statistics, company reports, weather reports, treasury data, etc. One problem which arises is that the information you have may be jaded or slanted in some way, or it may not be the latest data available in the marketplace. Further, people tend to buy on rumors and sell on facts in the marketplace, so the time of the data you have is crucial along with an understanding of how the marketplace will use that data. You may determine that a company is fundamentally sound, has a good image and marketplace for its products, employs a happy work force that works for a fair wage, and produces products for which there is a considerable consumer demand and little competition. However, even if this is all true, people will not necessarily buy into the company at this time due to other emotional issues.

A company's financial position can be determined through an analysis of its income statement(s) and balance sheet. These are generally published quarterly and are available through different publications or from the company itself. A successful analysis does require some knowledge of accounting rules and practices and the application of certain ratios, such as a break-even analysis, also known as the cost-volume-profit analysis. The value of your investments in terms of both present and future (potential) value is measured and compared to other companies in similar markets to determine the fundamental soundness of the company and its position in the marketplace. This type of analysis can become very complicated, and it occupies much time for many people in the economic community. A good financial analyst thoroughly understands terms like sales, revenue, accounts receivable, inventory, accounts payable, operating expenses, accrued expenses, depreciation, profit, tax accruals, cost of goods sold, return on equity, and many similar terms.

The disadvantage to fundamental analysis is that it takes many years of practice to understand how to properly conduct this type of inquiry, as well as much specialized schooling and learning. The greatest drawback, however, is that all people in the marketplace potentially have access to the same data and not all of them will interpret it in the same way. Thus, your opinion of what is a sound fundamantal and another person's learned opinion of a fundamental may not agree. Therefore, this type of analysis, for all practical purposes today, is used more as a general guide than as an investment timing vehicle. Furthermore, much of the data available contains errors, either deliberate or accidental, and errors in a crucial number can make a considerable difference in the outcome of an analysis. To complicate matters even more, certain privileged people (called "insiders") know about other data which can affect the present fundamental values.

In **technical analysis**, none of these financial terms or perspectives is important. The technical analyst is only concerned with the momentum that is built into the price motion of the instrument on the markets. Is the stock going up? Or is the stock going down? Technical analysts have invented a variety of very clever ways to measure the current market placement of an instrument to obtain answers to these two questions, for they understand that you can make money in a rising market *and* a falling market. The key is to determine which way the market is headed in the future in order to make any money at all.

The primary purpose of technical analysis is to determine current market trends and select market turning points. Sometimes this selection is best done in retrospect or after the turning has become apparent, and this is a drawback to technical analysis. A person successful at selecting through analysis can make a lot of money in any market if s/he knows how to apply technical analysis. But herein lies another of the difficulties with any analysis. It takes one type of personality to be a good and accurate judge of technical indicators and direction, and it takes quite another type to use this information to achieve successful trades. In the first instance, the person must be a good analyst, but in the second instance the person must have a good psychic or sixth sense to use this information to trade appropriately. How this successful application of technical information is done is far, far beyond the scope of this chapter.

Technical analysts concern themselves with many factors, such as price movements, graph patterns, volume, interest rate trends, moving averages, momentum, breadth, sentiment indicators, line slopes, etc. Typically, a technical analyst will draw lines on a chart of price and volume movement for a stock and interpret the patterns of the price movement against these drawn lines. Certain lines will indicate "resistance levels" which show important forward ceilings for a price, while others will show "supports" or places where a falling price should encounter a "floor" or support. The activity of a series of trades or price movements in the pattern of these lines can tell much about the present activity of a stock.

Historians have observed that ancient priests would cut open the entrails of an animal and observe internal lines, forms, and dispositions. From this observation and analysis, they would forecast future movements and directions. This practice is called fortunetelling. Today, however, it is perfectly acceptable in the business community to use similar types of devices and interpretations on financial data utilizing lines, graphs, and patterns to make observations about future trends, directions, and activities. This practice is called technical analysis.

Technical analysis is a very important marketplace tool, and no serious trader should ignore its practices or principles for a very good reason—so many market participants use it that it becomes a self-fulfilling prophecy. At any moment in time, many thousands of people may be reading the same pattern and expecting the market to behave to that pattern in a standard way. Thus, they will participate in the market expecting that pattern, and the activity becomes self-fulfilling. There are many services available which will do much of the more difficult part of price plotting, etc.; hence, many people use the same data, but not all of them will interpret it in the same way.

What people generally look for in the marketplace is some way to forecast the technical trends of financially sound companies. This leads investors to learn and then use the third forecasting method, **cyclical analysis.** The great allure of cyclical analysis is that it potentially allows you to forecast the present technical trends. Thus, as you see the forecasted cyclical trends unfolding in the marketplace on fundamentally sound instruments, you are able to use your analyzed information to make money.

Cyclical analysts hold that all business activity—even all of life—works in cycles. There is a time to expand or be bullish, and there is a time to contract or be bearish. There is some impressive statistical evidence for this phenomena on both a general and a long-term basis. There have also been some impressive failures of this method to account for certain activities in the marketplace. However, cycles only help to show trends and are not generally used for serious daily investing purposes. Like fundamental analysis, no good trader will ignore the cycles of an instrument when deciding which instrument to trade, but few traders will use these cycles to determine the exact time to make a particular trade in the market.

People have noticed, over periods of time, that events tend to recur at regular intervals. Cycles are the study of events which recur at reasonably regular intervals. Cycles have been observed in biological, astronomical, geological, agricultural, social, political, and psychological realms. The most easily observable cycle is the day/night cycle. Cyclic patterns have been detected in stock prices, and many people have used these wisely in combination with fundamental and technical analysis to make profitable trades in the market. Cycles are real but we do not know what causes them. They are an outgrowth of rhythm, trend, and growth. However, cycles in the market and cycles of business activity are independent events. An intelligent guess is that the stock market tends to anticipate business cycles. Hence, business cycles tend to follow more established patterns than stock cycles. In recent years the Federal Reserve Board has attempted to artificially control business cycles with regulation of the money supply and credit system. They have achieved some success with this, but has also had some failures.

The last type of analysis is not a form of analysis at all, but it does have its place of importance within the overall scheme of market forecasting and instrument selection, and as a practice it cannot be ignored. This is **guessing**. Once you have studied your cycles and fundamentals and completed your technical analysis, you must use all of this information to make your trade. You "guess" at the proper moment to make your trade, and your guess, intuition, sixth sense, or whatever notion of deduction you wish is used to arrive at the moment and direction for the trade.

The Use of Computers and Computer-Based Models

There is a tendency to assume that all data output by computers provides very accurate answers to difficult problems. The name for this psychological phenomenon is "The Barnum and Bailey Syndrome." It originated because people are often so entranced with technique and method that they fail to observe the validity of the results. The use of computers in data analysis falls into this category. People will spend so much time gathering, entering, verifying, massaging and analyzing data that they will fail to ask themselves whether or not the results make any sense. Computer users say "garbage in, garbage out." And, garbage in any form, regardless of how well it is packaged, is still exactly that: garbage.

Just because a computer can analyze more data than a human or perform many fundamental or technical analyses quickly, one should not believe that the results obtained from a computer are any more valid than results obtained in a more simple manual fashion. Tying your latest computer to an on-line network and using the most sophisticated analysis software available simply allow you to arrive at your results more quickly and neatly, but not necessarily more accurately. This is an important distinction to understand. Using a computer to help you with your market decisions is only important if you must analyze a large amount of data, in which case the computer can relieve some tedium. If you must analyze data very quickly so that you can trade in and out of the market rapidly, computers can also help with this task.

A computer can be useful if your approach to market forecasting involves the gathering of large amounts of information which need to be correlated and analyzed either by programs special to your needs or by using commercially available software. There are commercial programs which provide various forms of fundamental, technical and cyclical analysis. If you use commercial software, realize that many other people will use the same programs and thus arrive at roughly the same decisions you do because they are analyzing the same data in the same way. This leads to self-fulfilling propositions. *The market at any moment represents the sum of the expectations of all of its participants.* Computers do not change this fact in any perceptible way. The market is still a market, and you are either an observer or a trader, with or without your computer.

Astrology as a Market Forecasting Tool

Astrology is a form of cyclical analysis which is very good at providing accurate information about market trends and also specific changes in market direction. Astrology is a practice which is difficult to rigidly define, but it involves using the planets and/or astronomical information, which is then analyzed by the rules of astrology, to help give insight into problems. Astrology is another tool available to the trader, just like advance-decline lines, call/put ratios, demand index and money supply statistics are tools. Astrology is complex, but it offers insight into the qualities of time at any particular moment which are difficult to obtain by other methods of analysis.

As a market observer, you are interested in knowing whether the information you have analyzed from your fundamental, technical, and cyclical analysis is accurate and correctly interpreted, and whether or not this is the best time to use this information in the marketplace. You also wish to see if the astrological cycles are bullish or bearish. For these two points, astrology can provide strong answers. My personal research has shown that the answers received can be treated with about 75% confidence. That is, about three times in four astrology will accurately answer the astrological trend or direction of the market. Astrology is equally accurate when answering a specific question like "Should I buy long 100 shares of General Motors at 10:30 A.M. today?"

There are 11 different schools of astrology, but only two are of primary importance to the market trader: **business astrology** and **horary astrology**. All 11 schools of astrology use a horoscope, and often this is their only point of commonalty. Business astrology is that school of thought which is concerned with analyzing market trends and directions, determining market turning points, and analyzing the potential of a company as an investment vehicle. Horary astrology is that school of astrology which deals strictly with the answering of the question asked, as in the question about the purchase of GM stock above. Horary astrology has many specialized rules, and while superficially easy to learn, it has twists and turns of nuances which take many years of practice to understand. Unless you are ready to devote a minimum of seven years to learning horary, I would recommend that you hire a good horary astrologer when you want to have your specific investment questions answered.

There are two other schools of astrology which peripherally hinge upon market practices, and these are **electional astrology** and **mundane astrology**. Electional astrology is used when a person wishes to determine a good or bad time to elect (*i.e.*, start) a process (*e.g.*, buy a car, start a new job, open a business, introduce a product line, etc.). For instance, there may be a time when you would want to incorporate a brokerage business and would need electional techniques.

Again, this is a very specialized field of study and it requires many years of learning and practice to gain proficiency. It is best to hire a good electional astrologer when you need one. Mundane astrology is the study of nations and political trends. There are times when understanding the destiny of a nation is important to making an investment. Again, it is best to hire a specialist in this area if you have questions of a mundane nature which require immediate answers.

BUSINESS ASTROLOGY

Central to all of astrology is the *horoscope*. A horoscope is a stylized map of the heavens and contains five equally important sources of information: the planets, signs, houses, personal sensitive points, and aspects (or harmonics). Astrologers consider both the Sun and the Moon to be planets, equal in their astrological value with Mercury, Venus, Mars, etc. There are two basic orientations to the horoscope: Sun-centered (heliocentric) or Earth-centered (geocentric). Both orientations are used in business astrology. There are three major analytical practices within business astrology: horoscopes, harmonic analysis of planetary positions, and cyclical analysis of planetary orbits.

The principle of the horoscope can be used in many ways by a business analyst. The horoscope of a corporation is created by using the date, time and place that a corporation becomes a legal entity. This is not as easy as it sounds, for corporations will merge, be bought out, change names, acquire companies larger than themselves which substantially alters their conception of the marketplace, etc. The horoscope of the corporation will reveal much information about the nature of the company and its internal practices. Some of this information can be useful in determining market trends for the company's stock.

The horoscope for a commodity will reveal information about that commodity during the life of its trades. There is the horoscope for the beginning of all aspects of a commodity, like the first trade for corn in an exchange which occurred in July 1888 in Chicago, and also the opening trade for the May 1989 corn futures contract. Both charts (horoscopes) are needed to gain an insight into the price direction for May 1989 corn futures at any particular moment.

The horoscope for the NYSE itself is helpful, as is the horoscope for the government, so you can see the trend of its reaction toward agricultural products in general. Historians show that the birth of the United States occurred at about 5 P.M. LMT in Philadelphia, PA on July 4, 1776. (*Ed. Note:* There is some controversy among astrologers as to the correct time for this chart.) Also important is the horoscope of the Federal Reserve Board, which is used to understand the overall direction of monetary policies. The horoscope for the exchange you wish to trade on will reveal information about the operation of the exchange and give additional insight into the daily pressures encountered there, disclosing whether these are increasing or decreasing.

The problem with using horoscopes is that more often the information revealed is about the nature of the company and not the direction of movement for the company's stock. A company may experience a reorganization as forecast by the horoscope, but the stock of the company may have no significant activity around that time. If you are a novice with these techniques, it is best to hire a knowledgeable consulting business astrologer for advice. Please refer to the organization list at the end of this article for companies or organizations which can be helpful in this specialized area.

Astrologers have learned that individual planets specifically relate to certain commodities. For instance, the Sun and Neptune are primarily important in determining the price trend of gold on the markets, etc. The same is true of companies in that certain planets will have more effect on the direction and practices of a company than other planets.

It takes experimentation and hard work to determine such specific factors.

Harmonic analysis of planetary positions is a very important trading tool. To apply this tool, the aspects or angles between every planetary pair are examined and analyzed according to a set of rules. In general, angles between planets which are 90°, or factors of 90° (like 45°), are negative in the market, while angles which are 120°, or factors of 120° (like 60°), between planets are positive to the market.

Through proper use of planetary harmonic analysis, you can determine the dates on which the markets should turn or reverse direction. If a market is already moving up, you can determine when the market may go down and vice versa. The problem with this type of analysis is that you cannot determine how far up or down a movement will go. Also, the probability of a correct forecast is only about 75%. However, money can be made even at this 75% accuracy if you determine that the Standard and Poor's 500 will move up for four days starting on _____ or whatever. There is much merit to this type of forecasting. These methods and procedures are not so straightforward when you consider that planets move in four dimensions (X, Y, Z, and time), however, and specialized computer software to do this type of analysis is required or else the calculations become too tedious and time consuming.

Cyclical analysis of planetary orbits is a sophisticated tool which has been shown to be very good at determining major trends within the markets themselves and as such is a complement to harmonic analysis. The two methods offer very different results. Cyclical analysis gives the long-range view, and harmonic analysis provides a short-range view of market activities. Cyclical analysis uses the market's past historical movements during combinations of planetary cycles to forecast future market motion. For instance, the synodic period of Mars and Jupiter is about 2.2 years, and these periods or cycles can be examined over 50 or so years of market activity to determine the impact of the relationship of Mars to Jupiter during various phases of their cycles.

A *synodic period* is the interval of time, usually expressed in Earth years, between the successive alignments of the Earth and two other bodies (such as Mars and Jupiter). Certain synodic periods are highly significant in reflecting market activity. For example, Mars and Jupiter will conjunct at the beginning of their synodic cycle and proceed through phases where they are 90°, 120°, 180°, etc., from each other. As the planets make these angles in their orbits, the markets on Earth are affected in various, but definite, ways. Use of this information can be important to both the observer and the trader.

There are several small nuances to astrological theory that are separate in concept, but can only be lumped into a general category of "other." These include ideas such as: void of course (both planets and the Moon); Moon cycles and phases; eclipses; lunations; and new issue studies. *Void of course* is a term borrowed from horary astrology and relates to the passage of a planet, primarily the Moon, but also other planets, through a zodiacal sign. As the Moon travels in space through a sign of the zodiac like Libra, it will reach a point in its travels where it has formed the last significant aspect in the sign of Libra. Let us assume that this was a conjunction to Mars and occurred at 26° 34′ of Libra. The time it takes the Moon to travel through the rest of Libra (to 29° 59′ Libra) before it enters the following sign of Scorpio (at 00° 00′), the Moon is considered to be void of course. Since the Moon travels an average of 13 degrees a day, the time to travel about three and a half degrees in the sky is between six and seven hours. The Moon will be void of course during that time. Studies have shown a statistical significance to market action when the Moon is void of course and in certain signs of the zodiac.

The Moon has an approximately 29-day synodic cycle and goes through various phases during this cycle. There seems to be some reaction, particularly at a New or Full Moon, which can be attributed to these phases. An eclipse occurs when the Earth, Sun and Moon align in certain ways. Eclipse studies have shown a complex but interesting set of effects among the planets and the markets. A lunation is a New Moon, and a horoscope erected for this moment at the location of a market is said to be very revealing of that market's activities for that lunar month. New issues which are traded during certain lunar cycles, phases or void-of-course periods have been shown to incur a statistically significant market reaction. Again, these methods all provide information which is potentially useful to a trader and should not be ignored just because they are not sufficiently accepted in general economic practice.

There are other occult methods such as I Ching, numerology, Tarot, pendulum, dowsing, and the methods put forth by Gann and the Elliott Wave theory which also incorporate techniques which are not usually considered to be acceptable within economic theory. However, each offers an unusual insight into market activity that is useful to certain traders. Again, study and practice of these methods is not particularly easy, and they may take several years to learn and master. However, each has some merit.

Conclusion: The Need for Balance

The secret to successful investing is to know yourself and your limitations. There is a psychology to the art of investing, and some people are naturally more adept at this practice than others. Knowing your faults and weaknesses in this area is important. If you are unsure of yourself when you begin investing, you will certainly learn a lot about yourself during your trading practices. All of the different tools and techniques discussed previously will give you superficial knowledge of where you are with your trade, but they will not help you make a successful trade if you lack any sort of a trading instinct. You also have a responsibility for budgeting and financial accountability; in fact, no trading program is complete without this. Finally, the relationship you have with your broker is also important and if used well can be most profitable to both of you.

There are no easy answers on how to invest. There are certain tools and techniques which can give you information about the markets and their trends. However, like gathering information beforehand on traffic patterns and flows in a busy street intersection, if you do not look both ways at the traffic before crossing this intersection, you run a substantial risk of getting hit by a vehicle. You are asked to supply prudence and judgment before committing yourself to any type of investing. Fundamentals, cycles, technicals and astrology simply provide information for you. It is your responsibility to use this information wisely for your own purposes. None of these methods provides investment answers—only investment information. Use them all, use them wisely and prosper with your activities in the financial markets and marketplaces of life.

References

The titles included here offer you a place to start in your quest for knowledge and are given for your reference only. You should not assume that I personally am endorsing any of these works or their methods by listing them. Some of these works are quite expensive. Works are listed alphabetically within the categories, and some are out of print. A partial list of organizations providing specialized services and software in the areas of astrology, business, and cycles is given at the end of the references.

Fundamental Analysis

Schwager, Jack D. *A Complete Guide to the Futures Markets: Fundamental Analysis, Technical Analysis, Trading, Spreads, & Options.* New York: John Wiley & Sons, Inc., 1984.

Shim, Jae K., Joel G. Siegal and Abraham J. Simon. *The Vest Pocket MBA.* Englewood Cliffs, NJ: Prentice-Hall, Inc., 1986.

Tracy, John A. *How to Read a Financial Report: Wringing Cash Flow & Other Vital Signs Out of the Numbers.* 2nd ed. New York: John Wiley & Sons, Inc., 1983.

Technical Analysis

Colby, Robert and Thomas A. Meyers. *The Encyclopedia of Technical Market Indicators.* Homewood, IL: Dow Jones-Irwin, Inc., 1987.

Edwards, Robert D. and John Magee. *Technical Analysis of Stock Trends.* Springfield, MA: John Magee, 198x.

Eng, William F. *The Technical Analysis of Stocks, Options, and Futures.* Chicago, IL: Probus Publishing Co., Inc., 1988.

Kaufman, Perry J. *The New Commodity Trading Systems and Methods.* New York: John Wiley & Sons, Inc., 1987.

Pring, Martin J. *Technical Analysis Explained.* 2nd ed. New York: McGraw-Hill Book Co., 1985.

Schwager, Jack D. *A Complete Guide to the Futures Markets: Fundamental Analysis, Technical Analysis, Trading, Spreads, & Options.* New York: John Wiley & Sons, Inc., 1984.

Cyclical Analysis

Dewey, Edward R. *Cycles: The Mysterious Forces that Trigger Events.* New York: Hawthorn Books, 1971.

Hayes, Michael. *The Dow Jones-Irwin Guide to Stock Market Cycles.* Homewood, IL: Dow Jones-Irwin, Inc., 1977.

Matlock, Clifford Charles. *Man and Cosmos.* Development Cycles Research Project, Box 886, Waynesville, NC 28786, 1977.

Astrology

Bradley, Donald. *The Stock Market Barometer.* The American Federation of Astrologers, Box 22040, Tempe, AZ 85282, 1949.

Eng, William F. *The Technical Analysis of Stock, Options, and Futures.* Chicago, IL: Probus Publishing Co., Inc., 1988.

Gillen, Jack. *The Key to Speculation on the New York Stock Exchange.* San Antonio, TX: Bear Publishers, Inc., 1979.

Jensen, L. J. *Astro-Cycles and Speculative Markets*. Lambert-Gann Pub., Inc., 1978. (available through: Halliker's Inc., Springfield, MO 800-641-4626, Ex. 221)

McWhirter, Louise. *Astrology and Stock Market Forecasting*. New York: ASI Publishers, Inc., 1980.

Williams, David. *Astro-Economics*. St. Paul, MN: Llewellyn Publications, 1974.

Other Titles of Interest

Damian-Knight, Guy. *The I CHING on Business and Decision Making*. Rochester, VT: Destiny Books, 1986.

Dreman, David N. *Psychology & the Stock Market*. New York: AMACOM, 1977.

Gann, W. D. *45 Years in Wall Street & New Stock Trend Detector*. Lambert-Gann Pub., Inc., 1949. (available through: Halliker's, Inc., Springfield, MO 800-641-4626, Ex. 221)

Gianturco, Michael. *The Stock Market Investor's Computer Guide*. New York: McGraw-Hill Book Co., 1987.

McLaren, William with Matthew J. Foreman. *Gann Made Easy*. Overland Park, KS: Gann Theory Publishing Co., 1988.

Phillips, Michael *et al. The Seven Laws of Money*. New York: Random House, Inc., 1974.

**Organizations Offering Special Astrological
Support and/or Software**

The American Federation of Astrologers, Box 22040, Tempe, AZ 85282

Astro Computing Services, P.O. Box 34487, San Diego, CA 92108

Astrolabe Software, Box 28, Orleans, MA 02653 (508-255-0510)

Llewellyn Publications, Inc., P.O. Box 64383, St. Paul, MN 55164 (800-THE-MOON)

Matrix Software, 315 Marion Ave., Big Rapids, MI 49307 (800-PLANETS)

The National Council for Geocosmic Research, Inc., 26 W. Susquehanna Ave., Baltimore, MD 21204-5278

Neological Systems, Inc., P.O. Box 6030, Falls Church, VA 22046-0821

(You may contact the author through this company.)

Pat Esclavon Hardy

Pat is a highly respected consultant in financial and business astrology and in geocosmic cycles analysis. She's the former publisher of "Energies, Trends, Cycles" newsletter—a financial market letter using planetary cycles to forecast markets. She has worked with the National Geological Survey Department in forecasting Earth disturbances.

An article in *Registered Representative*, a national stockbrokers magazine, named Pat as one of the top five Wall Street astrologers.

Writer, teacher and lecturer at many financial/business conferences, she is an annual contributing writer to Llewellyn's *Moon Sign Book*, writing the "Stock Market Forecasts" section.

Recently, her focus has been on personal trading with commodities, stocks and options.

CHARTING THE UNITED STATES
and
THE NEW YORK STOCK EXCHANGE

New York Stock Exchange Roots

New York grew in the late 1780s and into early 1790. Population in the 1790s was 33,131, making it the largest city in the United States. At the close of George Washington's first administration, New York appeared to be a new city. There had been a major fire in 1776 which destroyed a large part of the "old city" bordered by Broad and Whitehall Streets and Broadway and Rector Streets. The city rapidly grew north.

New York was a bustling port, surpassing Philadelphia in total shipping tonnage by 1794. It had the finest harbor in America and a satisfactory road system. It was a natural for New York to become the commercial center of the North. Skiffs from the upper Hudson River would dock and unload their commodities on the west side, and drovers would stop at taverns for one last drink before entering the city proper.

Robert Sobel's book *Panic on Wall Street: A History of America's Financial Disasters* describes the drovers entering the city:

"... the drovers would then continue down Broadway for seven blocks until they reached Trinity Church, at Wall Street. Should they turn left, they would walk past the City Hall, rows of banks and mercantile establishments, and many taverns and inns. The Merchant's Exchange and

39

the Government House were below Wall Street, but this narrow lane was the center of the city in 1790.

"Wall Street was also the seat of American Government. Alexander Hamilton, the Secretary of the Treasury, resided at the corner of Wall and Water Streets in a small house not far from the Coffee House Slip on the East River. The City Hall, renamed Federal Hall, was the temporary center of government. Washington's original New York residence, Number 3 Cherry Street, was in Franklin Square, then a fashionable section not far from Wall Street. The city's social elite were clustered in mansions around Bowling Green, but the men would usually be found at noontime two blocks farther north, on Wall Street."

One must realize that buying and selling activity was already taking place on Wall Street. The exchange or barter system was in effect, and the wealthy financial community was already speculating before 1792.

It was the **Buttonwood Agreement** that produced the first effort to organize trading. This agreement was literally born out of a crisis already in progress. A speculator by the name of William Duer accelerated the "paper speculation" that produced the 1792 financial panic.

On May 17, 1792, a group of merchants and auctioneers met to rectify this situation. They decided to meet daily at regular hours to buy and sell securities under an old buttonwood tree on Wall Street, only a few blocks from the present site of the Stock Exchange. So it was on May 17, 1792, " . . . twenty-four men signed a document in which they agreed to trade securities only among themselves, to maintain fixed commission rates, and to avoid other auctions. These men are considered to be the original members of the New York Stock Exchange." (*Understanding Wall Street*, Little and Rhodes, 1978)

Wall Street was once the political capital of the United

States, just as it is a financial center of the world today. The 1789-90 Congress authorized an issue of $80 million in stock to help pay for the costs of the Revolutionary War. There was a scattered market for this government stock as well as for the shares of newborn banks and insurance companies. Trading was carried on in various coffee houses, auction rooms and offices, but it was largely unorganized and unregulated, factors which frightened away most potential investors.

For a short time, the brokers' union met under the aging buttonwood tree facing 68 Wall Street, but they soon moved indoors when the Tontine Coffee House was completed a year later in 1793 at the corner of Wall and William Streets. They prospered and moved to larger quarters in 1825 in what is now known as 40 Wall Street.

On March 8, 1817, the members adopted a formal constitution creating the New York Stock and Exchange Board. To start the day, " . . . a list of all the stocks to be auctioned was read to the assembled board members who would then make bids and offers while seated. Only members were allowed to trade, and the privilege to sit at the auction cost $400." (*Understanding Wall Street*, Little and Rhodes, 1978)

Many people feel the chart for the NYSE concerns only its members, but keep in mind that some of the nation's major brokerage houses who buy and sell for the public have seats on this Exchange, and therefore it affects the public!

NYSE Planetary Patterns

Two major planetary patterns in Chart A provide clues to its future:

Pattern #1—Jupiter conjunct Neptune in opposition to the Moon conjunct Saturn

Pattern #2—Uranus opposing Pluto

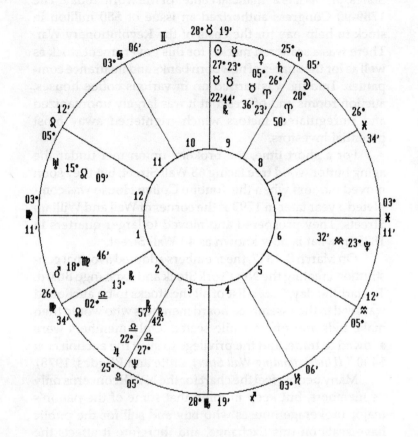

New York Stock Exchange
May 17, 1792   11:56 AM LMT
40N45   74W01
New York, New York
Source: Author's Research

Chart A — Placidus Houses

By progression, these planetary patterns get tighter and tighter, and combined with transits, they reveal the true release of this stored-up energy!

Using the following format of planets with earlier degrees to late degrees, you may also get an idea of how the energies are contacting, working and blending from one to the other. It is strictly a procession of degrees. This simple exercise reveals a tremendous amount of focused energy that can be released through progressions and transits.

Uranus	- 15 degrees	Uranus applies to a TRINE to the Moon.
Moon	- 20 degrees	Moon applies to an OPPOSITION to Jupiter.
Jupiter	- 22 degrees	Jupiter applies to a TRINE to Pluto.
Pluto	- 23 degrees	Pluto applies to a SEXTILE to Saturn.
Saturn	- 26 degrees	Saturn applies to an OPPOSITION to Neptune.
Neptune	- 27 degrees	

A planet enters a sign at 0 degrees and works toward the end of that sign at 30 degrees, whereby the path of that transiting or progressed planet for the New York Stock Exchange chart triggers the two major planetary patterns beginning with Uranus and ending with Neptune. It starts with a Uranus/Moon trine (harmonious) aspect and completes its phase with a Saturn/Neptune opposition (challenging/blending) aspect. This would be the final result of how all these energies play out a "story" of the planetary patterns above.

Note: This writing occurs during an historical time

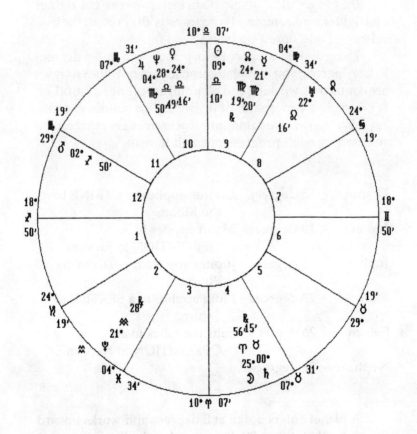

New York Stock Exchange
Progressed to 1929

Chart B — Placidus Houses

window where the people of the United States have just elected George Bush of the Republican Party as President for the next four years.

Astrological Chronology

Progressing the NYSE Chart

Reflect for a moment on the major benchmarks today's investors use as reference. I would like to narrow them down to the 1929 crash chart, the Record High/Top of the stock market in August 1987, and the October 19, 1987 crash.

NYSE Chart Progressed to 1929

Stock market crash and panic . . . financial panics are truly unusual phenomena, and anyone who has ever been through one never forgets it! There is a difference between a market sell-off in an uncomfortable manner and a major emotional, dramatic sell-off, such as that of 1929. *Panic* is defined in *Webster's Dictionary* as: 1. a sudden, extreme fright. 2. rapidly spreading alarm, especially in financial circles.

Market prices crashed beginning Tuesday, October 24th, following a drop in U.S. iron and steel production and a rise in British interest rates to 6.5%. The latter pulled European capital out of the U.S. financial markets. Recovery did not start until 1937, a full 7.5 years after that fatal day.

There were only two Solar Eclipses in 1929. The May 9th Solar Eclipse at 18 degrees Taurus widely squared natal Uranus and trined natal Mars. The other Solar Eclipse at 9 degrees Scorpio was on November 1st, within two days (48 hours) of the CRASH! It was exactly semi-sextile the progressed Sun at 9 degrees Libra (see Chart B).

Progressed Pluto was opposite progressed Uranus (Planetary Pattern #2), being squared widely by the 18 degrees Taurus Solar Eclipse. (A wide orb, but blended

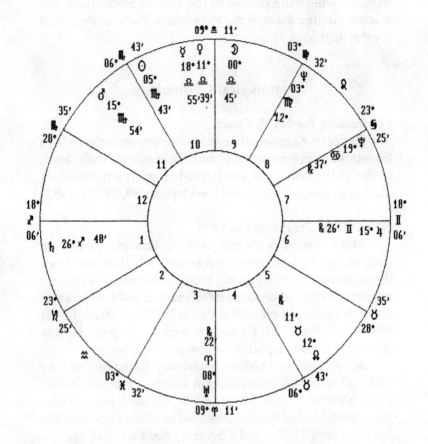

New York Stock Exchange
Transit Chart for the Day of the Crash
October 29, 1929

Chart C — Placidus Houses

with other aspects, it remained through the mid-'30s.) Progressed Mercury (buying and selling) was exactly inconjunct progressed Pluto. The progressed Moon was conjunct progressed Saturn on November 1st, the eclipse date. The progressed Ascendant was exactly square natal Mars!

Transit Chart for the Day of the Crash: October 29, 1929
The best timer was transiting Neptune at 3 Virgo 12 (Chart C) exactly conjunct the natal Ascendant. I have repeatedly seen where Neptune played an important part in the outcome of the market. To me, Neptune rules the market!

Transiting Pluto was stationary retrograde on October 20th at 20 degrees Cancer, exactly square the natal Moon. The North Node in October was 12 degrees Taurus, approaching a square to natal Uranus. Transiting Mars was passing over the transiting South Node, exactly square natal Uranus. Transiting Uranus at 8 degrees Aries was opposite the progressed Sun at 9 degrees Libra. Even the rising sign on the day of the crash was 18 degrees Sagittarius, exactly square natal Mars, and the transiting Midheaven was exactly conjunct the progressed Sun. The transiting Sun was on progressed Jupiter and transiting Saturn was inconjunct the natal Sun. WHAT A DAY!

Transiting Neptune in Virgo was in the natal 1st House and remained there the next five years. Progressed Venus was applying to a conjunction to progressed Neptune in the 10th House of the progressed chart. This denoted the period when the depression was at its worst. It has been stated that Neptune in Earth signs contracts the economy. With other planetary modifiers and factors, this added extra energy to an already crisis situation.

Record High and Crash for the Year 1987
In viewing the progressed chart for 1987 (Chart D), focus, if you will, on Planetary Pattern #2 of Uranus/Pluto.

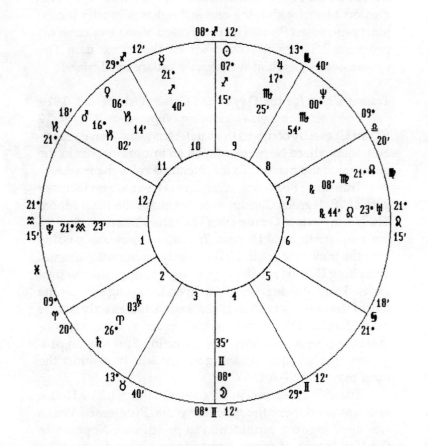

New York Stock Exchange
Progressed to 1987

Chart D — Placidus Houses

Progressed Pluto was exactly on the Ascendant opposing progressed Uranus. The progressed nodes were squared by progressed Mercury. In April 1986, transiting Neptune at 5 degrees Capricorn set off a Grand Trine with natal Venus and the natal Ascendant. This transiting planetary pattern stayed with the chart until Neptune's station at 5 degrees Capricorn (Earth sign) in September 1987! Transiting Pluto opposed natal Venus in 1985-86, setting up a slow transformation of some kind within the structure of the NYSE.

Note: Planetary Pattern #2 of Uranus/Pluto became exactly opposed by progression in 1914-'15. This was the year the stock market closed due to war on July 31, 1914, and re-opened on December 12, 1914. Transiting Jupiter conjuncted the progressed and natal Pluto in early 1915, representing a re-evaluation aspect of the growth of the Exchange. The industrials went from trading 12 to 20 stocks as an average, and a statistical change took place in 1915 whereby the Dow-Jones Industrial Averages were calculated differently.

Uranus/Pluto Opposition

The "Pressure-Release Valve" Aspect
This aspect basically indicates that events and deeds from the past begin to produce consequences that revolutionize! It is time to make sweeping changes. A new birth of awareness is due to the breaking of old patterns that have been limiting. Flexibility is needed, letting go of circumstances, rules and issues that no longer apply or have any *real* function to the system. The key is to recognize that this process is *not bad*; upsetting, yes! But it must capture our attention to produce an awareness of going into the flow of events to bring about a badly needed change. Usually

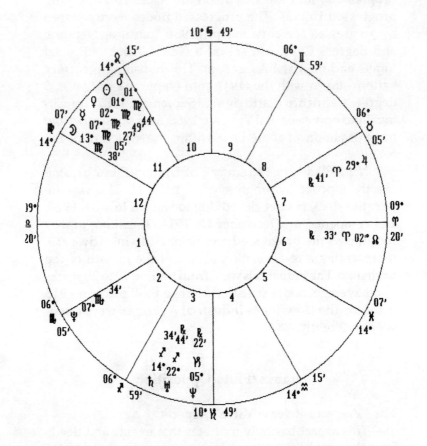

New York Stock Exchange
Highest Day on Wall Street
August 25, 1987
DJIA reached 2744.8 points

Chart E — Placidus Houses

a crisis, then a re-evaluation and reorganization process come from the sudden release of this energy.

The 1987-88 progressed Ascendant conjunct progressed Pluto brought a badly needed change, and if the Stock Exchange didn't take matters into its own hands, the government would have. Pluto—the power coming from within. Hence, "power plays" were brought to the surface (Pluto) where large volume players, program players with new computers and ideas (Uranus), were capitalizing on old rules and breaking them in the form of overloading or crisis. Exposing the "hidden talents" of these operations (Oct. 19, 1987) and being forced by the government to freeze trading, to reorganize, and to come up with some new rules that would prevent another similar occurrence— "circuit breaker" rules—had to be done before the government imposed rules that were inappropriate to the system. The New York Stock Exchange and Chicago Exchanges did this beautifully with combined efforts.

But we are still not finished with this aspect, as it is only in the transition/processing phase. This planetary pattern is in effect until 1990. The progressed chart of 1989-90 will expose another expression of these energies, and the NYSE will emerge into the transformation phase as the progressed Ascendant exactly opposes progressed Uranus for the finale.

Highest Day on Wall Street

The Dow Jones Industrials printed 2722.6 for an hourly reading on August 25, 1987! Intra-day figures were 2744.8, but statisticians use an hourly reading to apply to formulas. Chart E is truly interesting in that Neptune again is a major factor in setting up a "bubble-bursting" effect. Neptune trined the stellium in Virgo just as the transiting Moon was passing over this stellium. What a beautiful display of the Moon as a trigger! This whole stellium sat on the Ascendant

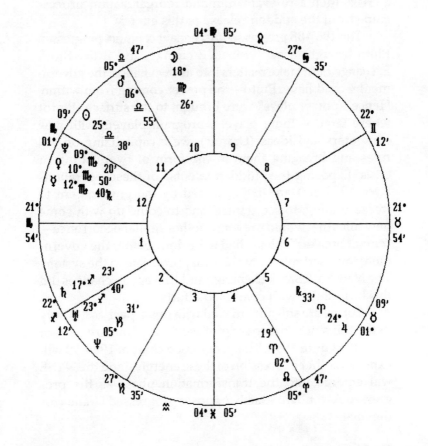

New York Stock Exchange
Transit Chart for the October 19, 1987 Crash
DJIA dropped 508 points

Chart F — Placidus Houses

of the natal NYSE chart. The 1987 progressed chart has a progressed Full Moon at 8 degrees Gemini, and this transiting stellium applied as a square to it for several days, inflating the market with high ideals and promises of a 3000 Dow. Mergers everywhere and prosperity, the best ever in our country's history. You may also remember that this was the period of *The Harmonic Convergence*, whereby the Mayan Calendar completed its approximate 2500-year cycle of the Age of Darkness and started the *Age of Light*.

Within 7.5 weeks, a new phenomenon was occurring; interest rates were headed higher and insider selling became apparent. Two eclipses had occurred, a Solar at 29 degrees Virgo and a Lunar at 13 degrees Aries. The markets reacted with heavy selling. The week prior to the crash the DJIA lost as much as 100+/- points per day. The Friday before the major crash the DJIA was 2248, shaving close to 500 points from the record high. Then came that fatal Monday morning when program-selling buttons were pushed and the market never looked back—straight down 508 points at the end of the day to a DJIA of 1743! The following day took the market down to an unbelievable DJIA low of 1706.90 before it started back up. This shook Wall Street like never before, as this became the worst crash in the history of the stock market. In reflection at the end of the day, you had the feeling that this was truly the end of an era!

The Day of the Crash: October 19, 1987

The transit chart (F) shows this fatal day with transiting Saturn on the horizon squaring the NYSE natal Mars. The transiting Moon was in exact conjunction with natal Mars. The Moon was in Virgo for a high on August 25th, but the same transiting Moon in Virgo (after a September Virgo Solar Eclipse) on October 19th squared transiting Saturn, and this is what burst the bubble. Reality was upon us! Everything had gotten blown out of proportion, even as transiting Neptune was trining natal Venus. Both transiting Jupiter and the Sun were setting off the natal Planetary Pattern #1 of Jupiter/Neptune opposing the Moon/Saturn.

Where Do We Go From Here?

Let us imagine for a moment that we can see into time, not the details, but time windows that allow us to get an idea of what the focus may be. We will try to do this with progressions of the New York Stock Exchange chart. Progressions set a theme for the year, and the transits activate the players in the theme.

NYSE Chart Progressed to 1988-89

1988 was a presidential election year, revealing the continuation of the Republican administration for the next four years. The NYSE is still under Planetary Pattern #2 that was activated in 1987. To reiterate, the progressed Ascendant crossed over progressed Pluto at exactly 21 degrees Aquarius and is applying to an opposition of progressed Uranus at 23 degrees Leo by 1990.

The progressed Ascendant in Chart G is at 22 degrees Aquarius, separating from the conjunction with Pluto, but it is still available for "action" due to the tight opposition to progressed Uranus. This represents a time window where the NYSE is being called upon to take care of issues that are of significant magnitude. Pluto represents control or powers that are larger or stronger than our own and forces one to make changes because of some long-unresolved issues that have been swept under the rug or ignored. The NYSE is being called on the carpet by others who are concerned and have the power, control or manipulative energy to make these types of demands with an "or else" attitude.

I think that the rules and regulations of the NYSE will

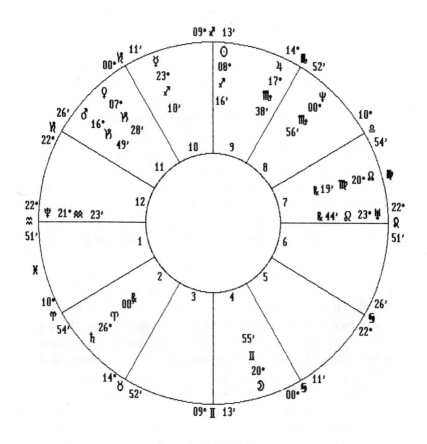

New York Stock Exchange
Progressed to 1987-89

Chart G — Placidus Houses

still go through another phase of changes, fine-tuning the procedures on how trading orders are carried out on the market floor, especially with the futures and options exchanges. Priorities will need to be set up to distribute the buy and sell orders without special treatments. The public needs more consideration from the exchanges if they are to continue to put their monies into speculation and investments. In the past, the larger blocks and corporations have taken precedence over the private individual, and many times his or her orders would be filled at higher prices, giving the "big guys" more advantages. The exchanges will come to realize, WE THE PEOPLE make the difference in the markets.

This is astrologically confirmed with the progressed Ascendant applying to square natal Mercury retrograde for the next 18 months. You will probably see some news concerning these Pluto issues during the months of fixed signs—April/May, July/August, October/November and January/February.

1989 will commence the transiting Saturn/Neptune cycle of 35.87 years. This particular cycle comes on the heels of the 1988 Saturn/Uranus cycle of 45.363 years. For these two cycles (which usually occur approximately ten years apart) to manifest in this time window only one year from one another announces significant CHANGE associated with the energies of Saturn, Neptune, and Uranus.

There have been only two other times in this century that this Saturn/Neptune conjunction occurred—1917 and 1953. In the past, the economy entered a recessionary period and the stock market declined, confirming a true Bear Market in both years. The Saturn/Neptune cycle seems to correlate with a contraction in the economy (this time deflationary) and is recession oriented.

The Saturn/Neptune conjunction will occur three times in 1989 due to stationary positions: March 3rd, June 23rd and November 13th. I think the economy could accelerate reces-

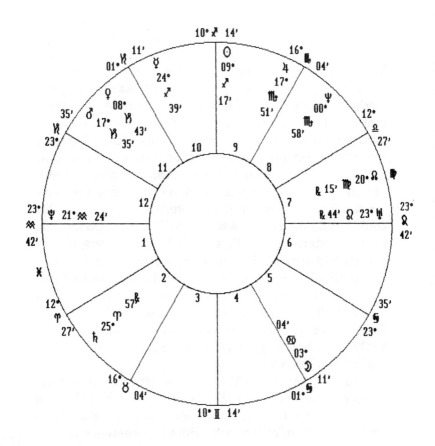

New York Stock Exchange
Progressed to 1989-90

Chart H — Placidus Houses

sionary attitudes and believe we are in a Bear Market (down) as of this writing. October 19, 1987 was the first clue! The major Bull Market (up) topped out on August 25, 1987.

There will be a sensitive time window of approximately 120 days from February through May 1989. If there was ever a time that major problems with the economy and markets could arise, it will be then! Send out positive energy that we find alternative ways of taking care of these important issues without financial pain for the majority. We need to see/visualize/imagine America actively working out the problems in order to have a beneficial and positive outcome. The constructive side of this aspect can be the ability to make extraordinary self-sacrifices or attitude/belief changes that could be common sense actions that EACH OF US must do for the betterment of all, a more balanced conservative approach in our daily lives to help the economy get back on its feet for all of us. The emphasis is that we must all participate in the betterment of our material Universe! After all, our reality is what we make it. If we don't take the initiative and act, we cannot blame those who do—and do it badly! Are you going to let unqualified people decide your reality? Get involved!

Pay attention to the Moon cycles as they act like a timer to Saturn/Neptune. The Moon in the cardinal signs of Aries, Cancer, Libra, and Capricorn will activate this planetary conjunction, particularly adding its influence around the above-mentioned dates when Saturn/Neptune become exact. We are embarking on a new 35.87-year cycle taking us into the year 2024!

NYSE Chart Progressed to 1989-90

The progressed Ascendant exactly opposes progressed Uranus at 23 degrees Aquarius/Leo in Chart H. With Pluto, the changes come in forms of transition and transformation and take longer to emerge as the energy unfolds slowly, focusing on priority issues. With Uranus, the changes are more sudden and unexpected and come in the forms of the unusual, unique and the least expected, particularly in regard to finance and opportunities for making money in unusual ways. This is a time window when you can truly be profound in saying "Expect the unexpected!"

It has been said that Saturn makes the laws and Uranus breaks them. More legal disputes could come into play during 1989 with some pretty outrageous high finance schemes fueling them. This should wane into the 1990s as such disputes won't be as appealing. The government by this time will have set some rules or laws concerning this type of action. Big business is truly getting bigger. Bond markets may be in focus during 1989-90 due to interest rates, and the transiting Saturn/Neptune aspect in 1989 heralds a deflationary economy that can be "bubble bursting." If done positively, it will occur with the Pluto energy in a transformative manner that is not overwhelming and destructive. Basically, a redefinition of the New York Stock Exchange could be in order, especially if we are to cope with the world economy—new structures being applied to deal with the enormous advent of the World Financial Markets! Circumstances are being created under this progressed Planetary Pattern #2 to initiate changes and modifications for our economic structures to remain healthy in the long run, but with Uranus you can never be sure of the outcome.

The progressed Moon is in Cancer, making a strong connection with the United States chart. The public may be making demands on the government to take action on issues that seem very emotional in this time frame. Strikes and embargos could run some commodity prices wild, both ways.

Again, we should focus on the transiting Sun in the fixed signs of Taurus, Leo, Scorpio and Aquarius—April/May, July/August, October/November, and January/February. These time windows may be more sensitive than

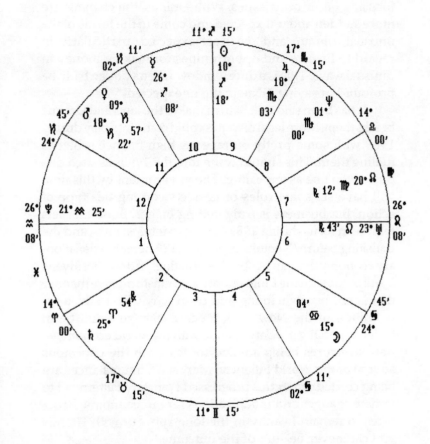

New York Stock Exchange
Progressed to 1990-91

Chart I — Placidus Houses

other periods in the year to express the above-described energies.

NYSE Chart Progressed to 1990-91

Progressed Mercury at 26 degrees Sagittarius trine natal Saturn (Chart I) is a time for serious thinking and important concerns as this is a good problem-solving aspect. I tend to think that buying and selling (Mercury) volume on the Exchange will have dropped (as compared to the latter 1980s) and stabilized, falling into a suppressed market attitude. The wild speculative/gambling attitude that we've seen in the past few years will give way to a new reservation. Conservatism and caution are the key words this year! Contraction in the economy is supportive here in the USA chart also. The NYSE may realize that it will regain the people when its approach is more like what it used to be before the Great Bull Market and it is a place where people can *invest* their money for decent profits and feel relatively secure.

The progressed Moon in Cancer is still activating the USA chart, and there seems to be much emotion connected between it and the New York Stock Exchange chart. Since the Moon rules Cancer, it is stronger here than usual. Moon/Cancer is also connected with the energies of cycles. I think that more of the public will come into contact with cycle studies than ever before, and **The Foundation for the Study of Cycles** (3333 Michelson Drive, Suite 210, Irvine, CA 92715) should be on everyone's list to obtain this kind of information.

Progressed Mars trine natal Mars shows vigorous assertion on behalf of the NYSE. It is a good time for the Exchange to take the initiative and start a new project or make some kind of effort for the small investor. This is an opportune time for the NYSE to prove its worth as a confident Exchange for the people of this country and the world to do business with.

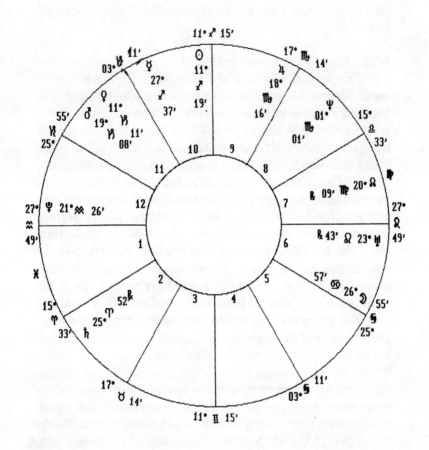

New York Stock Exchange
Progressed to 1991-92

Chart J — Placidus Houses

NYSE Chart Progressed to 1991-92

Mars is applying as a square to the natal Moon (Chart J), setting up a period of several years (at least seven) where Planetary Pattern #1 will be activated. The behavior of the NYSE will seem somewhat erratic and unfamiliar. Since it must become more world oriented, the Exchange will go through some growing pains. And this could be the period when this will happen. We will find out that we (USA) are not the leading economy anymore. This could provide a fighting attitude, making for some pretty intense situations.

Transiting Neptune will conjunct the transiting North Node in Capricorn around November 1991, and transiting Uranus will be following right behind. In past history, Neptune/North Node have produced significant lows in the markets, usually a bottom to recessions or Bear Markets. Other dates of this phenomenon were October 1924, mid-1941, February 1958, and December 1974.

Transiting planets that pass through cardinal signs of Aries, Cancer, Libra or Capricorn will affect these energies and may produce issues for the NYSE to deal with.

THE UNITED STATES OF AMERICA

Let us pause for a moment and bring another factor into play—the chart of the United States of America. I am not going to debate which is the correct U.S. chart. Books have been written on this subject alone. There are many, and you choose which one you like to work with. I have chosen the 7 Sagittarius rising chart as I find it works for me.

Planetary cycles play the most important part in our lives as applied to whatever charts you choose. One form is the **Sidereal Period** (star period). This is the time it takes a celestial body to make one complete revolution in its orbit, measured by its recurrent alignment to a particular star. The following measurements refer to alignment to the Sun:

Mercury	=	88 days
Venus	=	224.5 days
Earth	=	365 days
Moon	=	29.53 days
Lunar Nodes	=	18.6 years
Mars	=	1 year, 322 days
Jupiter	=	11 years, 315 days
Saturn	=	29 years, 167 days
Uranus	=	84 years, 5 days
Neptune	=	164 years, 288 days
Pluto	=	248 years, 157 days

When Neptune entered Virgo in July 1929, this initiated the first Neptune Return in the chart of the United States (see Chart 1). Neptune took approximately 14 years to transit this sign. America, just prior to its birth, was breaking away from its Mother country, England, because of the people's inspirations, dreams and ideals (Neptune) of a better country—*our* new country. This inner re-orientation led to the American Revolution.

In 1929 and the '30s when Neptune approached its birth position (Neptune Return), we see some of the same traits of idealism. The Federal Reserve Board had forced credit into the system just a few years prior, and most of this newly created money went into the stock market because of the enormous rate of return. (That is, as long as it continued to go up!) In widespread areas, people began to borrow money to speculate in the markets because they could get back more than they invested in such a short time. This was called *margin*. Money went into paper assets such as stocks and bonds. The Fed created credit so that money could be put back into the economy for productivity, since it was rapidly failing. But America was literally gambling it away on the markets! Hence, other countries who had money in our banks pulled out due to the "house of cards" they saw

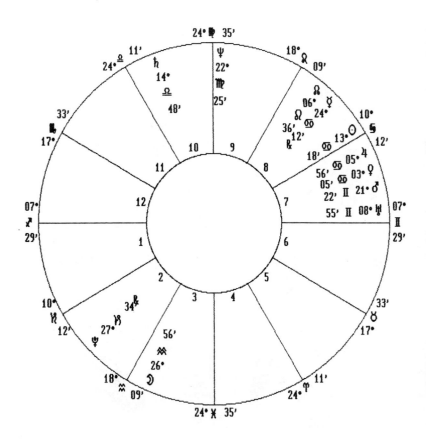

United States of America
July 4, 1776   4:47 PM LMT
39N57   75W10
Philadelphia, Pennsylvania
Source: Barry Lynes

Chart 1 — Placidus Houses

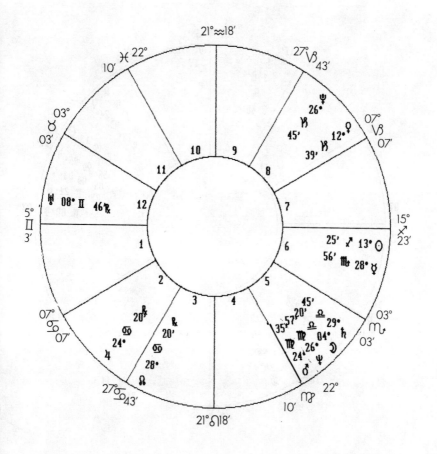

United States of America
Progressed to 1929

Chart 2 — Placidus Houses

beginning to fall. The result was a temporary collapse of our economic system—a re-orientation of these Neptune energies!

The tightest and most exact aspect in the chart of the United States is the natal **Mars square Neptune**, and Neptune conjuncts the Midheaven. Mars is applying to this square by 1 degree, 3 minutes. So you can surely say Neptune has a strong influence on the U.S. chart as well as the New York Stock Exchange. What a coincidence! The Kondratieff Wave of approximately 54 years is linked to the Neptune cycle (in Earth signs).

Even the chart of the Federal Reserve Board has a strong Neptune! (The Fed has the power to control and create money.) So I believe that Neptune is strongly linked to economic phases and changes.

In the 1929 progressed U.S. chart (Chart 2), you will see that progressed Mars in Virgo triggered natal Neptune and the Midheaven for a few years. The natal Neptune square Mars is a very strong energy by itself, but it truly has a "bubble-bursting" effect when activated. All that idealism had to be turned into active (Mars) reality, and it simply didn't work. America was betting on a dream that could not be activated into our economy/society. The progressed Ascendant at 15 degrees Gemini was on the natal Mars/ Uranus midpoint applying to natal Mars for the next several years. It was World War II that encouraged people to believe in America again, and the War produced the dollars to get our economy back on its feet. The next Neptune Return is in the year 2094!

The Uranus Return—Can It Be a War Cycle?

Uranus returns to its natal position every 84 years and seems to be related to rebellion, which thus far has been seen as war. This could be the "cycle of war" in the U.S. chart. The first Uranus Return was in 1860, the Civil War. The second one was in 1944; this was the War of Wars, World War II. The third Uranus Return arrives in 2028.

Uranus represents a revolutionary America and usually is associated with wars of liberation to help others find identity. **Freedom with responsibility** that paves the road to freedom of speech, choice of associations, and movements against self-incrimination is accented. Wars and space exploration (also Uranus-ruled) have helped America with technological advances.

Basically, the Uranus cycle helps us to break free of outworn or outdated limitations. Rebelliousness could be the catalyst, but is not always. Information and knowledge (Uranus) of new ways of doing things can also be the tools for constructive change.

The Road to the Pluto Return

The United States' first Pluto Return in the year 2024 will come very close to the Uranus Return! This Pluto cycle takes longer to reach our awareness since it happens so slowly. Only at "power points" do the Pluto energies manifest an issue or crisis on which we must focus.

Pluto represents transition/transformation; the opposition (half of the Pluto 248.6-year cycle) occurred just after 1900. The Uranus opposition was also involved. Following a century of steam, the century of electricity began. The Industrial Revolution era, with the advent of the automobile and machines, transformed America. New roads and bridges were built, new corporations were made since machines could help do the work of many people, and companies became larger. Based on these observations, I would venture to say that the Pluto Return will force us to re-evaluate and update our roads, bridges and buildings as they could be in pretty bad shape after so many years. Pluto represents the masses and new eras, so another quantum leap in the ascent of man should come upon us just after we enter the 21st century.

In the 1950s, transiting Pluto was trine to the USA natal Pluto representing power for America! The Baby Boom resulted and there are more people in America than ever before. This was the dawning of a new era since the war was over and our patriotism was stronger than ever; so were our exports. Everyone looked to America to see what was in vogue—from finance to consumer products. America was booming.

Transiting Pluto arrived at the waning square (270 degrees) to natal Pluto in 1972 through 1984. Richard Nixon was re-elected President in 1972, and the Watergate affair led to his resignation in 1974. Worldwide inflation helped cause dramatic increases in the cost of fuel, food, and materials. In the early '70s, we were in economic recession. The DJIA fell to 663! OPEC and the oil crisis brought higher gasoline prices. By the close of the 1970s we had deep problems with the economy; inflation and interest rates were out of hand in double digits. On a more positive note, the USSR and USA signed a treaty banning nuclear weapons on the ocean floor.

The exact square between transiting Pluto and natal Pluto occurred during October 1982 to September 1983. This transit signifies changes that are inherent within the hidden depths of things, and it brought a period of regeneration, with all the advantages and consequences. Ronald Reagan was elected President in 1980, and the Bull Market started in August 1982 after a minor recession and interest rates peaking in 1981 at 21% (an aftermath of the Carter administration). A new Prosperity era started in 1982! This country has seen six years (plus) of economic recovery, American prosperity and the re-election of President Reagan.

Unfortunately, a budget deficit in the trillions must now be addressed! It can no longer wait. The new administration is faced with this very serious problem as we finish the '80s and enter the '90s.

Transiting Pluto and Jupiter will exactly sextile the USA natal Pluto November/December of 1994. The sextile offers an opportunity, and transiting Jupiter conjunct Pluto is a re-evaluation aspect. The waning sextile can bring benefits from awareness and efforts applied before this aspect occurs. It brings to the surface some "fruits of labor" and a sense of moving toward our goals by simply allowing the current energies to play themselves out. This should be a period of stability within change. The transition of the '80s is now being transformed and maturing in the '90s.

Where Do We Go From Here?

USA Chart Progressed to 1989-90

As explained in the New York Stock Exchange progressions, the transiting Saturn/Neptune cycle of 35.87 years is upon us in the sign of Capricorn, applying to an opposition to the USA natal Sun. It will become more exact during November/December 1990. This is a time when America's creativity will be at an all-time low and adversities may appear overwhelming. Minor events could get blown out of proportion mainly from a lack of accurate information, overdramatization by the news media, or just the inability to locate the proper people to do the research on solving problems. Other nations/leaders may point the finger at America and ask us to redefine our goals in connection with the rest of the world. We also need to define our goals to ourselves. It will be a period to keep things simple and to deal with the many problems as they come our way. They can be workable. Applying effort and focus to

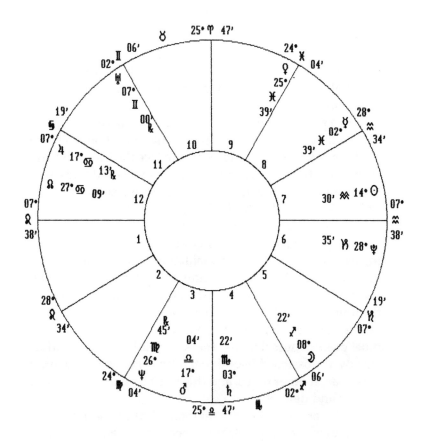

United States of America
Progressed to 1989-90

Chart 3 — Placidus Houses

achieving solutions to the problems being presented is the key to success. Idealistically, this is an excellent time for America to get its act together. We must acknowledge and take responsibility for ourselves, saying no to others when necessary. Other countries may have to start doing for themselves as we cannot continue to spend what we don't have!

In a person's chart, this transit indicates a time when s/he will be financially strapped. S/he cannot obtain more credit or ask favors. It is necessary to face the issues at hand and deal with them. An ingenious person would find a way to consolidate, reorganize and simplify as a solution to the issues. America should do the same.

So conservatism will be back in style! There appears to be a contraction in the economy, and I think we will be dealing with inflation/deflation vacillation. Deflation more than inflation. America is in transition, and we are getting to the point where we need to remain healthy in order to accomplish the much-needed changes ahead of us. Other countries are asking that we define ourselves and our self-worth. We must present ourselves to others as clearly and straightforwardly as possible. Misunderstandings may develop more now than at other times, and this must be guarded against. Clarify and define!

Who are we? A nation in debt! That's how others see us. Japan is certainly a stronger economy than we are, and coming on stronger. We will see if the old saying "When America sneezes, the whole world catches a cold" is still in effect!

The progressed Sun trine natal Saturn energies (see Chart 3) should help give the USA the opportunity to know itself better, especially through our relationship with our environment. Emphasis may be on waste and contamination of our resources. A real fight against the abuse of drugs— both illegal and those from the medical profession—is needed as garbage may be presented in the name of a cure. When the economy is down, the underground surfaces more and more to make money illegally.

Spirituality is in! Meditation, New Age ideas (Neptune) and communication will blend into the work and corporate environment to raise the awareness of all who are on this planet. This is a time when spirituality (not necessarily religion) will dominate, and the positive thinkers will be the ones who help bring America to its redefinition. Metaphysics can help people to focus on their priorities both to themselves and to this nation. America needs the help of its people again. WE need to believe (Neptune) in her. That's how she became as great as she is! Patriotism . . . where is it today? Let us rekindle her strengths. America needs her people!

Possibly a new drug to help AIDS may be developed as the virus spreads even more. Prevention and communication must be achieved to stop this deadly virus. The plague of the '80s and '90s is upon us, and we must all fight it together.

USA Chart Progressed to 1990-91

Progressed Mercury trine natal Venus and applying to a trine with natal Jupiter points up foreign relations. Relationships that we cultivate now with other countries could benefit us in the long run. Since Venus rules finance and financial matters, they would also be in favorable focus. Business in this country should be on the incline as we activate our presence in a positive way throughout the world. It is an excellent time to negotiate with foreign dignitaries, and we may see various treaties, contracts and deals made with world leaders. Our country could be exposed to more new information and ideas than usual which will help broaden our understanding of the world.

Progressed Mercury trine progressed Saturn (see

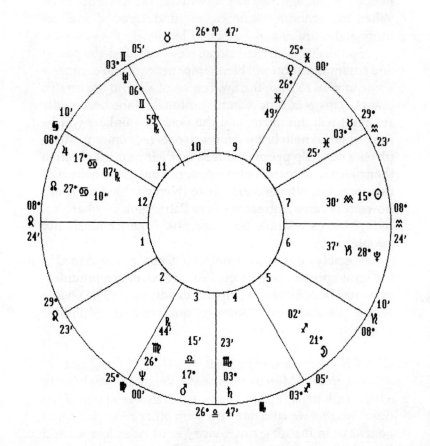

United States of America
Progressed to 1990-91

Chart 4 — Placidus Houses

Chart 4) will engender a serious-minded approach to all world affairs. Practical matters are spotlighted. Application of a methodical approach brings the "big picture" into focus, and details should not be overlooked. The government may take on very conservative, contractive policies which are needed to get through this period due to the huge mortgage on our future. The budget and trade deficits are still in focus, and the trine to Saturn points toward some slow but effective solutions. Part of the decision will involve time—time to let these energies play themselves out or time to deal with an immediate world focus that will distract from our dilemma. Let us hope that effective decisions will be made with positive results!

Progressed Venus sextile natal Pluto supports the relationship and finance issues of this time frame. Possible confrontations could occur that result in a deeper meaning to our quest. Diplomatic relationships are very important under this influence.

Progressed Mars square progressed Jupiter will be activated by transits, and the important time frames will be February 1990, June 1990 (very positive), April/May 1991, and September 1991. These dates will show both results and consequences. Military issues concerning foreign governments could arise with a military re-evaluation of what we own/lease from other countries. Our military bases throughout the world could go through a reorganization period and weeding out of unnecessary installations, shifting military power strategically to where it counts. Satellites can now take the place of actual ground control, except where fuel stops or strategic areas are needed.

This Mars/Jupiter aspect can be one of speculation and gambling with positive results. What if a National Lottery was started to be used to help pay off the National Debt? Splitting the proceeds between the winner and lowering the National Debt! Just a thought . . . .

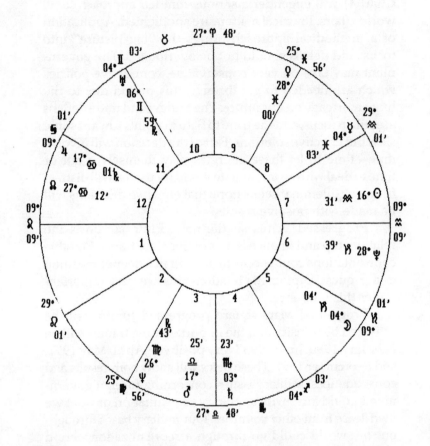

United States of America
Progressed to 1991-92

Chart 5 — Placidus Houses

USA Chart Progressed to 1991-92

Progressed Mercury will be making a station within the next 18 months trine the natal Venus/Jupiter midpoint (see Chart 5)! Whatever long-range plans, projects, negotiations, deals or actions initiated now will reap results at the time of the stationary retrograde. Any projects not completed by that time will probably not amount to any significance as these energies wane quickly after the station is made.

In September 1992, transiting Jupiter will conjunct natal and progressed Neptune and apply to a trine with natal Pluto and the progressed South Node. Idealism and spiritual, religious and mystical philosophy are likely to grow at this time. Issues relating to the homeless, needy, and aged of our own country could be strongly focused. Some results from past projects could come to fruition.

With this type of energy involving the South Node, America could be dazed with a false sense of happiness, living in a dream world with no basis in reality. Since USA natal Pluto is in Capricorn, the business world could be the major focus. Massive misrepresentation or major misunderstanding could lead to the desire to gamble, speculate or take risks with limited resources. Stock and bond markets may again be heavily in the news. Creative financial schemes may show up without real basis. It sounds impressive but is not functional in the long run.

SOLAR AND LUNAR ECLIPSE DATES

These dates are important keys to the release of planetary energies that bring specific issues into focus. The stock and financial markets are excellent barometers to watch around eclipse dates. Apply these dates to charts, cycles, trends, technical data or whatever forecasting tools you use. They offer timely and rewarding information. Make

note of them on your calendar or personal files to remind
you. Become aware of eclipses!

January 26, 1990	- Solar at 6 AQU 35	
February 9, 1990	- Lunar at 20 LEO 47	
July 21, 1990	- Solar at 29 CAN 04	
August 6, 1990	- Lunar at 13 AQU 52	

*1991 has 6 eclipses indicating a very busy year. Changes are
prominent.*

January 15, 1991	- Solar at 25 CAP 20	
January 30, 1991	- Lunar at 9 LEO 51	Be very cautious
June 26, 1991	- Lunar at 4 CAP 59 ⎫	as 3 eclipses occur
July 11, 1991	- Solar at 18 CAN 59 ⎬	within 6 weeks!
July 26, 1991	- Lunar at 3 AQU 16 ⎭	Very sensitive
December 21, 1991- Lunar at 29 GEM 03		time window!

January 4, 1992	- Solar at 13 CAP 51
June 14, 1992	- Lunar at 24 SAG 20
June 30, 1992	- Solar at 8 CAN 57
December 9, 1992	- Lunar at 18 GEM 10
December 23, 1992- Solar at 2 CAP 28	

References

Bolles, Albert. *Financial History of the United States.* 3 vols. New York: Augustus M. Kelley Publishers, 1949.

"The Buttonwood Agreement," New York Stock Exchange, New York, 1953.

Commodity Quote Graphics, Inc., Computer for Applied Technical Analysis.

The Dow Jones Averages 1885-1980. Ed. Phyllis Pierce. Homewood, IL: Dow Jones-Irwin, 1981.

Little, Jeffrey B. and Lucien Rhodes. *Understanding Wall Street.* Cockeysville, MD: Liberty Publishing Co., Inc., 1978.

Sobel, Robert. *Panic on Wall Street.* New York: Macmillan Pub. Co., Inc., 1968.

Trager, James. *The People's Chronology.* New York: Holt, Rinehart & Winston, Inc., 1969.

"The Stock Market Under Stress." New York Stock Exchange, New York, 1953.

Jeanne Long

Jeanne Long was born in England and educated in England and Argentina. In 1957, she moved to the United States.

An international lecturer, instructor and consultant on market patterns and timing, she has 20 years experience as a professional astrologer, with six years as a professional futures trader.

Currently on the Board of Directors of The National Council for Geocosmic Research, she is now living in Florida and trading the futures market using specialized state-of-the-art computer equipment with customized software.

NEW CONCEPTS
FOR TRADING COMMODITIES
COMBINING ASTROLOGY AND
TECHNICAL ANALYSIS

The natural cycles of commodity prices correlate beautifully with the natural cycles of the planets. Each commodity has its own cycle. It is not surprising, especially to astrologers, that each individual commodity has a particular planet that it favors. For example, gold responds to the Sun. Consequently, all commodity prices do not rise and fall simultaneously. Groups of commodities, such as the "financial group" or the "agricultural group," will more often than not respond in tandem with their particular group, however.

Two different areas of study are blended in this chapter, therefore some of the terminology may be new to you. A recommended reading list completes this chapter, and these books cover the basic principles of both astrology and the futures market.

THE HARMONIOUS RELATIONSHIP
OF PRICES & PLANETS

In order to trade or invest successfully, it is necessary to have an intimate knowledge of the commodity you wish to trade—to have your finger on its pulse or to be in tune with it. Therefore, it is important to understand that each commodity, while naturally unfolding within its cycle, will appear to be marching to the beat of its own drummer. The marching is the commodity cycle; the drummer is the planetary cycle. Simply put, the commodity prices are dancing while the planets are playing the tune.

Each combination of planets and commodities has its own special melody. Sometimes we do it one note at a time! Following this analogy a step further, we can think of one planetary aspect (two planets, of course) as a soloist, which translates price-wise into a minor short-term reversal of price. A whole orchestra, or multiple aspects, often creates a major long-term reversal of trend and price. For example, the top of the Dow Jones Industrial Averages (DJIA) in August 1987 was without a doubt the complete orchestra. (More details on this later.)

As commodity traders or investors, if we can occasionally hum the special melody of our favorite commodity in tune, we will be rewarded by profitable trades. Losing trades are a clear indication of singing off-key. Technical analysis of price patterns combined with planetary timing is one of the ways to avoid singing off-key. When a trader has a methodology that consistently makes a profit, we know s/he is definitely in tune with the market.

PLANETARY TIMING: "THE TOOL BOX"
Aspects

Two planets forming an aspect to each other have the potential to time a price reversal. The following geocentric as well as heliocentric aspects are used:

☌	0°	conjunction
✳	60°	sextile
□	90°	square
△	120°	trine
☍	180°	opposition

(45° semi-squares and 150° inconjuncts may also be used, but they are not a part of this discussion.)

Prices usually respond to an aspect by changing direction. The degree of the change varies from very minor to major, depending on the aspect, planet and commodity.

It is impossible to trade at every aspect presented, therefore we choose the aspects and planets that create the major turning points in our preferred commodity. We then combine our own special technical tools with these aspects. In other words, we pick up the major beat or rhythm of the commodity as it responds to certain aspects.

Example: Cocoa responds readily with all aspects to Venus. We can choose to use every aspect to Venus or to pick one pair in particular. If we select Venus and Mars in aspect (♂ ✳ □ △ ☍) to each other, we find they clearly time significant reversals of price. (See Chart 1.) This graphic illustrates geocentric Venus with Mars, as well as Venus in aspect to Pluto. The turning points in price are plainly visible at the time of each aspect. When these planetary timing tools are combined with technical tools, the result is a very profitable trading system. (For your observation, also look at heliocentric Venus aspecting Pluto and geocentric Mars changing signs using Chart 1.)

General Guidelines for Aspects and Planetary Movement

Single aspects = short-term, minor price reversals.

Multiple aspects = long-term, major price reversals, especially if the multiple aspects occur within a very short time frame. If multiple aspects are spread over a two-week period (or more), then congestion of price generally forms, but you must remember this is only a guideline because the energies of all aspects and planets pertaining to various commodities are not equal.

Retrograde and Direct: Planets changing direction often correlate with reversals in price of certain commodities, but again, only some commodities respond.

Example: Soybeans relate to Mercury. When Mercury

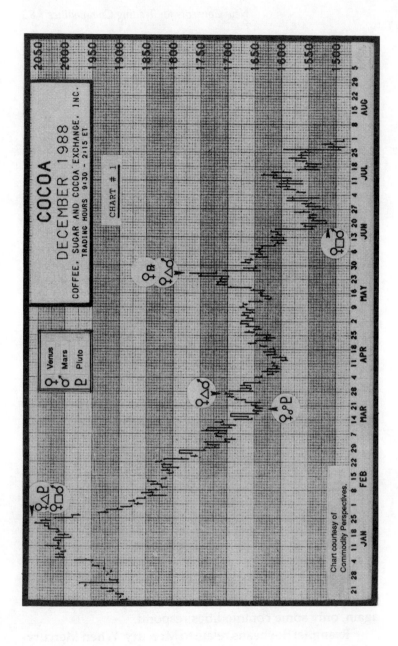

changes direction, powerful reversals in price are shown. The above can easily be used as a short-term trading tool, or it can be combined with heliocentric and geocentric aspects to Mercury along with technical tools for a super trading system.

Change of Signs: As planets change signs, either heliocentrically or geocentrically, prices may also reverse. If several planets move into new signs together or within just a few days of each other, this adds energy to the reversal. A dramatic example of this occurred August 24, 1987, when the DJIA reached an all-time high.

> *Geocentric Change of Signs:*
> August 21: Mercury into Virgo
> August 22: Mars into Virgo
> August 23: Sun, Moon, Venus into Virgo
>
> *Heliocentric Change of Signs:*
> August 20: Mercury into Virgo
> August 21: Mars into Virgo
> August 23: Venus into Virgo

Even without including aspects, retrogrades or direct motion of the planets, the above list is very impressive. We seldom find five geocentric planets changing signs together, while it is even more rare to find three heliocentric planets changing into the very same sign! This massive grouping, of course, created multiple aspects which stopped the DJIA dead in its tracks. The market then moved sideways until the October crash. Multiple aspects often cause congestion or sideways movement. The planet Jupiter also turned retrograde on August 19, 1987. The DJIA generally moves sideways or down when Jupiter is retrograde.

Moon Phases and Eclipses: Full and New Moons are often powerful energies that reverse price, especially if they fall within a day or two of a planetary aspect, in which case the price reversal will often occur at the lunation rather than on the date of the actual planetary aspect. Solar and Lunar Eclipses are also extremely important timing tools. A change of trend may occur on the actual eclipse date or at a later time when the eclipse degree is re-energized by the transit of another planet.

TECHNICAL: MORE TOOLS

Price charts are made up of constants. Take the *daily price chart*, for example. Each day there is a high price, a low price and a final price of the day, known as the *closing price*. These three daily constants, the high, low and close, form a bar. When price bars are strung together over a period of days, weeks, etc., they create patterns.

Certain patterns occur with regularity. Our awareness of these patterns gives us the ability to see them developing. The visual recognition of patterns unfolding offers a frame of reference as to where future price can go—the knowledge of what the possible completed pattern will be.

Technical tools monitor patterns and let you comfortably hold the hand of the price while it dances along. You now have an intimate knowledge of certain dance steps! Without this knowledge, you have no idea of where price is going or what it is doing. It's like being dragged along by a runaway horse. How can you possibly make a logical decision about a trade under these conditions?

Technical tools, therefore, allow you some element of control. (Not control over the markets, only control over yourself.) You can never tell the market what to do; you always let the market tell you what it is up to. Then with your technical tools, you monitor the action. It all boils down to *pattern recognition.*

Restated, the technical tools monitor price and set up a

framework within which the prices will fluctuate. *Planetary tools, however, give the timing for reversals of price.* When combined, these tools allow you to see the dance (visual patterns) and hear the beat (planetary timing) and therefore stay in tune with the market.

Both tools generate BUY or SELL signals which are utilized for trading or investing purposes. In other words, each time you trade, you are expecting two signals, one planetary and one technical.

Important: Do not take planetary signals without confirmation from technical signals. If, for example, an aspect occurs in a strong market, it may be the one time that price does not reverse as expected. (Aspect = reversal 75% of time.) In strong price moves, an aspect can just add energy to the forward thrust, and in this case there will be no confirming BUY or SELL signal from the technical tools. Hence, using technical signals to confirm planetary timing avoids stepping in front of a freight train.

Trend Lines

This is one of the most simple and most used technical tools. Therefore, it behooves us to utilize it with planetary timing.

In an up market, a trendline (TL) is drawn by connecting two or more lows. (See Chart 2.) By joining lows A and B, then projecting this line out into the future, it gives a line of support for future days/weeks/months, etc. In a down market, a TL is drawn by connecting two or more highs and projecting this line into the future, giving a line of resistance to the prices in future days.

Chart 2 illustrates a long-term TL that had been in effect since 1985. This line was not penetrated until the October 1987 crash.

If a market is to continue moving up, it should stop and reverse to the up side whenever it touches the TL. If it is a

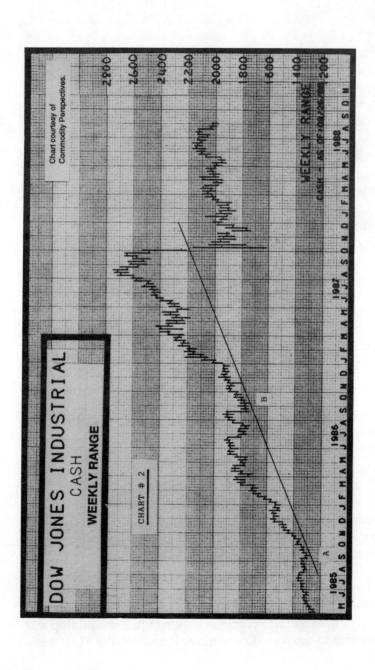

DOW JONES INDUSTRIAL
CASH
WEEKLY RANGE

CHART # 2

Chart courtesy of
Commodity Perspectives.

WEEKLY RANGE
CASH - AS OF 10/28/88

2800
2600
2400
2200
2000
1800
1600
1400
1200

1985 1986 1987 1988
M J J A S O N D J F M A M J J A S O N D J F M A M J J A S O N D J F M A M J J A S O N

strong market, the TL will support it and propel it up again, especially if important planetary signals form at the same time. In a weak market, as in October 1987, the TL did not support, thereby resulting in the TL failure.

Often, when a market falls through a TL, it will go back up to check out the TL again. At this time, the TL will become resistant and push the market down. Chart 2 illustrates the general weakness of the DJIA since it has never even been near the TL since the crash of '87.

Trend lines off *Lows* give *support*.
Trend lines off *Highs* give *resistance*.

Connecting high points A and B and extending that line out horizontally as in Chart 3 creates another support line. This line from 1986 is supporting the DJIA at C. The lows of the D, E, and F line supported the DJIA at G. The lows of H and I have given resistance to the Dow at J; in fact, for the last eight months the DJIA has traded between the upper resistance line and the lower support line. The Jupiter retrograde periods and importance of the black arrows will be discussed in the latter part of this chapter.

DJIA Daily With Planetary Aspects

Chart 4 gives an example of planetary aspects creating reversals as the DJIA reaches long-term resistance and support lines as shown on Chart 3. All aspects to Venus are shown as well as all aspects to the Sun. Note the longer term reversals of the Saturn/Uranus conjunction in February and June of 1988.

As a point of interest, the retrogrades of Saturn, Uranus Neptune are included. These retrogrades reversed the direction of the market before it even got to the support or resistance lines.

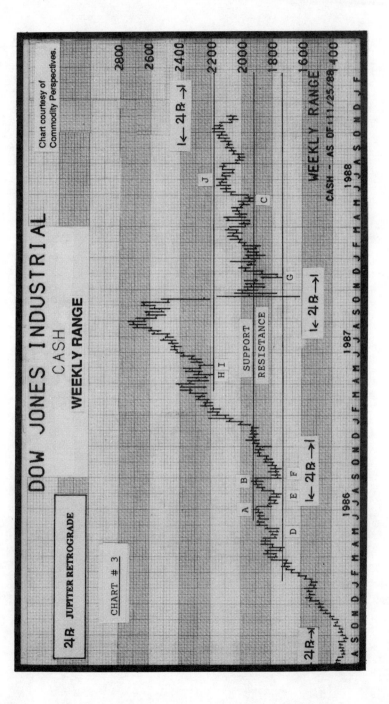

DOW JONES INDUSTRIAL
CASH
WEEKLY RANGE

2♃ JUPITER RETROGRADE

CHART # 3

Chart courtesy of
Commodity Perspectives.

WEEKLY RANGE

CASH — AS OF 11/25/88

2800
2600
2400
2200
2000
1800
1600
1400

|← 2♃ →|

|← 2♃ →|

|← 2♃ →|

2♃ →|

SUPPORT
RESISTANCE

A B
D E F
H I
J
C
G

A S O N D J F M A M J J A S O N D J F M A M J J A S O N D J F M A M J J A S O N D J F
1986   1987   1988

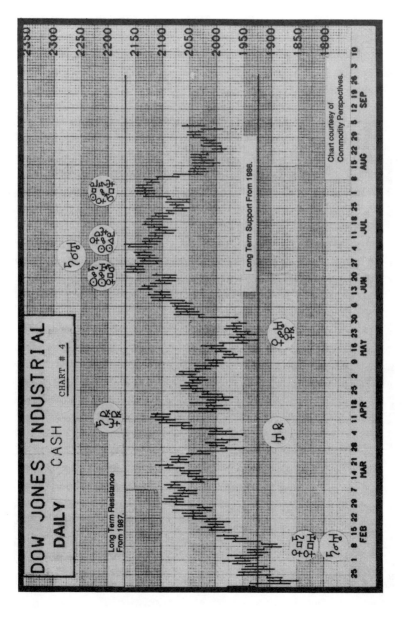

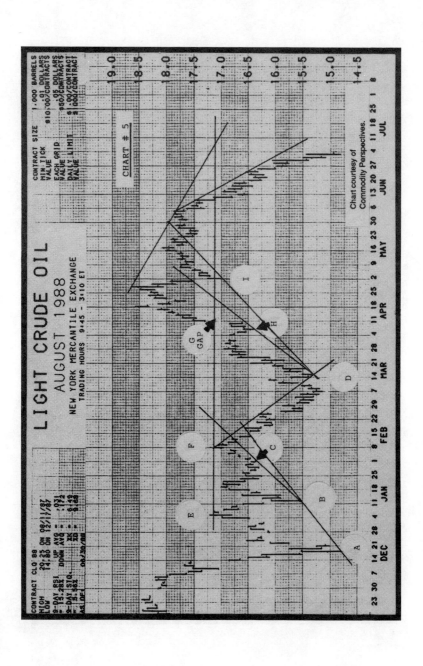

LIGHT CRUDE OIL
AUGUST 1988
NEW YORK MERCANTILE EXCHANGE
TRADING HOURS 9:45 - 3:10 ET

CHART # 5

Chart courtesy of
Commodity Perspectives.

Valid Trend Lines

The longer a TL has been intact, the more valid it becomes as support or resistance to future prices. The more times the price touches it without going through it, the stronger it becomes. The shorter the TL, the more easily it will be broken. For this very reason, you will shortly see why short-term TL's work well with planetary aspects.

As illustrated in Chart 5, any two low points or any two high points of ten days apart or more are connected to form short-term TL's. Point A is connected to point B to create the first TL. Point B is then joined to point C to make the second TL. How this B/C TL can be utilized for trading purposes will be shown in Chart 6.

E and F form a horizontal resistance line. Note how the price jumped (gapped) over this line at G. This line now becomes a support to future price. This support is clearly shown as the price comes down to touch it at I and is immediately propelled up again. You will notice that the price often jumps or gaps over support and resistance lines, or TL's. This is one of the easiest ways for price to deal with these hurdles.

Once a TL is penetrated, as in the case where the D/H TL failed as price went through to I, then the horizontal support line stopped price. It is now necessary to connect D to I for the new TL. The importance of updating TL's will become clear as we move on to Chart 6.

COMBINATION OF TOOLS

First, it is necessary to decide which planetary aspects to use with any commodity. For crude oil (Chart 6), I have chosen the following:
1. All aspects to the Sun
2. All aspects to Neptune

The choice of aspects to use is based on:

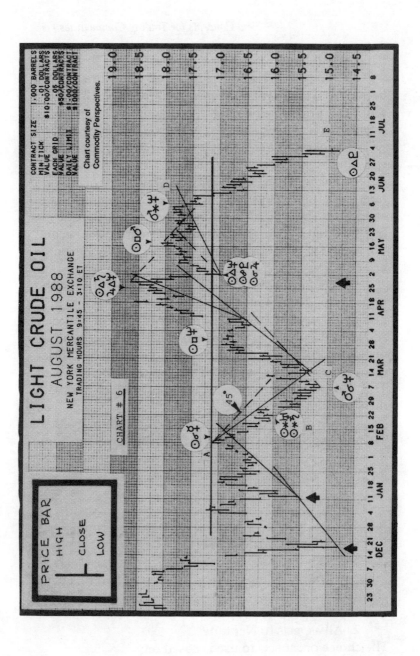

1. Whether you are trading for the Long or the Short term.

2. Which technical system you favor or are most familiar with.

The beauty of combining both astrological and technical tools is the many profitable ways to use them. In fact, from these tools a trading system can be designed to fit almost any trading personality. Techniques that encompass even the most sophisticated technical systems can be combined with every planetary energy, but that is a book in itself. The basic principles shown here are a steppingstone to the more advanced levels of Astro-trading, and they do stand on their own to produce a trading method with very satisfactory profits.

Trend Line Trading: A Walk Through Chart 6
Rules:
1. Use all TL's of ten days or more.
2. Use all aspects to the Sun.
3. Use all aspects to Neptune.
4. Take the first close under a TL following a Sun or Neptune aspect.

Monday, February 8, 1988 was the high point of a short-term trend run up. On February 10, the Sun was conjunct Mercury = take a trade on the first close (for representation, see the box in the left corner of Chart 6) under the TL, which happened February 10.

TRADE 1: Sell on Close Under TL at 16.75
(This is also known as a SHORT position)

Once in the market, you must immediately think about protecting yourself just in case the price should fly off in the opposite direction. This is done by a STOP LOSS. This stop loss is placed above the most recent high (which was on February 8). For oil only, the stop is always placed .15 above the high.

FIRM RULE: Never trade without a STOP LOSS.

Keep the STOP at the same place for three days following the entry into a trade. After three days, begin to follow the price as it moves down by moving the STOP down at a regulated rate. This is accomplished by adding a temporary TL at a 45° angle until a regular TL forms. After this, start placing the STOP at .15 above the regular TL each day.

If your STOP is hit in the first three days, you will incur a small loss. But the longer the trade is on, the more likely you are to break even or make a profit if the STOP is hit. STOPS are like insurance—you limit your loss from the first day.

Anyway, now we are in a trade, and the market is dancing while we are tripping nicely along by its side. Then on February 19, two aspects occur at B—the Sun sextiles Uranus and the Sun sextiles Saturn. Following these aspects the price begins to move up towards the 45° TL. This is a signal to watch for a possible reversal. But after a small pause, the price continues down. A new high point has now been made which allows us to draw in our regular TL = A to C.

On February 28, the Sun sextiles Neptune. Again, we are alerted to a possible change of trend, but after a small blip up, the price continues down.

On March 7, Mars conjuncts Neptune. Immediately the price reverses, and by the fourth day it has gone through the TL, hitting the STOP, which was at .15 over the TL. This means we are now out of our short position. On that same day, the price closes over the TL = BUY on close.

Profit from Trade 1
February 10: Short at 16.75
March 10: Out at 15.70 = profit of $1050.00

TRADE 2: March 10: Buy on Close Above TL at 15.85, STOP .15 Under Previous Low (March 7) at 15.00 for the Next Three Days

Three days after the trade is initiated we add the 45° TL. Upon doing this, we see that the price the day we added the 45° TL. has come down to close on top of it. This makes us a little nervous! The following day (at C), the price trades within .05 of the STOP! But then continues up! As with Trade 1, we move our STOP up daily at .15 under the 45° TL.

On March 21 and 22, the Sun squares Uranus and Saturn. We are watching and prepared just in case the price should penetrate the 45° TL. The price stumbles slightly, then continues up.

We are still unable to add the regular TL since we cannot connect two lows less than ten days apart. Hence, the 45° TL continues as our support line.

On March 30, the Sun squares Neptune. This reverses the price before it reaches the horizontal resistance line at 17.10. The price then moves down toward the 45° TL but reverses up before it touches it. Now we can add the regular TL off C.

Next, the price gaps over the horizontal resistance line, and it continues up through April 18 before any down days occur.

On April 20, the Sun trines Uranus and the Sun conjuncts Mercury, sending the price up. The low of April 20 now provides another TL.

On April 22, the Sun trines Saturn and Jupiter trines Neptune. The big guns send the market crashing through the TL on April 27. We are stopped out at our LONG position.

Profit from Trade 2
    March 10: Long at 15.85
    April 27: Out at 18.10 = profit of $2,250.00

TRADE 3: April 27: Sell on Close Below TL at 18.15, STOP .15 Over High of April 27 at 18.55

The price immediately dropped down through the horizontal support line. (Once the price is under it, it becomes a resistance line.)

Three major aspects occur over three days: on April 30, the Sun trines Neptune; on May 1, the Sun opposes Pluto; and on May 2, the Sun conjuncts Jupiter.

The price reverses and bounces right back up through the horizontal line and closes above it. We reverse our position from SHORT TO LONG on the close above this line.

Profit from Trade 3
    April 27: Short at 18.15
    May 3: Out at 17.45 = profit of $700.00

TRADE 4: May 3: Long on Close Over TL at 17.45, STOP .15 Under Low May 2 at 16.85

On May 17, the Sun square Mars forces the price down through the 45° TL. We are out of the long trade.

Profit from Trade 4
    May 3: Long at 17.45
    May 23: Out at 17.60 = profit of $150.00

TRADE 5: May 23: Short on Close Under TL at 17.55, STOP .15 Over High on May 17 at 18.20

We get stopped out of this trade on May 27 as the price trades .15 over the 45° TL.

Loss from Trade 5

May 23: Short at 17.55
May 27: Out at 17.80 = loss of $250.00

Important: There is none of our required aspects to the Sun or Neptune at the low on May 25, (or within two days either side of May 25), therefore we cannot take a long position on the May 26/27 close above the 45° line. We must now wait for the next aspect before we can take a position. Mars sextile Neptune occurs June 6.

TRADE 6: June 6: Short on Close Under TL at 17.35

Follow all the rules from previous trades. This trade was finally stopped out on July 7 following a Sun trine Pluto aspect.

Profit from Trade 6

June 6: Short at 17.35
July 7: Out at 15.80 = profit of $1550.00

From February 10, 1988 to July 7, 1988 = 6 trades, 5 wins and 1 loss.

5 winning trades = profit of	$ 5,700.00
1 losing trade = loss of	$ 250.00
Total profit trading one contract	$ 5,450.00
Total profit trading two contracts	$10,900.00
Total profit trading ten contracts	$54,500.00

(This does not include a deduction of commissions paid to a

broker as these commissions vary depending upon the broker.)

Note: The black arrows on Chart 6 will be discussed shortly.

Additional Insight

If we added all the aspects to Pluto on the Crude Oil chart, we would have seen valid turning points, but they would not have changed any of the trading decisions.

Finally, it is important to remember that price goes down as well as up. People generally seem more comfortable when price is going up. *When trading the futures market, it does not matter which direction price is moving.* Up or down can be equally profitable. In fact, it generally takes price twice as long to move up as it does for it to fall down. This means that profit is made twice as fast on the downside, therefore we LOVE to see price go down as the price fell from D to E in Chart 6.

Note: The 45° lines were first used by W. D. Gann who used planetary information as one of his main trading tools. He wrote several books on his methods of trading.

ADDITIONAL TECHNICAL TOOLS

There are two other simple technical tools that work well with planetary aspects. They are:

1. A key reversal signal (KR)
2. A two day reversal up or down signal (2DRU or 2DRD)

Key Reversals

An example of a KR day is shown in the left box on Chart 7.

A **KR Up** is a bar with a lower low than previous days

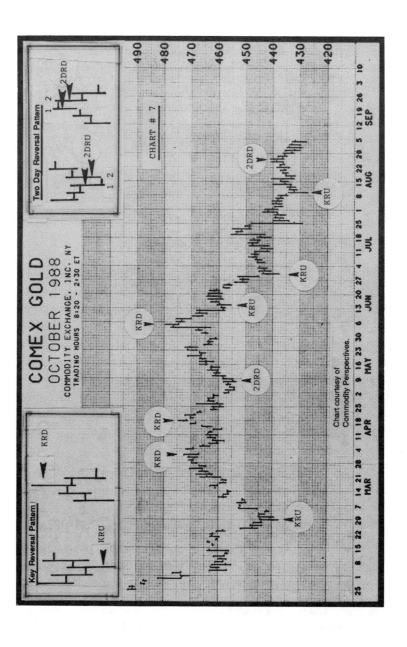

COMEX GOLD
OCTOBER 1988
COMMODITY EXCHANGE, INC., NY
TRADING HOURS 8:20 - 2:30 ET

CHART # 7

Key Reversal Pattern
KRD
KRU

Two Day Reversal Pattern
2DRD
2DRU

Chart courtesy of
Commodity Perspectives.

490
480
470
460
450
440
430
420

25 1 8 15 22 29 7 14 21 28 4 11 18 25 2 9 16 23 30 6 13 20 27 4 11 18 25 1 8 15 22 29 5 12 19 26 3 10
      MAR   APR   MAY   JUN   JUL   AUG   SEP

with the close towards the top of the bar (**KRU**).

A **KR Down** is a bar with a higher high than previous days with a close towards the bottom of the bar (**KRD**).

In general, KR days work about 50% of the time. The percentage of success increases to 75% when there is also a planetary aspect nearby. Note how the KR days on Chart 7 reverse the trend. On Crude Oil Chart 6, the KR days are marked with small arrows.

KR's are most valid when the following conditions apply:

1. The KR day's range has been wider than the previous day.

2. There has been higher volume than previous days.

3. Planetary aspects occur within the three-to-five-day range, depending on the commodity.

Two Day Reversals

An example of 2DRU and 2DRD is shown in the right box on Chart 7.

A **2DRU** is formed when on day one the bar makes a new low and closes on the low, while on day two it closes on the high.

A **2DRD** is created when on day one the bar makes a new high and closes on the high. The next day (day two), the bar closes on the low.

A 2DRU and a 2DRD are shown within Chart 7.

For further examples of 2DR's, turn to Crude Oil Chart 6, and check out June 22 and 23, 1988. An example of a Two Week Reversal (same pattern as daily) is clearly visible on the DJIA Chart 3.

TRADING WITH ALL THE TOOLS

A Walk Through Chart 8

Our first job is to set the parameters for the technical

tools. Secondly, we must define the aspects to be used with gold. Remember, we can choose different aspects and technical tools for each commodity. For gold, I have chosen the aspects listed below, but you may decide, after studying and trading gold, to use entirely different aspects as well as technical tools. The beauty of Astrotech trading is its many variables enabling everyone to dovetail his or her personal system to his or her own taste and personality. I personally use the information given, and I combine it with more sophisticated technical techniques that cannot be covered in this short chapter.

Planetary Aspects for Gold

1. Sun aspecting Mars, Jupiter, Saturn, Uranus, Neptune and Pluto only.

2. Neptune in aspect to all planets except the Moon.

3. Neptune and Pluto retrograde and direct.

4. Aspects to be used: conjunction, sextile, square, trine and opposition.

5. Heliocentric Mercury changing into the sign of Sagittarius.

Technical Tools for Gold

1. A KR or 2DR is only used when one of the required planetary aspects occurs. Otherwise, do not take a KR or 2DR. The range or orb for a KR is two days before to three days after the aspect. This means two trading days (the market is closed on Saturday and Sunday). Therefore, if an aspect falls on a Monday, the two trading days before would be Thursday and Friday of the previous week.

KRU =   BUY the day following the KR at $.50 above the high of the KR day, but only if the KR range is larger than the previous day's range.

KRD =   SELL the day following the KR at $.50 below the

low of the KR day, but only if the KR range is
larger than the previous day's range.

2DRU = BUY the second day of the 2 DR pattern on a close
at the top of the bar.

2DRD = SELL the second day of the 2DR pattern on a
close at the low of the bar.

2. Use horizontal support and resistance lines (HL) as
shown on Chart 8 at A to Z.

3. Use 45° TL's. Place this TL off the most recent low/
high after the close on the fourth day of your trade.

4. Use regular TL's. Connect any two points of more
than 12 days apart to create a TL.

5. When trading gold using TL's and HL's, if the price
reverses through the same TL three times when you are
stopped out for a third time, STAND ASIDE. Wait for the
price to go through a different TL before taking another
position. Be sure that the planetary aspects are also in effect.
See Trade 11 on Gold Chart 8.

6. STOPS: During the first four days after a trade is
initiated, your stop will be placed:

A. $.50 under the most recent low if you are
long.

B. $.50 over the most recent high if you are
short.

C. $.50 under/over the 45° TL after the fourth
day.

D. $.50 under/over the regular TL when it forms
after the twelfth day.

Where to Take Trades at TL's

45° TL Up =   You will SELL only on a close of 1.00 or
more under this TL if there have been the

appropriate planetary aspects at the preceding high.

You will be stopped out of your long trade
any time the price trades $.50 or more
below this 45° line while it is in effect. It is
not in effect once a regular TL has formed.

45° TL Down = Reverse the above rules.

Regular TL Up = Follow all rules of 45° TLU.

Regular TL Down = Reverse all rules of 45° TLU.

Horizontal Support Lines = Follow all rules of 45° TLU.

Horizontal Resistance Lines = Reverse all rules of 45° TLU.

Important: Once you have defined your parameters
and rules, you must stick to them. Never trade with a little of
this and a bit of that; it is a sure way to lose money. This is a
very disciplined exercise.

TRADE 1: Chart 8

On February 28 (Sunday), the Sun is sextiling Neptune. February 29 (Monday) = KRU. Take position tomorrow
at $.50 above today's high. March 1 (Tuesday) = Long at
445.00 ($.50 above yesterday's high).

(For those who have not traded before, call your broker
on Monday, February 29 after the close and tell him or her to
BUY one futures contract gold on March 1 at 445.00.)

STOP LOSS: Place your STOP at $.50 below the last
previous low, which was on February 29. The low was at
437.50. Your STOP LOSS point is at 437.00. Keep your
STOP at 437.00 for four days.

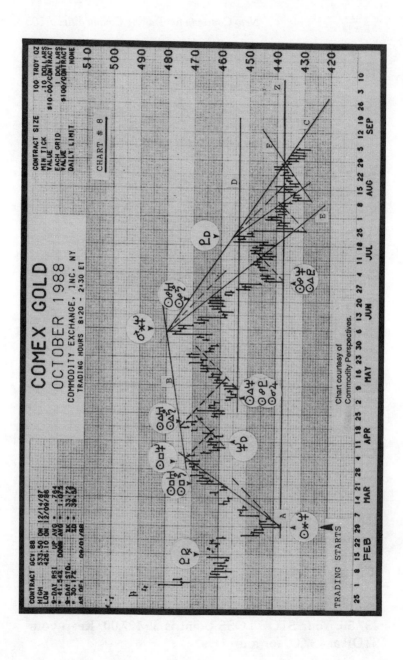

45° TLU: After the close on the fourth day, add your 45° line. The next day before gold starts trading, put your STOP LOSS at $.50 under this line. Every day thereafter, move your stop up at $1.00 per day (which will keep it $.50 under the 45° line). When the regular TL forms, then put your STOP LOSS at $.50 under this line each day.

After the Sun trines Pluto March 2 (the price kept going up), none of the required aspects now present themselves until March 21. Lack of aspects does not mean that you can walk off and forget your trade until an aspect turns up. Quite the opposite. Whenever you are in a trade, you must pay attention and monitor every day with a STOP LOSS. Always be prepared in case something unexpected happens, such as the market going crazy for a day or two before settling down again. For example, news of war, hijacking, riots, etc., can cause gold to respond and possibly overreact.

On March 21/22, the Sun square Uranus and the Sun square Saturn = KRD. You will put an order in for March 23 to SELL at $.50 below this KR at 461.50. This SELL order was not initiated as the price continued up. We now have a low point to connect our regular TL to (see TL at A).

On March 30, the Sun squares Neptune. On this day, the price trades below the TL. We are stopped out $.50 under at 467.00.

Profit from Trade 1

March 1: Long at 445.00

March 30: Out at 468.00 = profit of $2,300.00. Thank You Very Much!

TRADE 2

March 31 = KRD with a close under the TL = Short on the close at 467.00. STOP LOSS = 473.00, which is $.50 above the March 31 high. Keep at 473.00 for four days.

45° TLD: Start on the close of the fourth day with your STOP LOSS $.50 over it each day.

April 7: KRU. This is two trading days before Neptune retrogrades. BUY next day at $.50 above the KR = 462.50. This trade is initiated.

Profit from Trade 2

March 31: Short at 467.00
April 7: Out at 462.50 = profit of $450.00

TRADE 3

April 7 = Long at 462.50 at $.50 over the KRU. STOP LOSS = 457.50, at $.50 under the low. Keep this STOP LOSS for four days.

45° TLU = Start on the close of the fourth day. (Notice that the close of this fourth day was well under the 45° line. That was a little scary. The next day it must go up or you are out.) The price goes up! Whenever a KR occurs before the aspect, you must always be prepared for the price to reverse in the opposite direction at the aspect. Therefore, at the close of the fourth day, this was one of the possible scenarios we were thinking of even though it did not happen.

April 18 = KRD. Two days later the Sun trines Uranus = SELL at $.50 under the KRD at 470.50.

Profit from Trade 3

April 7; Long at 462.50
April 19: Out at 470.00 = profit of $750.00

TRADE 4

April 19 = Short at 470.00. *Note:* Our order was SELL at 470.50. On April 19 at the start of the trading day, (the Open) price started trading at 470.00, BELOW where our order was placed. Therefore, we are SHORT at 470.00, not 470.50. The close under the 45° TL on April 21 also confirmed our short trade.

STOP LOSS at $.50 over the high for four days. On April 22, the Sun trines Saturn, and the price continues down. Concerning the 45° TL, add as usual on the fourth day.

On April 26, there's a strong blip up as heliocentric Mars is in conjunction to Uranus, but there is none of our required aspects. The price does not go through the 45° line. Continue in short position.

On April 30, the Sun trines Neptune. On May 1, the Sun opposes Pluto with a Full Moon. The Sun conjuncts Jupiter on May 2.

Generally, when several aspects occur together, the price will congest (move sideways) for a few days. Watch for this pattern and watch for either a KR or a 2DR pattern forming within this congestion or at the end of it as it does here.

On May 6, the fourth day after the final aspect of the Sun conjunct Jupiter, a KRD forms. We are short anyway, so the KRD confirms our short. But the next trading day a close on the high of the bar forms a 2DRU and we BUY on close!

Profit from Trade 4

April 19: Short at 470.00
May 9 Out at 458.00 = profit of $1,200.00

TRADE 5

May 9 = long at 458.00 on 2DRU. STOP LOSS at $.50 under the low for the next four days. Add a 45° line on the fourth day.

On May 17, the Sun squares Mars, and this gives a KRD, but the range of this day is not larger than the previous day, which is one of our requirements for a trade.

Notice that since late May we have not been able to add any of our regular TL's. This is because the general trend is in congestion. You will find that congestion is where most losses occur.

On May 25, the price trades under the 45° TL. We are stopped out on the Open of May 25 under the TL at 465.00.

Profit from Trade 5

May 9: Long at 458.00
May 25: Out at 465.00 = profit of $700.00

None of our required aspects occurs until June 6 when Mars sextiles Neptune, therefore no new position can be taken here (May 25) at the close under the TL. We must STAND ASIDE until two days before June 6 to look for patterns.

June 3 (one trading day before June 6) = KRD. This day the price touched resistance line B of previous highs. Then the price came tumbling down.

TRADE 6

June 3 = KRD. On June 6, SELL at $.50 under the low of June 3 = 474.00. STOP LOSS at $.50 over the high for the next four days. Add a 45° line on the fourth day after the close.

Note: On June 4, heliocentric Mercury went into Sagittarius.

Use KRU/KRD, 2DR's or a TL to take a long or a short. (75% of the time that heliocentric Mercury enters Sagittarius, the price of gold goes up; 25% of the time, the price goes down. By using the TL, KR and 2DR when Mercury enters Sagittarius and also when it leaves 11 days later, you can make excellent profits. For example, in trading on Mercury in Sagittarius only since January 1986 to September 1988, the profit would have been $12,950.00 on a one-contract basis!)

On June 15, heliocentric Mercury moves into Capricorn. June 14 gave a KRU. More often than not when Mercury changes into Capricorn, if the price has been moving down, the lowest point will be the day before the change as it was here. If price has been moving up, the highest point will also be the day before the change. Certainly then, if you were just trading the Mercury in Sagittarius phenomenon, you would want to take your profit on the day before Mercury changes signs! Meanwhile, the system we are trading here calls for us to reverse our position June 15 when the price passes the high of the KRU by $.50.

Profit From Trade 6
> June 6: Short at 474.00
> June 15: Out at 461.50 = profit of $1,250.00

TRADE 7
> June 15 = Long at 461.50 at $.50 past KRU of June 14 with a STOP LOSS under the low of the 14th for the next four days.

June 16 looked like a KRD, but the next day did not trade by $.50 under the low of the 16th. Therefore, we are still long. June 17 looked like a 2DRU, which was fine with us since we are long anyway.

On June 20, the Sun is opposing Uranus and Saturn, and a 2DRD forms = a reverse and short.

Loss from Trade 7
> June 15: Long at 461.50
> June 20: Out at 460.00 = loss of $150.00

TRADE 8

On June 18, SELL at 460.00 on the 2DRD. STOP LOSS at $.50 over the high of June 17.

There's no need to add a 45° line here as we have a regular TL in effect off the June 6 high (line E). Price now falls sharply to the June 29 low. The horizontal support line stops the price, and a KRU forms. This occurs on the Full Moon of June 29. The Sun opposes Neptune on June 30, but when Full Moons occur near aspects, the Moon often times the reversal. We are now out of short on June 29 at a close of 443.50.

Profit on Trade 8
> June 18: Short at 460.00
> June 29: Out at 443.50 = profit of $1,650.00

TRADE 9

June 29 = long at 443.50.

We are stopped out of this trade on July 11 at 444.00 as the price trades by more than $.50 under the 45° TL = profit of $50.00.

There are no qualifying aspects now, hence we STAND ASIDE until one presents itself. The next one is on July 19 as Pluto goes direct.

TRADE 10

On July 20, the price closed under resistance line D = Short on the close at 452.00. STOP LOSS above the previous high.

Note: July 25 reveals an extremely large move. My personal rule is: Whenever the price of gold moves more than $1,000.00 per day, take all contracts off except one. This is just good money management. Here we have only one contract on, so we will stay with it.

Now we can also add a long-term regular TL from the high of June 6 to July 21 = TL C. Trading under this indicates that the general trend is down.

On July 26, the price is trading above the horizontal TL A which moves us out of short position.

Profit from Trade 10

July 20: Short at 452.00
July 26: Out at 438.00 = profit of $1,400.00

TRADE 11

July 27 = Long at 439.00 on the aspect of June 28 when the Sun trines Mars along with a Full Moon. STOP LOSS under the low of July 25 for four days. Add 45° TL.

On August 2, the price goes under the 45° TL and HL and knocks out the stop at 437.00 = a Loss on the trade of $200.00. The price does not close by the required $1.00 below the TL; consequently, we cannot put on a short position.

TRADE 12

A close over the TL on August 3 from aspects of the past two days of the Sun square Pluto and Mars square Neptune = Long again at 439.00. On August 5, we are knocked out again under the TL at 436 = Loss of $300.00. No short positions can be initiated now until August 8 when there is a close of over $1.00 under the TL. BUT, this is the third close past the same TL = STAND ASIDE.

Important: The last two weeks have traded around the horizontal trend line. The price has been back and forth over it. Anytime the price stays glued to a TL for a period of time, we have CONGESTION. Most money is lost in congestion. It makes sense, therefore, to stand aside until congestion is over. Rule: After taking a trade on a close over the TL, then taking another on a close under the same line, next time you are stopped out at this line, stand aside. DO NOT initiate any more trades at KR, 2DR, or HL. Take a trade only past new TL's of 12 days or more or past a different TL such as C. These closes must be past the TL by at least $1.00. (When prices trade back and forth over one particular TL, it nullifies it for trading purposes. (It does not nullify the line; obviously, this horizontal line has great power since the price is stuck to it.)

On August 26, the price finally closes under TL F after two attempts to go above the TL C, but it could not close above it by the required $1.00 or more. We are now back in and short.

9 winning trades = profit of	$ 9,750.00
3 losing trades = loss of	$ 650.00
Total profit trading one contract	$ 9,100.00
Total profit trading two contracts	$18,200.00
Total profit trading ten contracts	$91,000.00

JUPITER RETROGRADE AND OTHER GOODIES

The following points pertain to Chart 3 of the DJIA.

1. Notice that the periods of Jupiter in retrograde motion seem to move the market sideways or down. Dates of Jupiter retrograde:

1985: June 4 to October 3
1986: July 12 to November 8
1987: August 19 to December 15
1988: September 24 to January 20, 1989
1989: October 28 to February 24, 1990

You can now see how the highs and lows from the Jupiter retrograde period in 1986 created the support line A to B and the resistance line D to F. These very lines were the net that caught the falling DJIA in October 1987 while Jupiter was again retrograde! Note how on a weekly basis at the time of the crash, the DJIA never closed below the 1986 Jupiter retrograde support line. Also note that the A to C Jupiter line from 1986 has supported the DJIA all of 1988!

2. Remember that the DJIA cannot go up until there is a close above the current resistance line of H to J at around 2200. The DJIA cannot go down without first closing under the current support line A to C at approximately 1900, and secondly under support line D to G near 1750. You can monitor the DJIA within this framework, and at the same time, add any new trend lines that develop. Watch especially closely when planetary aspects form while the DJIA is near the support and resistance lines. This could mean a reversal.

3. Observe the two-week reversal patterns as shown by the arrows. These patterns work on weekly (monthly, yearly) charts in exactly the same way they work on the daily charts.

SUMMARY
Briefly, I have tried to show how profitable Astrotech trading can be. If you take the time and effort to walk through the charts, I think you will appreciate the results. Obviously, the more market and astrological knowledge you have, the easier this will be. To prepare yourself, I

highly recommend a complete study of the entire reading list, and practice, practice, practice! That is the only way to get to Carnegie Hall.

For your further investigation of Astro timing with Technical, I suggest you look at Moving Averages, the Elliott Wave Theory, Fibonacci Retracements and combinations thereof.

Disclaimer

All information given is based on original research methods of Jeanne Long. It is written and shared with sincere and reliable intent. The purpose of the information is to inform and report, not to mislead. Although these methods have proved reliable in the past, there can be, and therefore is, NO guarantee they will work in the future. Therefore, neither the author, the publisher or any other persons connected with this writing assumes any responsibility whatsoever for the readers' activities in the markets. Any such activity must solely be the responsibility of that person alone who chooses to be active in the markets.

References

Suggested Reading List

Drummond, Charles. *How to Make Money in the Futures Markets, & Lots of It.* Ontario, Canada, 1979.

Long, Jeanne. *Astrotech.* Fort Lauderdale, FL: Professional Astrology Service, Inc., 1988.

McLaren, William with Matthew J. Foreman. *Gann Made Easy.* Overland Park, KS: Gann Theory Publishing Co., 1988.

March, Marion and Joan McEvers. *The Only Way to . . . Learn Astrology.* Vols. I-IV. San Diego, CA: ACS Publications, Inc., 1981-1988.

Merriman, Raymond. *The Gold Book: Geocosmic Correlations to Gold Price Cycles.* Birmingham, MI: Seek-It Publications, 1982.

Michelson, Neil. *The American Ephemeris for the 20th Century.* San Diego, CA: ACS Publications, Inc., 1980.

Murphy, John J. *Technical Analysis of the Futures Markets.* New York: NYIF Corp., 1986.

Powers, Mark J. *Getting Started in the Futures Market.* Brightwaters, NY: Windsor Books.

Computer Programs and Services

Astro Computing Services, P.O. Box 34487, San Diego, CA 92108.

Astrotech Trading Programs. Available spring 1989. Professional Astrology Service, Inc., 2215 South Federal Hwy., #22, Fort Lauderdale, FL 33316.

NOVA: Astrological Program and *Astro Analyst Market Program.* Available from: P.O. Box 28, Orleans, MA 02653.

Georgia Stathis

Georgia Stathis received her Bachelor of Science degree from Northwestern University in 1970 where she majored in Speech and Theater. In 1978 she received her M.B.A. from Pepperdine University in Malibu, California.

After settling in California in 1971, she worked in public relations in San Francisco and handled major as well as campaign accounts. During the following years, she pursued the sales profession in advertising and real estate.

From 1971, she was actively involved in astrology. While she was pursuing her degree, she began counseling individuals and small businesses with a strong emphasis on business and investment.

Since April of 1977, she has been a full-time professional astrologer and lecturer. She is a member of The National Speakers Association. She has appeared on KSFO radio and has written for several publications as well as having her own column "Sign of the Times" in *Aquarius Rising* newspaper.

THE REAL ESTATE PROCESS

It has been said that the base of all wealth is real estate. As we look at the horoscope, this stands out visibly. The condition of wealth suggests many things—much money or property, abundance and well-being. The ability to process, purchase, sell, and develop pieces of property, as well as indicators of being in the real estate profession itself, are all seen in the horoscope. This process uses both masculine and feminine energy. Such energy is found in the chart, and all the planets are involved in this process.

The masculine planets are the Sun, Mars, Jupiter and Uranus. Feminine planets are the Moon, Venus, Saturn, Neptune, and Pluto. Mercury, the planet that rules agents, communication, contracts, and sales, has no particular male or female affinity.

The natural Cancer 4th House, which usually depicts the early home life and family, is ruled by the **Moon**, the designated ruler of property. Moving vertically towards the top of this natural axis, we find Capricorn, the natural 10th House sign, ruled by Saturn. **Saturn** is the designated ruler of real estate. It is an appropriate choice for real estate since *real estate* is defined in the dictionary as land, including the buildings and improvements on it, and its natural assets, such as minerals, water, petroleum, etc.

Saturn is the outward structural manifestation of the lunar (Moon) principle of containment. Both the Moon and Saturn are feminine, but they operate in different ways. The

Moon is the more conceptual of the two planets—it incubates, it reigns over fertile territory, it is movable and mobile (*i.e.* watery). Saturn is more finite, structured and concrete.

NODES

The Moon's Nodes transit through one complete cycle in about 18.3 years. The real estate industry calls this the Brenner cycle. Astrologers call it the Nodal Cycle. It is important to remember that the nodes are points formed from the intersection of the ecliptic of the Earth and the Moon and have to do with the public pulse. The Moon relates to public response.

When the North Node is in Cancer for approximately one and a half years, generally prices are high along with interest rates. The demand for property escalates, and there is a larger inventory of available homes. Cancer rules property, and the North Node shows abundance. As the node moves backward toward Capricorn (approximately nine years later), interest rates, prices and activity decline. Inventory of available housing is low. Witness the burgeoning homeless and less and less available and affordable housing.

The most recent example of how this works was when the North Node moved into Cancer in late fall of 1981 and interest rates were 20%+. At this time, many real estate agents left the industry; there was a correction in activity. This was also the beginning of the Republican administration and Reaganomics!

As the North Node moves closer and closer to Capricorn, if cash is available it is a good time to buy property and hold it for future investment. When the North Node is in Cancer, it is a good time to liquidate since people tend to pay higher prices for property and are willing to pay the high interest.

When Jupiter is in Cancer (property), Capricorn (real

estate), Scorpio or Taurus (the natural 8th and 2nd House signs), activity is high and people are willing to pay higher prices. The same is true when Jupiter conjuncts, trines or sextiles the North Node. There might be more activity since the public feels pushed to buy and act.

The converse is true if Saturn is aspecting the North Node. Activity may decline and fear may intercede and prevent the public from buying unless, of course, they have cash and can purchase at an excellent price or pick up distressed property (*i.e.* foreclosures).

In times when the North Node is in Capricorn or there is a strong Saturn influence, there is a possibility that properties will be available from the banks at a good price because they have gone into foreclosure.

TRANSACTIONS

Real estate transactions require the use of both masculine and feminine energies. After a period of incubation, the buyer of property—particularly residential property—has to look at several economic factors as to the feasibility of a real estate purchase.

Is there enough income to support the purchase? Where will work be available? Are the schools the right ones for the children? Upon deciding this, a real estate professional is engaged. The qualified agent must possess both assertive and receptive qualities. He or she must know his or her property inventory (a 6th House matter), the market, prices, and existing interest rates. Both sides of the brain are used: the logical, rational left-brain which is called the masculine side of the brain, and the right-brained intuitive, feminine function. (Both men and women have equal access to either the left or right brain.)

The intuitive ability is primarily a right-brained, feminine activity. The agent must know which questions to ask about income, outstanding debts, and how many bedrooms, baths, etc., the buyer requires. This is called the **probe**—a Pluto process.

The search begins and masculine Mars is engaged. Much time is spent moving about from one property to the next in an automobile. Interesting point—automobiles are ruled by Mars and are an integral part of real estate sales. (*Ed. Note*: We feel Mercury and the 3rd House have some jurisdiction over cars since they represent means of transportation.)

The agent must know when and how to close the deal so that when s/he finds a property that is best suited to the buyer and the buyer's qualifications, s/he must ask the question "Do you want to buy this property?" This process has a true Mars orientation!

Ultimately, however, the final decision about a piece of property is *not* logical but a gut-level response. The intuitive mode comes into play after the decision is made and the numbers and closing costs are calculated and taken into consideration. Thus the end result is intuitive. Remember, the Moon rules property: it represents the feminine and quite often it is the more receptive, intuitive members of the family who make the final decision about the property.

The neutral Mercury principle then blends in as escrows are opened and/or lawyers are consulted. (On the East Coast, attorneys generally process the transaction, whereas on the West Coast, the processing of a transaction takes place through a title company and its escrow department.)

THE PLANETS AND REAL ESTATE

The **Sun** usually represents speculative matters and conditions that represent some type of gamble due to its relationship to the 5th House. If the Sun is prominent and well placed by natal position or well aspected by transit, then the time might be appropriate to take a "gamble" on a piece of property.

The **Moon** reflects how you are seen by the public. If, for example, the Moon is in the 10th House at birth, the public might see you as one who deals in property, particularly if the Moon also rules the natal 4th House.

Even the progressed secondary Moon has a great bearing on moves and home changes in some capacity. The other progressions are also significant, but you primarily use the progressed secondary Moon because it moves so rapidly and it aspects the natal chart frequently. Particularly watch when the secondary Moon moves from one sign to the next. This often indicates a change in residence or the home situation. A progression moving over one of the angles can also trigger a move.

Aspects to the Moon may move you, change the way your home might look or create an emotional explosion or change in the home. The Moon may involve one particular property—occupied or leased—while Saturn can involve several properties as well as the sale, purchase or development of property.

Mercury, the fastest moving planet and the one closest to the Sun, rules communications, sales and written legal agreements—contracts. A successful transaction must have a well-placed Mercury. Individuals who do well in sales transactions usually have Mercury well-aspected.

If there are negative aspects to Mercury, the contract may be difficult to negotiate. For example, if transiting Mercury is opposing or squaring natal Jupiter or even transiting Jupiter, then you may pay too much for the property. Your judgment might be off. If Mercury is square transiting or natal Saturn, you may worry yourself needlessly concerning this particular real estate matter, no matter how long you own it! The other manifestation of Mercury square Saturn might be that something was forgotten in the contract at the time of its writing.

A good time to sign a contract is when either the Moon

(property) or Saturn (real estate) is well aspected by Mercury through a trine or a sextile. Always look at both the natal and the transiting planets and how they interact with each other.

If the Moon or Mercury is void of course at the time of the sale, the sale might not complete. When the move is scheduled, watch for challenging aspects to Mercury, particularly from Neptune or Jupiter, as there may be a tremendous disorientation.

Much has been said about *Mercury retrograde periods*, and they do have an effect on real estate transactions. If a new contract comes in during such a time, there may be a problem with finalizing the sale or purchase. Sometimes a particular word or paragraph is inadvertently left out when the contract is written. At other times, the intention of the purchaser to purchase may be based on some type of financial assistance from family or friends. When Mercury moves into direct motion, the missing paragraph is discovered or the funding is no longer available.

Mercury retrogrades approximately three times a year for about three weeks at a time. This is an excellent time to wrap up details in a contract or an escrow and uncover any problems about the property. One way Mercury retrograde "works" in a real estate transaction is perhaps the property was viewed prior to the retrograde, but the buyer or seller was not necessarily sure this was what he or she wanted. In presenting the offer, precautions still need to be exercised, but sometimes if care is taken this will work out during a Mercury retrograde period.

Even if Mercury is well aspected at the time of the retrograde, there could still be a delay in the transaction. Watch the degree and minute at which Mercury begins its retrograde motion. Watch when it returns to the direct position. Particularly watch when it returns to the original "shadow" position—the same degree and minute at which it went retrograde. This is when any differences or problems are usually resolved.

Venus, the natural ruler of the 2nd and 7th Houses, governs money, cash flow, legal papers, and contracts. If Venus is well placed, it often indicates a natural ability to make things happen, particularly if it is well aspected at the time of a transaction in either the natal or event chart. If it is moving in retrograde motion, it may indicate either a delay in receiving funds or an inability to get the funds necessary for a purchase. Luckily, Venus only retrogrades about once every two years for about six weeks. When it does, however, you must be cautious because the purchase you decide on may not be entirely appropriate to your needs, or the buyer or seller might change his or her mind. Venus retrograde may also indicate that you settle for less than you really want.

Mars is the planet that triggers the gun. The entire sky can be set up for action, but action only occurs when Mars comes along and sets it off. Where Mars is placed in the event chart is where stress will be experienced or where action takes place. For example, if it is placed in the 1st House of the chart, the seller might be agitated. Placed in the 4th House, the final outcome, the deal might not close or there may be trouble with the structure or the plumbing. Placed in the 2nd House of cash flow and resources, there could be difficulty in raising the capital to purchase the property.

This is not to say that wherever Mars is placed, you will find trouble. The other side of Mars' energy is that of courage and confidence. Mars placements in the chart may indicate areas in which you keep your nose to the grindstone.

Mars in the 2nd House, while it can indicate difficulty in getting funds, may also indicate your all-out effort to pursue and obtain those funds for a successful completion of purchase.

In a horary chart, if a question is asked about signing a contract and the Moon's last aspect was to Mars, some feel it is not a good time to close. If transiting Saturn is squaring Mars, people might easily be upset or angered.

Jupiter well-aspected to the 4th House ruler or placed in the 4th House of the horoscope can indicate luck in real estate matters. If this is found in a chart for a transaction, it might indicate a successful consummation of the deal. If transiting Jupiter is positively aspecting natal Saturn or the ruler of the 4th House, it often indicates a positive move in a real estate transaction.

Jupiter in flowing aspect to the Sun or Moon often indicates a positive outcome for a transaction. With the Moon (property) and Mercury (contracts) well-aspected, it is an indication of a good contract—a good buy. Mercury rules sales, so if Jupiter is in negative aspect to Mercury, you should check to see that you are not paying too much for the property.

Saturn was mentioned earlier as the ruler of real estate. It invariably takes an aspect to Saturn to purchase or let go of real estate or to enter a career in the building or real estate industry.

Positive aspects by transit or natally between Saturn and Jupiter indicate positive real estate potential. Transiting Jupiter conjuncting, trining or sextiling Saturn indicates great times for property purchase.

Prior to telescopes and the discovery of the outer planets, Saturn was also assigned the rulership of Aquarius. In modern times the rulership of Aquarius has been given to Uranus. **Uranus** also has its place in the delineation of real estate matters. It rules the "big dealers": subdivisions, developments, commercial property, REITS (real estate investment trusts) and leasing specialists, particularly if strong Pluto energy is also indicated.

Uranus prominent in the horoscope indicates an individual who has the ability to put together, in an innovative way, groups of people who collaborate on large real estate projects and work with syndications. Transiting Jupiter conjuncting, trining, or sextiling Uranus could indicate a very lucky, almost windfall-like possibility for any large project, development or leasing.

Neptune has had a lot of bad press concerning financial transactions. It may show confused judgment, misinformation and looking at deals through rose-colored glasses, particularly if it is poorly aspected by transit at the time of the transaction. A property may be overinflated price-wise, or you as the purchaser may misjudge what you can afford to pay. You could purchase at a time when things are beyond your current means.

The positive side of Neptune is the ability to visualize the potential in a property and to realize your vision. In a lecture about the pre-natal eclipse, Buz Meyers talks about Neptune/Pisces energy. He states that the nature of this energy is to act as a bridge and to reprocess negative into positive. A strong Neptune placement well-aspected natally or by transit can give those involved in the transaction insight into how to improve the property, but favorable aspects to Saturn or Pluto must also be operating. Transiting Jupiter positively aspecting Neptune can help you realize your vision and aid in your inspiration.

A prominent **Pluto** might indicate a talent in renovating large shopping centers or building complexes that need refurbishing before they exhibit profitability.

Strong aspects to Uranus or Pluto can indicate the development or transformation of pieces of property. Strong, positive aspects to Pluto by itself may also enhance the ability to acquire loans and funding. The converse is also true. If there are negative aspects to Pluto, you may miss out on the opportunity to acquire funds or even have to declare bankruptcy if other factors in the horoscope confirm this.

THE HOUSES

In defining the houses, both the natal horoscope and the event chart can be used. The time to set up a chart for the real estate transaction, the event, can be found on the final contract. When a transaction is consummated, the date and time are recorded next to the signatures of the purchasers and the sellers. At that moment, the **event chart** can be erected.

The **1st House** represents the seller—how he or she sees the transaction and how others see him or her.

The **2nd House** is the immediate cash at hand—the cash flow. It also represents other resources that are available in a transaction in other property for trade; tangible assets like valued stones, furniture, refrigerators can be compensation for a transaction.

The **3rd House** represents the signing of the contract, the communication in the transaction. Negatively it shows the loss of property (the 12th House from the natal 4th).

The **4th House** represents the property itself as well as how one deals with it. It also indicates vacant property and property damage particularly in the plumbing. In corporation charts it represents warehouses and factories held by a company. As in horary astrology, the 4th House can also indicate the outcome of the event.

Many planets in your 4th House often suggest that real estate might be a suitable choice for your profession or that you could profit from real estate holdings. This is particularly true if natal Pluto is placed here and is well aspected.

Traditionally, the **5th House** signifies speculation or taking a gamble on property. It is also an indicator of income from real estate (the 2nd from the 4th House). Sometimes recreational property is suggested by this house or income from recreational property.

For example, a man was part owner of a duck club, and

the income generated from the club plus the pleasure the individual received from going to his "investment" was a perfect combination of how this house works. When transiting Jupiter passed through his natal 5th House, the government offered to pay his group for NOT planting rice, which many clubs grow to attract the ducks, at which point they turned around and sold the surplus rice for profit!

The **6th House** of the chart reveals the agent, the tenants in a leasing situation, income property and the logistics of the real estate contract.

The **7th House** is simply the buyer of the property. It can also designate legal contracts.

The **8th House** represents the estate, a will, a settlement, or a business or marriage partnership's assets (the 2nd from the 7th). It depicts the joint holdings of a couple or a business partnership. In an individual's chart, it also indicates whether there is positive or negative financial support from the partner as well as inheritance possibilities. It can define the qualities of the mortgage, the interest rates, and the insurances required. Probate is represented by the 8th as well as the escrow itself, which includes the title search.

Taxes are also an important part of real estate transactions, and anything related to taxes comes from the 8th House. Jupiter in this house or Sagittarius on this cusp can indicate luck in investment matters with a partner, inheritance, or investments that prosper. So can Venus in or ruling this house.

The **9th House** shows the money that comes from an estate or settlement as well as the caretaking and any legal situations surrounding property.

The **10th House** indicates landowners, landlords, land developers, land dealers, and land in general.

The **11th House** designates money that comes from the individual's business or career, the treasury, and it can

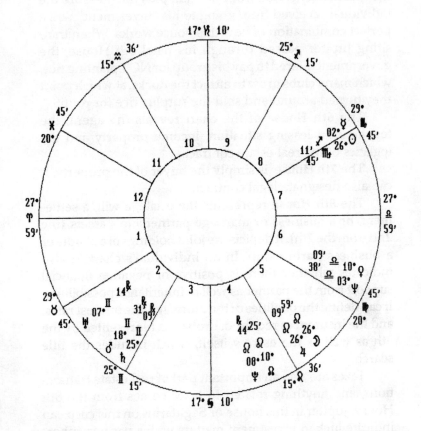

Natal Chart A
November 19, 1943   4:15 PM PWT
34N04   118W15
Los Angeles, California

Koch Houses

also indicate, if negatively aspected, the loss of property. Sometimes loss is also assigned to the 12th House.

The **12th House** denotes property in foreign countries (in the Hindu system, the 12th is the house of gestation and foreigners), or it can indicate the end of a situation.

RULERSHIPS, TRANSITS, AND DELINEATION

One of the most important delineation devices that can be used when interpreting a horoscope is to observe the planets, the houses they rule and the house in which they are placed. This is particularly true concerning real estate matters. Transits to these points set the wheels in motion.

The following are some case studies that demonstrate this concept. All charts shown in this article use the Koch House system. The first chart presents a way to interpret a real estate event. This person (Chart A) is a woman born November 19, 1943, at 4:15 P.M. Pacific War Time in Los Angeles, California.

For several years she has been a manufacturers' representative for various furniture lines. Energetic and industrious, she decided two and a half years before the following event that she wanted to purchase old properties, then gut and refurbish them. This is an excellent choice with natal Pluto in the 4th House sextile Venus and Uranus, indicating an uncanny ability to work hard (Venus in the 6th) and fix property, turning it around to make it financially profitable (Uranus in the 2nd). The high degree of the Fire element in her chart gives her the much-needed physical stamina required to refurbish.

In 1987 she purchased a huge, older home with a large amount of square footage, tremendous character and true potential. Note her Leo Moon which loves elegance.

For one year, she and a friend tore down walls, tore out floors, refinished, repainted, restored, and built new decks.

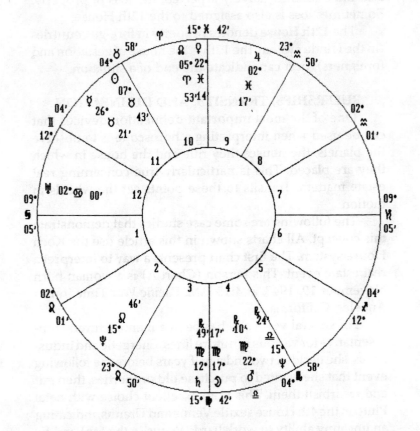

Natal Chart B
April 28, 1950   9:16 AM EST
42N30   83W09
Royal Oak, Michigan

Koch Houses

The home turned out to be an exquisite piece of art, which she had truly produced with love and her own hands. Note Moon (property and ruler of her 4th) conjunct Jupiter (luck) in the 5th House of artistic ability.

Even though she had purchased her materials wholesale, did the work herself and budgeted carefully, she found herself needing funds at the end of this incredible project and was prompted to sell the property. However, her heart was not really in it.

An offer came in at the time transiting Venus, her 2nd and 7th House ruler, was just turning retrograde. A few weeks later, Mercury went retrograde; both Venus and Mercury were in Gemini.

When Venus had just begun retrograde motion, she had second thoughts about selling the property, but this was shortly after she had accepted an offer. (Venus rules the 7th House, representative of the buyer.)

When I looked at her horoscope, I told her I felt that the buyer was going to ask for some type of change in the contract when Mercury (contracts) also turned retrograde. This would, of course, void the original contract, allowing her to back out of her legal obligation and keep the property. The buyer did indeed come back with a demand for an additional $6500 off the selling price. This, of course, changed the contract, and she finally said in a letter to me a few weeks later, "Sometimes you have to come close to losing something before you can decide to commit to it!" This was an appropriate Scorpio/Pluto response.

Another way to look at this transaction was to see whether the 4th House, her property, was stronger at the time of the contract than the 7th, representative of the buyer. If the 4th House is stronger at the time of a transaction, one often keeps the property.

Another woman whose birth date is April 28, 1950, at 9:16 A.M. Eastern Standard Time in Royal Oak, Michigan (see Chart B) was involved in the following transaction. Note the loaded 4th House with Saturn, the Moon (the chart ruler) and Mars in Virgo and Neptune in Libra. When transiting Uranus opposed her natal Uranus and natal Saturn in early 1988, she suddenly inherited a house from a friend who had died. Uranus often rules windfall opportunities. When Jupiter transited over her natal Mercury in Taurus (ruler of her 4th House of real estate), title was transferred to her, and she could either move into the house or choose to allow the current renter to stay there until the end of that year.

Because the client also happened to be a pilot and her schedule was very involved, she chose to delay the move until January of 1989 when transiting Jupiter would turn stationary direct at about 26 degrees of Taurus. Again, this was quite close to her Mercury at 26 degrees Taurus, the ruler of her 4th House of property.

This seemed to be the more appropriate date because there was an exact Lunar Eclipse on her Moon at 17 degrees Virgo on September 10, 1988.

When an eclipse hits a planet at an exact degree in the natal horoscope and in a certain area of the chart, there is sometimes change around that area and the house the planet rules. As noted earlier, the Moon signifies the property or the home. The change occurs either within a few days of the eclipse, or change can occur about 90 to 100 days later (about 90 degrees), or when the first square aspect by transit hits the point of the eclipse. It may also trigger off an event about six months after the eclipse.

In her case, it felt like it would be three to four months later or at the beginning of 1989. Looking at her secondary progressions for July 1, 1988, her progressed secondary Moon (the ruler of her chart as well as the assigned ruler of the home and property) was at 24 degrees Aquarius. Since the progressed secondary Moon moves at about one degree per month, six months equals six degrees, so when the progressed Moon moved into Pisces it suggested the intended move.

In the case of the progression, if the progressed Moon is changing signs, there is usually a move or a change in the way the home looks or, literally, a change in the structure of the home at the time it shifts energy or signs.

At the time this woman sought out advice, the transiting North Node in Pisces was traveling through her 10th House and soon would enter her 9th.

The transiting South Node in Virgo was moving through her natal 4th House. She had started her Uranus opposition. Note her natal Uranus at two degrees Cancer in the 12th House. Uranus rules Aquarius, and this is the sign in her 8th House of investments and inheritance.

When Uranus opposes Uranus at about age 38 or 39, the individual awakens to the soul's purpose, and often new and bigger opportunities can be presented.

Since Uranus rules her 8th House, the transiting opposition was already signaling thoughts of investing, transforming property, and then leasing or selling, thereby profiting for her future retirement security. This is an excellent example of positive use of Uranus transits. Since Uranus is the "antenna," when experiencing Uranus transits, there is a need to visualize them in a positive light. Many things fall into place in life when visions are followed.

Since Uranus can denote sudden, unexpected windfalls, receiving this piece of property quite unexpectedly was quite remarkable. Her instinct was operating on a higher level. She manifested what she envisioned!

REAL ESTATE VOCATIONAL INDICATORS
The following are charts of individuals involved in the profession of real estate in different positions. Included are

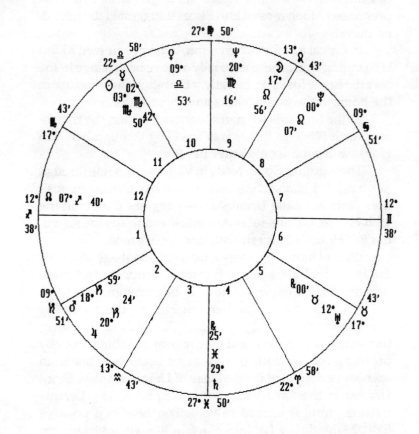

Natal Chart C
October 27, 1937   10:17 AM CST
35N13   101W50
Amarillo, Texas

Koch Houses

a manager who started out as an agent, an investor who is still an agent, a real estate marketing expert, and two people who work with subdivisions—one sells and one owns and sells.

The first example is a woman born Oct. 27, 1937, 10:17 A.M. Central Standard Time, in Amarillo, Texas (see Chart C). Her Ascendant is Sagittarius, ruled by Jupiter, an excellent rising sign for people in the sales profession. She has natal Saturn (ruler of real estate) in her 4th House. This placement seems to be fairly common in the real estate profession since Saturn rules real estate, but it also rules any career or profession. Most of her 4th House is Aries, ruled by Mars which falls in her 2nd House of cash flow, earned income and money. It conjuncts Jupiter, her chart ruler. She was a high-powered agent when she first began her career. Venus, the ruler of money and funds, falls in her 10th House of career; it is also the ruler of her 6th House of work. This is another indicator of professional involvement in tangible assets.

Notice the high concentration of Earth and Water elements in this chart. The Earth planets form a Grand Trine, and Saturn opposes Venus, another indicator of a structured profession. This opposition indicates someone who can manage quite unemotionally but effectively. She can also persuade people to cooperate with her because Venus falls in the 10th House of how the public sees her. She is viewed as structured and effective and is also well liked.

Chart D is of a man who is both an agent and an investor, but not a broker. He was born June 19, 1941, at 8:58 P.M. Pacific Standard Time in Berkeley, California. In the early '40s Saturn and Uranus were conjunct in Taurus, which is ruled by Venus, along with Jupiter in Gemini. There is a strong Earth concentration in this chart, particularly in the 4th House of property. His Ascendant is Capricorn, ruled

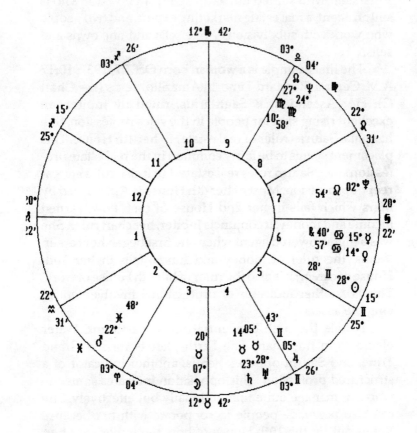

Natal Chart D
June 19, 1941   8:58 PM PST
37N52   122W16
Berkeley, California

Koch Houses

by Saturn, which also falls in his 4th House. Land, property and real estate are a very integral part of his life. Since Uranus is also in his 4th, forming a Grand Earth Trine with the Ascendant and Neptune in the 8th House of investments, this indicates excellent intuition about money and property matters.

Natal Jupiter in the 5th House of speculation rules both Sagittarius and Pisces. Pisces is intercepted in his 2nd House of cash flow. His Moon is also in Taurus. The Moon rules property, but in his chart it also rules his 7th House of how he deals with other people. It is placed in his 3rd House of communication/sales.

The Sun in Gemini, the sign of communication, Mercury, the planet of sales, and Venus, ruler of money, are all placed in the 6th House of service and work. He operates in a service profession which involves a tremendous amount of detail work (6th House), but he is also an agent. The 6th signifies the agent and also income property. He and his family own income property that they lease. Note the Uranus placement (leasing) in the 4th House of both real estate and family.

As mentioned earlier, Uranus also rules the big deals and the developers. At the time that Jupiter transited through his 4th House, his family decided to invest in a very large piece of property that needed subdividing. As of this writing, the transaction is still continuing and should complete about January 1989, when transiting Jupiter goes direct at 26 degrees of Taurus, the exact midpoint of his Saturn/ Uranus conjunction.

A woman born December 31, 1937, at 8 P.M. Pacific Standard Time in Portland, Oregon (see Chart E) is a marketing expert. Note the high concentration of planets in her 9th House of professional sales people and marketing. Her 4th House cusp is Cancer (property), and her 10th House cusp is Capricorn. She is a real estate marketing expert for a

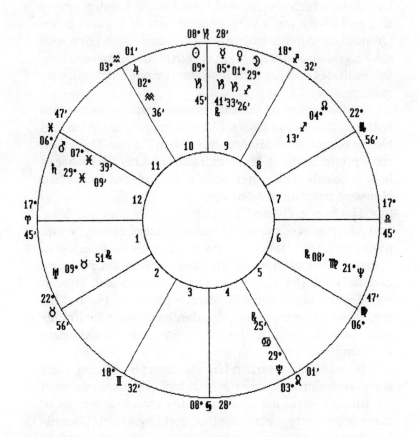

Natal Chart E
December 31, 1937   12:08 PM PST
45N32   122W37
Portland, Oregon

Koch Houses

very large developer. Uranus is in the 1st House in Taurus. Venus, which rules her 2nd House, is conjunct Mercury in the 9th House of marketing. She is able to communicate effectively and promote sales. Venus, Mercury, and the Sun in Capricorn all trine Uranus in Taurus—excellent aspects for big projects.

On a more personal note, she has natal Pluto in her 4th House in Cancer. She has bought and sold a lot of property. Each time she sells her property she profits. She refurbishes each property herself (Aries rising) through painting, building decks, and reconstructing rooms. The refurbishing offers her a tremendous amount of profit over a fairly short period of time.

Natal Pluto trines Saturn—an excellent aspect for making money with real estate, particularly since Pluto rules Scorpio, her 8th House of investments.

Chart F is of a young woman born July 31, 1952, at 11:17 P.M. at Whittier, California, who sells subdivisions. Note her Aries Ascendant with the ruler Mars in the 7th House of buyers trining her natal Uranus which rules subdivisions. Uranus is angular in her 4th House in Cancer, the sign representative of property. Her Sun is in Leo and is also in her 4th. Leo is on the cusp of her 5th House of speculation and also takes up some space in her 4th.

The property signs Cancer and Capricorn are on the 4th and 10th House cusps, respectively. The rulers, the Moon and Saturn, are sextile. The Moon is in the 8th House of other peoples' monies, and Saturn is in the 6th House of the agent conjunct Neptune. She helps people to achieve their vision.

A potent Jupiter is one indicator of strong sales abilities. It is in her 1st House and has challenging squares to Venus, Pluto and widely to Mercury, all in Leo in the speculative 5th House.

One of the future ventures she is considering is specu-

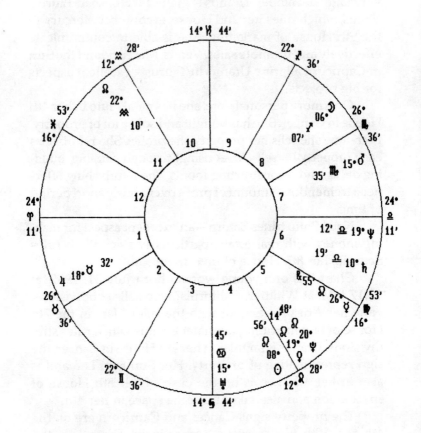

Natal Chart F
July 31, 1952   11:17 PM PDT
33N58   118W03
Whittier, California

Koch Houses

lating on recreational property, buying properties that need work, fixing them and using them as healing and health facilities. Note the above-mentioned concentration of Leo planets in the 5th House of speculation, fun and recreation. Note also the wide Saturn conjunction to natal Neptune in the 6th House. She has a strong interest in healing, and when transiting Saturn and Neptune conjunct in 1989 and 1990, her 6th House may be activated for the first time since birth so that she can integrate her investment knowledge with her healing interests.

The last chart is that of a woman born September 18, 1934, at 7:45 A.M. Central Standard Time in San Antonio, Texas (see Chart G). She sells subdivisions, but also OWNS them. Libra is rising, again giving Cancer/Capricorn 10th/4th House cusps. This time the cusps are reversed with Cancer on the 10th and Capricorn on the 4th. The ruler of her 10th, the Moon in Capricorn, is in her 4th House of real estate. The trine between the Moon and the Sun suggests fortunate speculation.

The ruler of her chart is Venus, and it trines natal Uranus, indicator of subdivisions, again angular. Saturn, the ruler of real estate and her 4th House, is in Aquarius in the 5th House of speculation. Saturn forms a trine to natal Jupiter in Libra in the 1st House—an excellent combination for success in real estate. Jupiter again is placed in the 1st House of the seller. So is Mercury, indicative of communication and sales ability.

She too has an angular Pluto in Cancer in the 10th House of career. She is a very powerful woman in the eyes of the public (10th House) and also very aggressive—note the angular Mars, ruler of her 7th House of buyers. Mars represents buyers and contracts in her chart and sextiles her natal Mercury, ruler of communications and contracts—an excellent configuration for successful consummation of transactions.

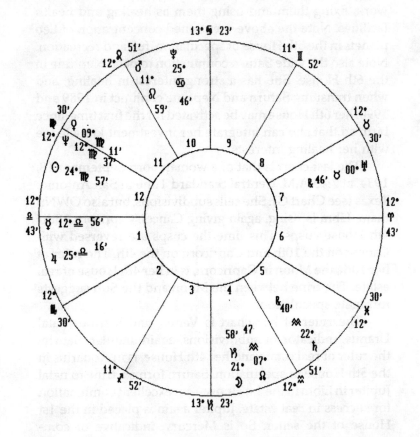

Natal Chart G
September 18, 1934   7:45 AM CST
29N25   98W30
San Antonio, Texas

Koch Houses

These are just a few examples of charts of people in various levels of the real estate industry and are presented here as an example of how to discover vocational potential in this particular industry.

LONG-TERM PROJECTIONS
FOR THE REAL ESTATE INDUSTRY

The outer planets (Uranus, Neptune and Pluto) are beyond physical sight and have much to do with future and outer trends in various industries. They are beyond the beyond, and for this reason we look at them as particular markers in the road for future change.

For example, in the last few years there have been a series of different synodic cycles particularly involving the planet Saturn, the ruler of real estate. By synodic, we mean rare line-ups of the outlying planets that only occur once every so many years. In 1981, Saturn and Jupiter lined up in Libra; in 1982, Saturn lined up with Pluto also in Libra; and in 1988, Saturn conjuncted Uranus three different times in Sagittarius and Capricorn. As we move into the late '80s and early '90s, Saturn will be conjuncting Neptune in Capricorn.

When Saturn conjuncted Jupiter in the early '80s, interest rates and property values went out of sight in terms of affordability, and since Jupiter can sometimes represent the sales profession, many real estate agents fled, weeding out the industry! The same was true in the following years as banks tightened their belts and loans for property ended up being as difficult to obtain as water in the desert.

Whenever Saturn conjuncts Uranus, major changes occur in the real estate industry; this occurred during the early 1940s when they were conjunct in Taurus. During that period in history, we saw some marvelous new ways of looking at housing. Contractors moved from building one home at a time to building tract housing to accommodate the influx of the post-war population.

Saturn also rules the elderly, and it is quite conceivable that there will be some revolutionary new housing approaches for the elderly with Saturn conjuncting Uranus. Around the end of 1986, there were even some newspaper articles that spoke about "theme parks" where the elderly might live! Part of the requirement of living in a "Wild West" park or a "Tudor Manor" park was to contribute some time and energy to community involvement as part of the payment to live in such an adult-oriented "fantasy" kind of place. (There was an article in the *San Francisco Examiner* in December of 1986 about this issue.) How appropriate since Uranus rules innovation—invention—"find a need and fill it." Saturn rules real esate, Uranus multiples.

Since the Saturn/Uranus conjunction in the early 1940s was in Taurus and Gemini, we not only saw tract housing developing at that time but a brand new idea that would improve travel—the interstate highway system. It was developed to accommodate the growing population.

Now we are in a new cycle of Saturn conjuncting Uranus in late Sagittarius/early Capricorn, which suggests some major changes in the real estate industry itself and in the loan industry. Negative amortization and adjustable mortgages are just some of the new financing methods available for real estate purchases.

In the industry itself, there is more and more need for "official education." For years there has been talk of making a real estate license a four-year degree and grandfathering in those agents who already have licenses.

The paperwork involved in real estate transactions has become so complicated that it easily compares to the paperwork required of a qualified attorney. In California, future real estate agents are now required to have 18 hours of college credit in order to take the real estate licensing exam. Typically, this has happened quite suddenly with 1988's conjunction of Saturn and Uranus in Sagittarius, which rules education.

Since Uranus, the planet of innovation, is involved in this conjunction, the education required is somewhat different from conventional education. The idea of an advanced bachelor or master's degree in real estate is not as inconceivable as it has sounded in the past. Imagine a master's thesis on the subject!

Since Uranus rules commissions, one of the things we could be seeing is a massive change in the commission structure in the industry. Most companies carry errors and omission insurance for their agents so that if there is any conflict at all the company as well as the agent are protected. For this, the broker usually takes half of the commission on one side or the other of the transaction. The commissions are negotiable, but generally speaking the agent receives roughly a one-quarter division of the total commission. The possibility of giving the real estate agent a larger piece of the pie along with more of the responsibility is a possibility in real estate companies in the coming years. More and more agents may even begin to charge a per hour fee for the information they now give free in order to make a sale. Remember, Uranus rules public information, consulting and commissions!

Uranus also rules awakening, invention, and revolutionary new ways of doing things, and with Saturn, which also rules construction, conjuncting it, we should be seeing new materials that are more easily put together and more durable.

Uranus also has an affinity with computers and electronics, and the entire industry has been on computers for many years, but now local boards of realtors are making it possible for an agent who is a member to hook up to the main computer line at the board and bring that information into the agent's home via a modem in a home computer.

This allows more freedom so that the agent can have more flexibility in the business! Along with this idea, we see more and more car phones being installed in agents' automobiles so that time is not wasted while on the road.

Even the signs that are posted in front of a residence to announce that it is available for sale are changing. There are now some "drive by" signs that are on a radio frequency, and an agent driving by in his or her car with the necessary equipment can immediately hook up to that sign and get the details about this particular piece of property!

Small portable computers are being presented to the real estate industry and its participants so that if a salesperson is on the road s/he has accessibility to information and net sheets, closing costs, and loans and interest information. A new real estate agent entering the industry is being challenged in quite a different way. In many areas, the agent is now required to input all the new sales data directly into the computer in the office, which in turn connects to the main computer bank, making the information instantly available to the entire real estate community.

In the past in Northern California Boards, there has been what they call a "DAILY HOT SHEET" that has come out listing the properties available in the last 24-hour period. This precludes the weekly basis, but the large Multiple Listing Services books continue to be published. This practice was recently disbanded, and now an agent can directly access into the main bank computer with the latest available data. This requires that a real estate agent learn different skills involving the ability to work with equipment and input information.

The industry is becoming more and more computerized, and it is foreseeable that in the next seven years with Uranus in Capricorn computer hookups may occur between states. This would be an ingenious setup because more and more states are honoring the real estate licenses from other states, especially if their current residents hold licenses from California.

The statute is called the Non-resident Reciprocity Statute. The states of Washington (Scorpio), Florida (Pisces), Alabama (Sagittarius), and Alaska (Capricorn) now allow California licenses for their state residents. It would be interesting to see which of the other states that have early Capricorn energies in their charts hop onto this computerized bandwagon.

The above statute might imply that an agent or buyer could travel from one state to the next looking for investments and then hook into the main computer information center for available properties, doing business anywhere in the USA. We could be looking at a global real estate market!

Mary B. Downing

Mary B. Downing is equal parts astrologer and designer/ advertising/public relations consultant, a combination she feels to be totally synergistic. "Astrology is *the great tool* for understanding and using the cyclic nature of our environment. It enables one to meet life with a minimum of wheel-spinning, and *it applies to everything*."

Her approach to financial investments is flavored by her experiences as business/marketing consultant, fellow investor, and long-range cycles researcher. Her approach to astrology is thoroughly pragmatic. She selects the most efficient tools for a specific job.

She is the Executive Secretary of NCGR, the National Council for Geocosmic Research, and a principal of Mercury House, Inc. She resides in Stamford, Connecticut.

AN INVESTOR'S GUIDE
TO FINANCIAL ASTROLOGY

Analyzing market realities is unfortunately more complex than the simple delineation of a natal chart. It is no more difficult—only more detailed and many-layered. There is no "silver bullet" event chart that, however brilliantly analyzed, will cough up pertinent and profitable market projections in a reliable fashion on an "investable" time scale. Instead, we must use different approaches for different purposes, occasionally substituting *volume* of analyzed material for elegance and subtlety of interpretive technique.

True market-oriented astrology is only just a-borning. Certainly attempts have been made to isolate relevant cycles by Dewey *et al.*, but these were pure smoothed waves not hinged on planetary configurations. It's been an ill-kept secret that many financial moguls have used astrology, but—and this is a very important caveat—these are people of schooled instinct who intimately understand market workings and the influence of broader affairs on the speculative psyche. Astrology is the icing on their money cake. Those of us who haven't got MBAs and haven't spent a good portion of our lives "on the street" first need to go to school, as it were, and learn our market ABC's. Astrology alone won't do it. Indeed, astrology as it is generally practiced will offer very little assistance.

Astrology-assisted investment is a four-pronged process that:

1. Needs the proper astro tools.
2. Needs long-, intermediate- and short-term cyclic orientation.
3. Needs to isolate individual investment opportunities.
4. Needs an understanding by the astrologer of the "rest of the (financial) story."

TOOLS: THEIR PROPER CARE AND USE

When I first confronted the market, I innocently thought either the New York Stock Exchange or United States chart would offer the practical type of information usually available from any institutional chart. I wasn't disappointed; they do. They are, however, devoid of up/down indicators. The NYSE chart will predict an outbreak of measles among the floor traders, show volume surges, and perhaps indicate major changes in administrative structure. It has enough connection with overall market health to warrant study, but not to predict trends. The USA chart is equally good for a general checkup. The Federal Reserve's map is more fruitful, since it reliably shows changes in Fed policy. Yet, none will indicate a rally or route (at the present state of astro art).

Corporate and municipal charts (and bank charters) are an investor must. They don't show market movements either per se. What they *do* show is the internal health of the corporation, its future batterings or blessings, its liability to takeover or bankruptcy, and what kind of press it's getting.

See Chart 1 of American Can Company's transit bi-wheel and 45° graphic ephemeris. When Neptune transited American Can Company's mid-mutable configuration, the company changed from a container/forest products manufacturer to a financial, mail-order and music enterprise. It also became involved in that music company's legal woes (record pirating), which led to the trial and imprisonment of two executives. With the final transit of Saturn/

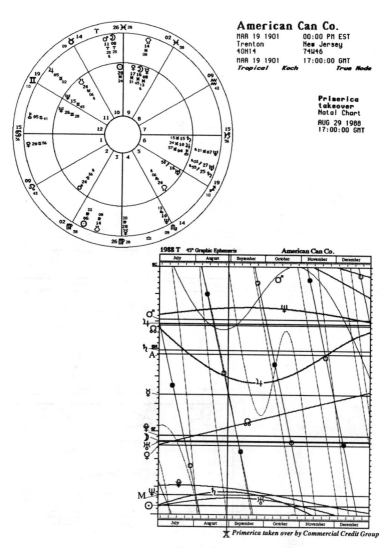

American Can Co.
MAR 19 1901   00:00 PM EST
Trenton   New Jersey
40N14   74W46
MAR 19 1901   17:00:00 GMT
Tropical   *Koch*   *True Node*

Primerica
takeover
Natal Chart
AUG 29 1988
17:00:00 GMT

1988 T   45° Graphic Ephemeris   American Can Co.

✕ *Primerica taken over by Commercial Credit Group*

Chart 1

Biwheel chart and 45° graphic ephemeris are courtesy of Graphic Astrology, Times Cycles Research, 27 Dimmock Rd., Waterford, CT 06385.

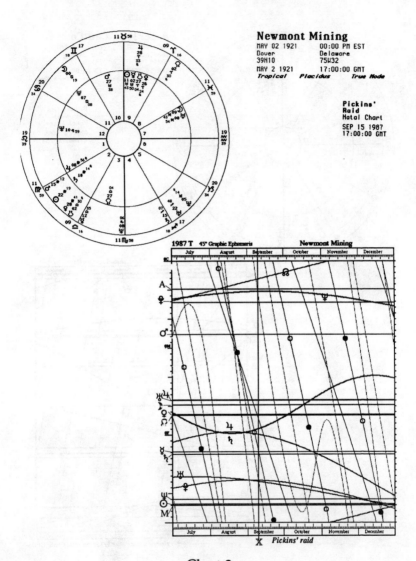

Newmont Mining
MAY 02 1921   00:00 PM EST
Dover   Delaware
39N10   75W32
MAY 2 1921   17:00:00 GMT
Tropical   Placidus   True Mode

Pickins'
Raid
Natal Chart
SEP 15 1987
17:00:00 GMT

1987 T   45° Graphic Ephemeris   Newmont Mining

Ⓧ *Pickins' raid*

Chart 2

Biwheel chart and 45° graphic ephemeris are courtesy of Graphic Astrology,
Times Cycles Research, 27 Dimmock Rd., Waterford, CT 06385.

Uranus semi-square transiting Pluto afflicting its natal Sun, the company "died." It had lost too much in the stock market meltdown to recoup.

Chart 2 of Newmont Mining presents another example of the use of these charts. With transiting Pluto opposing the natal Sun and squaring natal Neptune, and transiting Neptune opposing natal Pluto, Newmont Mining was visited with the unwelcome attentions of T. Boone Pickins, forcing 50% of it into the arms of Goldfields, Inc., a "white knight" who already owned 31% of the company. Newmont issued a $35-per-share dividend to remove (by stripping its coffers) any further takeover incentives. At last report Newmont has announced the shutdown of its New York headquarters and Danbury, Connecticut and Tucson, Arizona centers and is repairing to Denver to await the further treats Saturn, Uranus and Neptune have in store for it.

Both of the above happenings were eminently predictable from the corporation chart using transits alone. Solar arc directions would have made things even clearer. The most efficient method to transit-track a corporation chart is the **graphic ephemeris**(Chart 3), and the simplest method of combining multiple charts (for essential comparisons) is the **90° dial** (Figure 1). *These are "must" tools for serious financial work.*

In the graphic ephemeris format, transits are presented in a left-to-right time line in exactly the same presentation as market graphs. It is possible to see not only approaching major aspects, but the entire sequence of build-up, exact formation, and subsequent co-transits. *The whole picture presents itself.*

Chart 4 shows the extraordinary visual pattern of the simultaneous Jupiter/Saturn stations and the subsequent "convergence" of 1987. Though other indicators suggested that this was an exceptional year, prone to major market reversals, the station and its "convergent" transits would

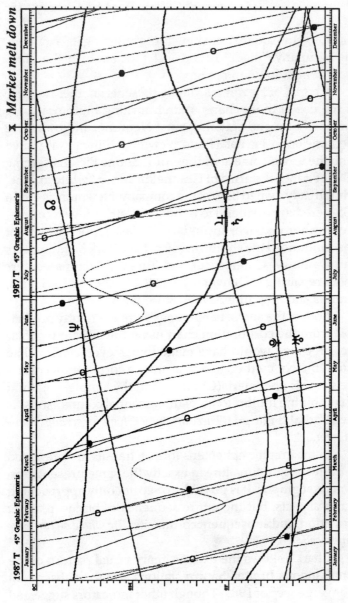

This 45° graph is generated electronically using Graphic Astrology software from Times Cycles Research, 27 Dimmock Rd. Waterford, Ct. 06385

Chart 3

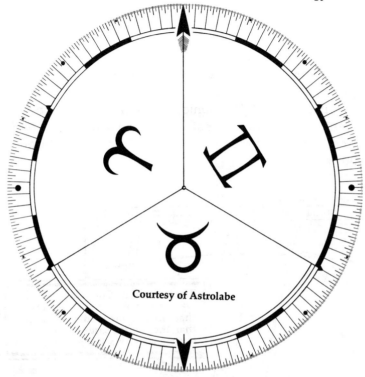

Courtesy of Astrolabe

Figure 1

still attract attention *if you saw them.*

Graphic ephemerides work on a concept of "overlays." See Chart 5. In the 45° 8th Harmonic graphic, 0° of the *cardinal* signs marks the top of the graph, which descends through 0° *fixed* to bottom at 15° *fixed*. The chart then wraps over itself and restarts with 15° *fixed* at the top, descends to 0° *mutable*, and finally ends at the 30° *mutable* bottom. As a result, any planet in conjunction, opposition, square, semi-square or sesquiquadrate will be "conjunct" on the graph. The 45° aspect is both easily missed and exceedingly important, particularly when it is combining the delights of Saturn, Uranus and Pluto as in 1988. Missing the Pluto link could mean missing a potential bankruptcy or hostile take-over.

In the 30° 12th Harmonic graphic, all signs overlay all other signs. Any planet at 5° will relate to any other 5° planet regardless of sign.

In the 40° 9th Harmonic graphic, the division is by element, starting with 0° *fire* at the top, down through 9° *earth*; from 10° *earth* through 19° *air*; and from 20° *air* through 30° *water*.

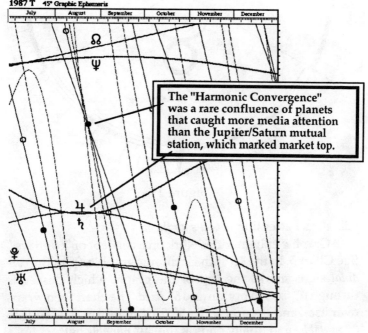

The "Harmonic Convergence" was a rare confluence of planets that caught more media attention than the Jupiter/Saturn mutual station, which marked market top.

This 45° graph is generated electronically using Graphic Astrology software from Times Cycles Research, 27 Dimmock Rd. Waterford, Ct. 06385

Chart 4

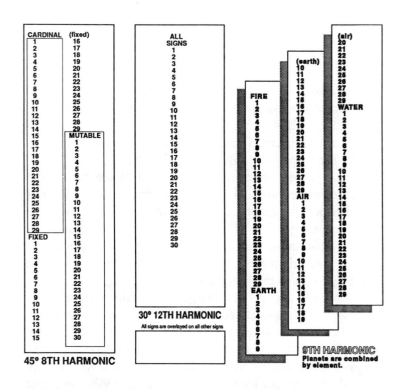

Chart 5

While the 45° (semi-square, sesquiquadrate or 8th Harmonic) is most commonly used, 30° (semi-sextile or 12th Harmonic), 40° (novile, navamsa or 9th Harmonic), and 72° (quintile or 5th Harmonic) are available, being actively investigated by market analysts, and show definite promise.

Large format blank charts (11 x 17, both helio and geocentric) are published yearly by Astrolabe in 30° and 45° format. ACS offers individualized computer-plotted charts in any format you can conceive. *A-Year-at-a-Glance, the 45° Graphic Ephemeris for 101 Years: 1900-2001* by Roxana

Muise has sufficient 45° data for your initial research. If you have a Macintosh computer, *Graphic Astrology* from Times Cycles Research will generate individualized charts. Undoubtedly both Matrix and Astrolabe will have a PC version available in the not-too-distant future. A five-year 45° geocentric graphic (Mars, Jupiter, Saturn, Uranus, Neptune, Pluto and Node) for '80-85, '85-90, and '90-95 is available from Mercury House, Inc. This format is particularly useful for corporate long-range evaluations.

The "exotic" harmonics (9, 7, and 5) are mostly the province of researchers who are willing to generate their own heliocentric graphs. Helio positions have the advantage of being straight-line graphs, very suitable for do-it-yourselfers. Helio aspects can occur only once (no retrogradation). If they work adequately, this is an immense benefit. They at least "get you to the ball park."

Note: 45° aspects operate geocentrically and heliocentrically, but the geo aspects, along with lunations, stations and the like, are much more important on a short-term basis. The 40° (9th Harmonic) sequence seems much more impressive in a helio-only reference frame and will operate on a short-term projection! See Chart 6 of a 9th Harmonic helio chart. Planetary configurations in the 9th Harmonic are shown under the year in which they occur. This is a long-range outer-planet-only graph. Compare the corresponding market movement in Chart 7 of the DJIA. Chart 8 presents the 9th Harmonic aspects for the market crash of October 1987.

WHEELS IN WHEELS

The companion products to the graphic ephemerides are the 90° and 360° dials. Individual dials can be erected for the 12th, 5th, 7th and 9th Harmonics, but since a 360° dial can be marked to indicate all at once, it hardly seems profitable to bother with separate dials unless you want to

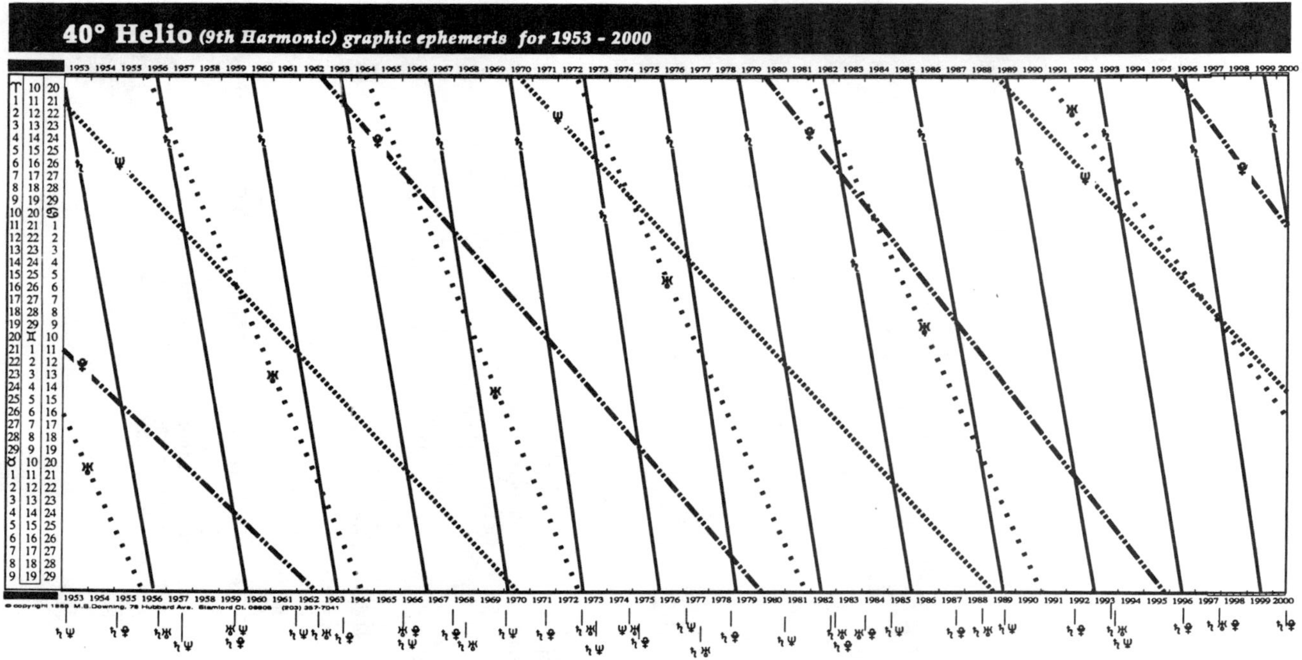

40° Helio (9th Harmonic) graphic ephemeris for 1953 - 2000

Chart 6

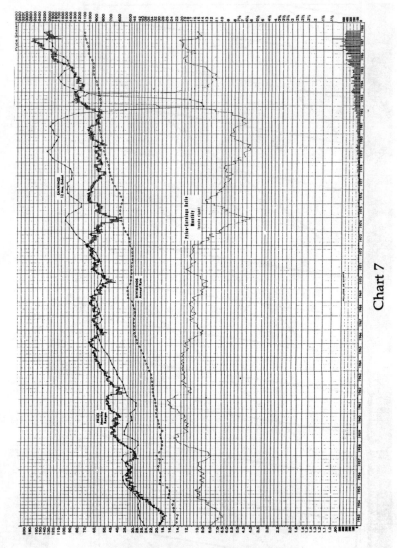

Chart 7

Courtesy of Securities Research Company, a
Division of Babson-United Investment Advisors,
Inc., 208 Newbury St., Boston MA 02116.

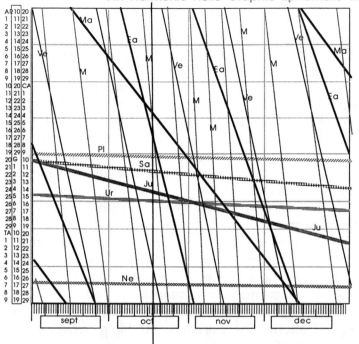

Chart 8

experiment with, say, solar arcs solely in that harmonic.

By itself, the 90° dial is a remarkable tool. It allows one to instantaneously inspect the 1st, 2nd, 4th, 8th and 16th Harmonics (seen as arms on a *cross*) while also checking any 3rd, 6th, 12th or 24th Harmonics (in the equally obvious *triangle* formation). Midpoints and harmonics to midpoints are just as immediately visible.

Solar arc directions can be marked on the dial and moved with it. *Any number of charts can be compared simultaneously.* In fact, the only limit on the number of charts handled at one time is the device used to separate them. I like colored markers. I also use concentric circles for printing purposes which are admittedly neater if less aesthetic. Any method that works is right.

These ganged charts yield surprising dividends. If there is some shared activity, the charts will connect. Subsidiary companies will cluster around some configuration in the parent enterprise and create super populated bumps. Corporate officers will relate to each other *and* the company. Major industry competitors have charts that occupy the same segment of the zodiac or have comparable planetary aspect patterns. There are recognizable patterns for container manufacturers, mining companies, publishers, etc. This is a whole field for future study. Think how profitable it would be to spot the penny stocks that correspond with industry partners that have already made it!

Obviously, if all or most of a company's subsidiaries are receiving negative transits, something is afoot—perhaps divestiture. Should half the upper management be connected with a negative corporate transit, they may be leaving. If all the major companies in a given industry receive very negative transits at the same time, what does it say about that industry? Is there a new technology that will render the industry obsolete? What did buggy whip manufacturers look like when Ford was building his tin lizzies? Is it open takeover season in mining/publishing/food packaging? Ever notice that "runs" are made on not *just one* target but its competition as well? If one giant consumer food producer is "tasty," so must his competitor be.

If a corporation decides it's going to be a financial services giant instead of a can company, it should have a chart that looks like all the other financial services companies. If it is odd-man-out, it may be hustling after the wrong business. What happened to Primerica (née American Can) had an exact and prior parallel in Continental Can! Each decided that the answer to crumbling packaging lines was to challenge General Reinsurance.

Corporations aren't stuck with a birth chart. They can re-incorporate where and when they want. Unisys, originally Burroughs, Inc., re-incorporated as a Sun/Moon Gemini *before* they merged with Sperry. I love their current advertising tag, "The power of two."

Bangor Punta was a sugar producer in Cuba before the Castro expropriation of foreign assets. Its Cuban holdings were remarkable in that their corporate Suns, solar arc Suns and Mars/Saturn midpoints clustered in early cardinals and were being transited by Saturn at "grab" time. Later, as a U.S. manufacturer of recreational boats and firearms, BP became entwined with Chris Craft and Piper Aircraft in a very ill-fated business deal. All three solar arc Suns directed to the same mutable position and were hosting Neptune.

The 90° dial is most often connected with the Uranian and Cosmobiology schools of astrology. Its use was popularized by Reinhold Ebertin. His "bible" of midpoint interpretation, *The Combination of Stellar Influences* (American Federation of Astrologers), is still the best work on what its title suggests—multiple planet influences. It is arranged in cookbook fashion. One opens to a combination, like Mars/ Saturn, and *combines* it with a third influence—the Sun.

While this formula is traditionally used for midpoint interpretation, it is just as valid for aspect, solar arc or "contact"
delineation. In fact, since it delineates in outline form (positive, negative, possible manifestation, etc.), it encourages
the user (notice I didn't say reader) to extrapolate from the
text and apply it to his or her given situation. Ebertin also
wrote very practical books on transits, directions, and contact charts that I happily recommend.

The 90° dial is also a *layered* technique. All cardinal
planets are equally superimposed, as are all fixed and
mutables. (See Figure 2.) To properly erect a 90° dial chart:

1. Pin the dial to a work surface with either a thumb-
   tack or a screw post. File folders are an excellent
   medium for storage and chart combined.
2. Mark Aries—0° of the cardinals—at the *top* of the
   chart. Secure the dial with a piece of masking tape
   while entering the planets.
3. Starting at the "Aries" position, mark all cardinal
   (Aries, Cancer, Libra, Capricorn) planets pro-
   gressively down the left (counterclockwise).
4. At the 30° position, mark all fixed (Taurus, Leo,
   Scorpio, Aquarius) planets from right to left across
   the bottom.
5. At the 60° position, mark all mutable (Gemini,
   Virgo, Sagittarius, Pisces) planets counterclockwise from bottom up.
6. All conjunctions, squares, and oppositions will
   appear at the same spot on the dial.
7. All sextiles, semi-sextiles, inconjuncts and trines
   will appear at the 30° and 60° positions.
8. All semi-squares and sesquiquadrates will appear
   directly across from the pointer. Bi-octiles (22½°)
   appear on the "arms of the cross."
9. Transits and other comparative positions can be
   entered on the same chart by using some means of

separation (color coding, concentric circles).
10. Solar arc and reverse arc positions can be determined by marking the appropriate separation on the wheel.

Individual directed positions can be recorded on the chart or the arc simply marked on the wheel itself. In solar arc direction, all planets are advanced either one degree for each year or by another calculated increment. *The important consideration is that all planets are advanced by the same arc.* Typical methods of directing a chart are: degree-for-a-year, secondary progressed Sun arc, and naibod arc (mean solar movement). Cosmobiologists commonly use reverse arcs as

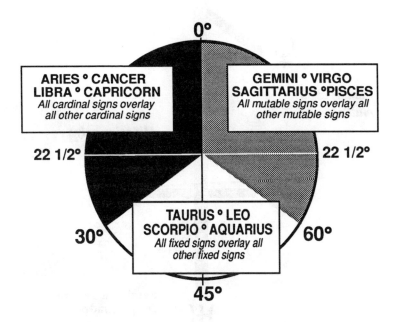

Figure 2

well and mark the wheel to both left and right of the pointer. Any number of solar arcs can be marked on the wheel at the same time provided some means is employed (color coding, numbering) to separate them.

Note-taking "tree"

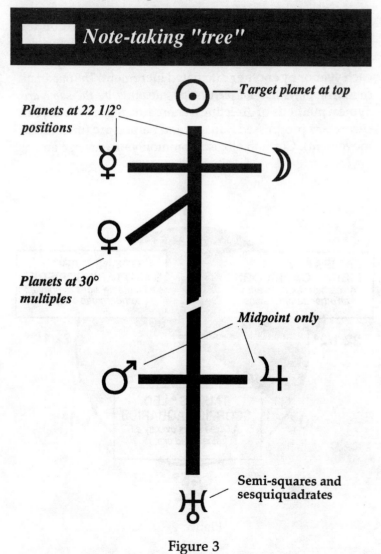

Figure 3

To analyze a planet, simply put the pointer on the planet and check the "cross arm" and "triangle" positions. Planets there (or within a degree or two) are in actual traditional aspect to the analyzed planet. See if the solar arc marker is contacting another planet. If it is, it is "directed" to that planet. If you are comparing the target chart to transits or another chart, see if the "contact" planets are involved. Finally, see if pairs of planets are equidistant on each side of the pointer. If they are, the target planet is their midpoint (or in aspect of 90°) to the actual midpoint.

NOTE-TAKING TREE

Cosmobiologists use a "tree" or "fishbone" note-taking device for recording their dial analysis. I use a modified version you may find useful. See Figure 3.

The target planet is at the top of the diagram. Any 45° planets are at the bottom. All 22½° positions are recorded with straight lines, and all 30°, 60°, 120° aspects with slanted lines. Following the actual aspects, all midpoint configurations are entered.

360° DIAL

The 360° dial doesn't require detailed explanation. It is a straightforward circle divided into degrees with 30° signs indicated. See Figure 4. One can mark the 360 with indicators for 9th (40°), 7th (51.43°), and 5th (72°) increments. Again I recommend color coding or numbering as an indicator. Polar paper (obtainable from commercial stationers and engineering/drafting supply houses) is a ready concentric-circled worksheet. The same surprising patterning discernible on the 90° is evident, but more so. You may not notice that all cardinal positions are strictly Cancer/Capricorn on a 90° dial, but you *definitely* will notice such sign-oriented patterns on the 360° dial.

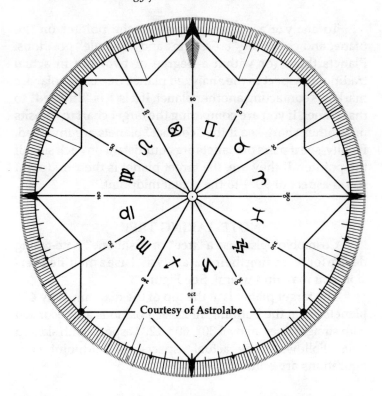

Courtesy of Astrolabe

Figure 4

NEW COMPUTER PROGRAMS

I am sure financial astrology has come into its own because personal computers have come into our offices. As I write, there are two major and completely different programs aimed at the financial/cyclic astrology market. I am most familiar with Bill Meridian's *Astro Analyst* from Astrolabe. This program was designed to please a technical market analyst who is also an astrologer. It has a resident Dow data base back to NYSE's beginnings (in a reconstructed format for earlier years). The *Astro Analyst* has powerful statistical routines, moving averages, 90° dials, pop-up astro charts that update themselves in four-minute ticks, and mainly the ability to analyze planetary combinations and relate them to the market data over any given time span. It then can present in graph form the combined history of all Saturn/ Uranus squares, Saturn/Neptune semi-squares, or Jupiter-through-the-signs, etc. Whatever combination you require, it will analyze the reaction of that selection on the given data base being researched, and the data bases can be edited! If I want the Jupiter/signs chart on only Bull Markets, I can doctor a Bull-only Market data base. Other data sets can be substituted for the Dow. Should I wish to examine earthquakes, pork bellies, or airplane crashes, I only have to provide the program with a data base and it will compare whatever planetary combinations I input.

Unfortunately, I haven't seen the *Matrix Cycles* program in action. It would seem a strong cycles tool with magnificent graphics.

TRENDS AND CYCLES
Long-Term Tools

I approached market cycles by default. My original interest was the internal operations of companies per se, not the fluctuation of their stock prices. My background is in advertising, nonprofits and trade associations. I have much experience in watching companies bring a product to market, make public relations gaffes and triumphs, and do direct mail promotions or any of the various and sundry public-connected motions a corporation makes. I've worked on start-up accounts of great companies with marvelous products that simply died. I've equally worked for slipshod, confused clients who couldn't have cared less—and they *still* made a killing. If you're an astrologer, it sets you thinking. Certainly what a company is doing internally *eventually* affects its public image, which in turn will, over time, affect stock prices. There are, however, shorter-term overriding factors.

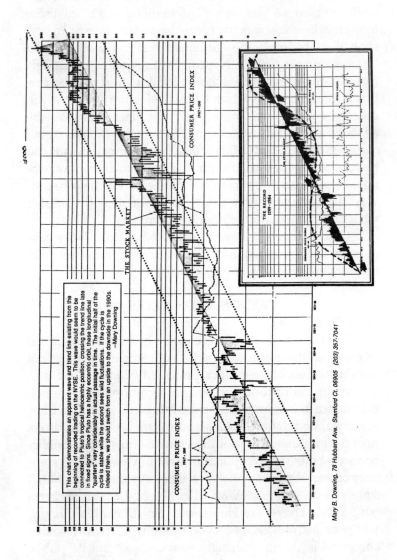

This chart demonstrates an apparent wave and trend line existing from the beginning of recorded trading on the NYSE. This wave would seem to be connected to Pluto's tropical heliocentric position, crossing the trend line late in fixed signs. Since Pluto has a highly eccentric orbit, these longitudinal "quarters" vary considerably in actual passage in time. The initial half of the cycle is stable while the second sees wild fluctuations. If the cycle is indeed there, we should switch from an upside to the downside in the 1990s.
—Mary Downing

THE STOCK MARKET

CONSUMER PRICE INDEX
1947=100

CONSUMER PRICE INDEX
1947=100

THE RECORD
1789-1984

Mary B. Downing, 78 Hubbard Ave. Stamford Ct. 06905 (203) 357-7041

Chart 9

Even the best managed of companies had a troubled future after October of 1929. There was a stronger force operating than the internal reality of the company. It's analogous to a far-sighted, frugal European stuck in Hitler's Germany during WWII. What good did his planning do him when the world was falling down around his ears? What good does it do to bring out a public offering when the Dow drops 500 points?

Chart 9 is a semi-logarithmic graph of the Dow's yearly action from the NYSE's inception. Obviously, the early figures have been converted from different indices. Semi-log graphs show proportional change.

There is a trend line that exists from the inception of the Dow that is steadily moving upward. Market movement snakes around it with first cyclic bottoms bouncing off the line, then tops. *These cyclic arcs cross the trend line when Pluto reaches 24-25 degrees of a fixed sign heliocentrically.*

Pluto possesses an extremely eccentric orbit. The "quarters" of its cycle are of radically different length. Our current square is the shortest of all—only 39 years. The first part of each quarter segment is marked by relatively stable business cycles. Sometime after Pluto passes the halfway point (and a semi-square to 24° fixed), the Dow explodes in a spectacular—if short-lived—Bull Market. This runaway speculation continues until the prices reach the upper trend parallel, which is currently around 2800. There seems to be some internal stability that manifests when the market reaches a specific proportional distance from the trend line.

We are on an upper arc now. The 1835 market collapse is the only other historical sample occurring from the *upper* position. For that matter, we have only two prior examples of my "bounce-off-the-top" theory. Hardly an impressive sample, but, short of time travel, I haven't any means of fattening it. The 1929 collapse had greater amplitude since it started from below the trend line. The reader will no doubt notice that the entire shape of the market since 1954 mimics that of the early 1800s. If we follow the 1835 template, we should have:

- Major banking problems with farm foreclosures.
- An economic downturn greatly affecting the South and West (caused in 1835 by a glut of cotton, not oil).
- Land speculation.
- The USA as a debtor nation with its currency and banking establishment in disarray. (In 1835 this was due to debt incurred during the War of 1812.)

I think there are sufficient similarities. Could the Pluto cycle be the real (though illusive) Kondratieff Wave? We shall certainly see soon enough.

We can demonstrate that in the Dow the trend line and parallels exist. We can equally demonstrate three examples of the "Pluto arc" with its stable-early and erratic-later pattern. The crossover points *do* coincide with Pluto at 23-25° of the fixed signs. What we *don't* have is sufficient repetitions to be confident that the pattern is consistent. However, I would carefully watch the market between now (11/88) and 1993. If the pattern does hold, the cyclic tops will be rebounding off a trend line skewering 1000 in '93-94.

Medium-length cycles

Saturn, Uranus, Neptune and Pluto in combination describe one set of major cycles. The actual movements occur, unfortunately, on geocentric combinations. They require triggering secondary aspects. A Pluto/Neptune aspect can go on for decades like the current one. The present Uranus/Pluto semi-square has been operative geocentrically since 1985. It was exact heliocentrically in October

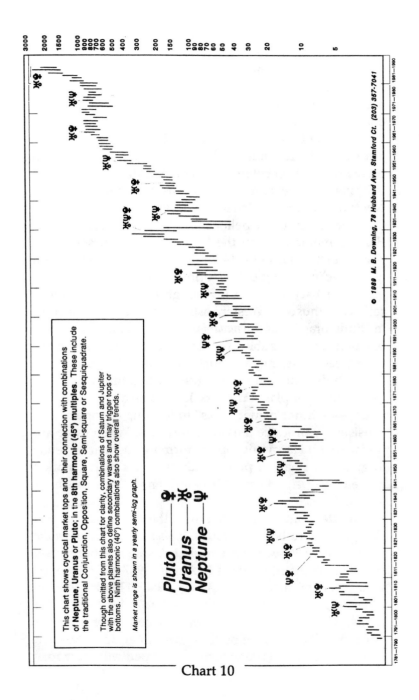

This chart shows cyclical market tops and their connection with combinations of **Neptune, Uranus** or **Pluto**; in the **8th harmonic (45°) multiples**. These include the traditional Conjunction, Opposition, Square, Semi-square or Sesquiquadrate.

Though omitted from this chart for clarity, combinations of Saturn and Jupiter with the above planets also define secondary waves and may trigger tops or bottoms. Ninth harmonic (40°) combinations also show overall trends.

Market range is shown in a yearly semi-log graph.

Pluto ——— ♇
Uranus ——— ♅
Neptune ——— ♆

© 1989 M. B. Downing, 78 Hubbard Ave. Stamford Ct. (203) 357-7041

Chart 10

of '87. That may be neat for our current crisis, but it really was a fluke. In 1929, the Neptune, Pluto, Uranus, Saturn configuration was just starting. It didn't break up until the end of 1933, just when the market began its recovery.

If a Bear Market is full blown, a Saturn/Neptune combination will often indicate the *bottom*. These bottoms often occur in the quarter before or after the actual aspect. However, if the market is developing downward momentum, Saturn/Neptune will only stabilize the decline.

See Chart 10 of heliocentric Neptune, Uranus, and Pluto combinations on the Dow. As you can see, these planets in 8th Harmonic (45°) patterns are associated with major cyclic turning points, primarily tops.

Refer back to Chart 6. Though the 9th Harmonic is relatively unused in Western astrology, it has a long history in Hindu practice as the *navamsa*. While 9th planetary combinations seem less able to indicate the relative strength of a market response, they are much more consistent in predicting both direction and pinpointing actual times, but they also need inner planet triggers. Indeed on a very short 24-hour basis, inner planet "ticks" to forming configurations consistently produce measurable results. When there are no major 9th Harmonic aspects forming, the market tends to go *up*. We have a potent indicator of a major market movement if significant 8th helio's and 9th geo's simultaneously occur.

Jupiter combining with any of the above planets will also produce noticeable results. *Jupiter/Saturn has been the major financial bellwether in times past.* It is always there when anything important happens. In August 1987, they stationed semi-square of each other, and the great Bull Market topped. When Jupiter retrogrades, the market at least goes flat. Jupiter/Uranus can send the market bounding in either direction. The ratio seems to be two times down to each time up. Jupiter/Neptune comes equipped with very rosy

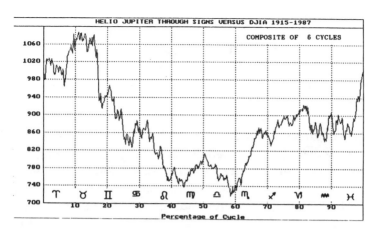

Chart 11A

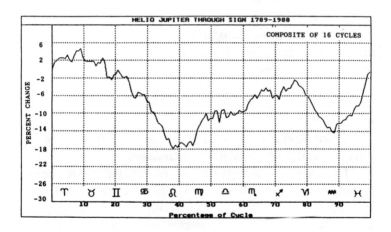

Chart 11B

Charts courtesy of
Astro Analyst **from**
Astrolabe.

glasses. It has an inflationary quality about it.

One of the first and exceedingly interesting products of the *Astro Analyst* program was a search of Jupiter through the zodiacal signs. See Charts 11A and 11B. As you can see (especially in 11A), Jupiter reaches its high in Taurus and quickly drops off in Gemini.

Barbara Watters used **declination cycles** in predicting commodity prices. She was particularly fond of the relationship between *gold and the Jupiter declination*. Considering the realities of gold futures trading, Jupiter at extreme position is an almost useless indicator—the metal is too volatile and the planet stays there too long. It would be fine for the collector of coins, however. We have a similar situation with Jupiter and Saturn in extreme north or south declination, as well as with Uranus, Pluto, and Neptune. If we were to take the same chart of yearly indicators that was used in the Uranus, Pluto, Neptune graph and mark it for Jupiter or Saturn in extreme north or south declination, we would hardly see a naked market top. Even the crossover north to south point is significant.

Chart 12 shows the actual short-time chart of Jupiter in extreme north, south and 0° declination.

Declinations have greater consistency than the outer planets *on a long-term basis*. But while the outer planet configurations respond to short-term daily transits with important market movements, the declinations only confirm that a major trend reversal is about to take place with some planetary configuration sparking the action. "About" is defined as within the next year or so. However, when we have semi-squares that play tag for four years, any added input is welcome—and they are certainly easy to research!

Short-Term Triggers

How can we reduce these millenial indicators into workable prediction tools? For short-term traders, the good

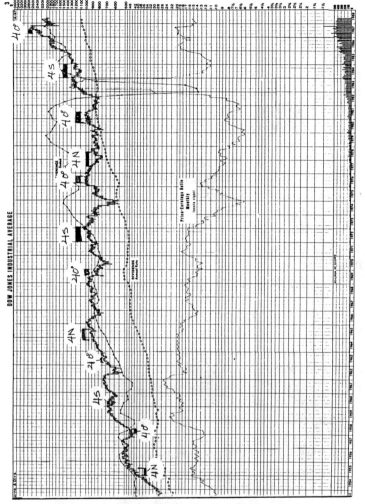

DOW JONES INDUSTRIAL AVERAGE

Chart 12

news is that daily the Sun, Mercury, Venus, Mars and the Earth on the 9th Harmonic act on forming outer-planet combinations with measurable results within a day at the most of their exact contact. These reactions may be even more profitable in futures and bond markets. If an investor uses a graphic ephemeris, it is relatively easy to isolate important short-term configurations. It will take some ret-rogressive research to properly apply them to your special speculative area, however. As I write this, the Japanese market, which is hovering at the equivalent of a 2800 Dow, is reacting much more strongly to the Saturn/Uranus/ Pluto configuration than is the NYSE. We may be seeing the demise of NYSE's premier position in world markets. In 1929, the British markets began to decline before we did, indicating our assumption of financial leadership.

Besides daily transit triggers watch:

Eclipses: *particularly when close to another aspect pattern*
Eclipses are often felt *before* the actual aspect. If an eclipse strikes an important configuration, that same grouping will likely be hosting a transit of the Moon's Nodes. Nodal contact suggests a public brouhaha involving whatever is signified by the other planets.

Lunations: *traditionally associated with strong emotional public response*
Again, linkage with a significant pattern is meaningful.

Retrograde periods: *deny smooth operation*
Mercury is particularly annoying, scrambling communication and encasing every communication in aspic.

Stations: *release the pent energy*
Mercury stations have triggered more than one market decline. Jupiter *direct* stations are often followed by a two-to-three-week market drop, and then (if there is no contraven-ing influence) an upsurge. One of the benefits of the new *Astro Analyst* program is its ability to describe a "footprint"

of specific planetary events, such as stations.

Sign Changes: *issue in a new agenda*

When a planet changes signs, it changes "priorities." Uranian and Cosmobiologists consider 0° of the cardinals particularly charged. It is the *world axis*. This observation is akin to the traditional astrological concept of essential dignities.

Fixed Stars*: galactic center, planetary nodes, asteroids, hypotheticals, and other extraordinary bodies and locations*

These must be investigated systematically in the future. The tendencies of planets in related industries to *group* in specific zodiacal locations indicates the importance of longitudinal position. Right now, we have only "ancient wisdom" to guide interpretation of these astral neighborhoods, but tomorrow is another story. One of the Uranian hypotheticals, Hades, has the nastiest habit of sitting on the Midheaven in the truly awful disasters. Juno and Chiron have demonstrable market correlation.

Note: Not only do outer planet aspects relate to market movement, they can—regardless of longitudinal position—connect with companies and countries. The Philippines and Central America will be in the headlines during Saturn/Uranus contacts no matter when or where zodiacally the aspect occurs.

SPOTTING POTENTIALS
IN THE CORPORATE CHART

Corporate entities exist *from the moment in time when they are stamped.* In some states, the filer can literally watch his or her creation come to legal life. Usually bureaucracy decrees that they are batch processed whenever efficiency dictates, which may or may not correspond with the time affixed to the papers. Since the 10th House cusp is the mundane corporate indicator, I recommend a universal corporate noon birth—even if I have a supposed timed chart.

Use the "timed" Moon and angles as supplemental information. Most of your corporations won't be timed, and your comparisons will be, at least, consistent.

Many traders use "first trade" charts which are timed accurately by computers. However, this again requires mixing properly timed with untimed charts.

The business corporation, bank charter, or municipal corporation's birth data is public property. All the researcher has to do is consult the proper information source.

Publicly Traded

If a reasonably large USA or Canadian corporation, it will be listed in *Moody's* or *Standard and Poor's* manuals. *Moody's* breaks listings into Industrials, Financial (two volumes: banks and others, *i.e.*, insurance companies, etc.), Transportation, Utilities, International, Municipal, and OTC.

The Secretary of State's office in each state will have a phone-in service that will give the date of incorporation. New Jersey charges $7.00 per inquiry.

If the enterprise is a "foreign" corporation (*i.e.*, from another state) doing business in your state, your call-in number will be able to tell you at least when it filed locally and perhaps when it was incorporated. If not, they will tell you its home state.

Privately Held

Information is available from the Secretary of State's office in its home state and in any state in which it is doing business as a "foreign corporation." Why would you be interested in a private company? It may be a crucial customer, supplier, property owner, etc.

Moody's and *Standard and Poor's* indexes offer an encapsulated history of the company, its major subsidiaries and acquisitions, and its bond rating which is a "quickie" glimpse into its fiscal health. You may find that a company is wholly owned by another and yet has never been integrated into the "mother" company. Equally, a company may have majority, but not total, control of another. In such cases, *both* the target company and the "mother" charts are important. What's been bought can be sold. Specific operations can be spun off at any time for any reason.

International companies often have separate corporations for operation in the USA. This may or may not be relevant to your situation. They are rarely traded separately, but the U.S. Corp. would be the contractor, property owner, employer, etc. The Secretary of State's office in the state where the international has its headquarters is the best source for information of any specific American subsidiary.

You may find acquisitions with only a year listed. Chances are the article will say, "For details of acquistions before 19xx, see Moody's Industrials 19xx." Most libraries maintain old copies. If you can't find the company at all, you may be looking under the wrong name. There are both Brand Name and Who Owns Whom directories. Companies change names as well. Recent name changes and acquisitions are listed in the blue-page introduction of *Moody's*. Also check the summaries of corporate news items and "warning" lists that are updated monthly. Make sure you understand the relationship of the target company to all its subsidiaries, holding companies, and internationals. Equally, when investigating the municipal bond market, remember that a city is not necessarily the same incorporation-wise as its sewer district or housing authority; you must check both.

There are more reasons to study a corporate chart than simply investing in its stock. We work for, sell to and buy from them. They may be the major employer and taxpayer of a target city whose bond issue you are considering. I became vitally interested in mergers when in rapid succession my major and three minor advertising clients went pouf in a takeover feeding frenzy.

THE PLANETS' FUNCTIONS
IN A CORPORATE CHART

The Sun—the company itself, its viability. It is particularly vulnerable by transit or direction to:

Pluto: need for extreme change (usually forced), bankruptcy.

Neptune: extremely political environment, potential mergers, redistribution/reinvestment of monies and resources.

Saturn: inherent problems (with *Uranus:* buried problems resurface, *i.e.*, tax audits, etc.; with *Mars*: energy is blocked, course of action aborted).

The Moon—the employees. By transit and direction:

Pluto and *Saturn:* both indicate separation/turnover.

Neptune: major morale problems, layoffs, reassignments, illness, dishonesty, drug and alcohol abuse.

Uranus: the presence of a major disruptive force, often connected with union activity.

Important in service, container, food and beverage industries.

Node—public connection by transit and direction.

Mercury—internal communication and sales.
Important in electronics, communications, publishing, advertising, light manufacturing, and vending operations.

Venus—physical comfort of the work place.
Important in clothing, decorative fabrics, entertainment, design, and housewares industries. (Statistically fewer companies than expected have retrograde Venus.)

Mars—quality of action performed. Particularly sensitive to:

Pluto: forced action, out of control, insurmountable difficulties, to be liable to or the source of "force."

Neptune: indecisive or fraudulent actions, or strategic planning and image-producing action.

Uranus: chaotic or original action, liability to accidents.

Saturn: blocked direction or extremely precise, deliberate work.

Jupiter: successful action, aggressive demeanor.

Venus: public magnetism.

Jupiter—profit and expansion. By transit, it increases traffic and opens opportunity. It can increase the disruptive inclinations of *Uranus* and the inflative qualities of *Neptune.*

Saturn—the administrative function, the corporate "blind spot," the presence of a "mentor" in individual connections, regulatory agencies, and the corporation itself. Saturn by aspect and direction separates.

Important in all municipal charts (govenment itself), building and land development, printing, mining and manufacturing.

Uranus—innovative and disruptive elements: research and development, computer operations, union activity. By transit and direction, it increases both energy level and accident risk.

Important in all electric, electronic, computer, research activities.

Neptune—all public relations, advertising, external sales, financial and strategic planning functions, and the distribution of working funds and resources. Neptune by transit or direction may indicate illegal or badly planned activities, divestiture, acquisitions and mergers.

Important in all advertising, entertainment, public relations, sales, financial, chemical, photographic, health care, drugs, oil and cosmetics.

Pluto—outside force requiring change, all rehabilitative and remodeling functions, and basic research. By transit and direction, Pluto forces major changes, often requiring the company to abandon existing products and industries or change locations. It may precipitate bankruptcy.

Important in mining, smelting, all raw material processing, heavy industry, refining, rehabilitation, and research.

Note: Jupiter, Saturn, Uranus, Neptune and *Pluto* are planets that by synodic periods mark the major planetary cycles. If these synods occur in aspect to natal corporate planets, it is an indicator of involvement by the corporation in the greater financial cycle.

Corporations respond in a primitive fashion to planetary transits. They are the response of the mass mind without the civilizing patina of society. "Business ethics" may be a wry contradiction in terms. They are the amoral spawn of commercial intercourse. To apply motives more elevated than raw survival is wishful.

A GUIDE TO THE PERPLEXED

How do you learn? Read a book(s). Take a class(es). Dry trade. Visit a big public library with a commercial section and acquaint yourself with the plethora of materials published almost hourly to update people who make a living by financial means. This is one of the most graphed, analyzed, and projected objects of study among civilized man. It also has theories, systems, and gurus enough to make astrology seem an old sobersides. Everybody's an expert. At least, if you learn the analytical basics and use the astrological techniques you already understand, you can blame the right person when things go bust.

Take a good look at your assets and liabilities, both financial and personal. The key word is *speculation*. It's a gamble. Don't bet the mortgage money. Consider what you are willing to invest in time. If you are a busy casual investor who wants a decent return with little time input, consider mutual funds and government-secured Ginnie Maes. Equally, if you inherited stock or have been waiting 20+ years for

Pan Am or A&P to regain their 1960s highs, *please* look at what these companies have been doing all these years and compute what the same money deposited in a S&L would have yielded in compound interest!

On the flip side, we have the market professional just wetting his toes in astrological waters. Where in all this literature devoted to karma, Jungian shadows and truly obscure techniques will the pilgrim find his grail? I've already recommended Ebertin and should include Witte, Jacobsen, Sherman, Niggeman and other Uranian (Hamburg school) astrologers. The Uranians use hypothetical planets that can confuse a neophyte; the Cosmobiologists (Ebertin, *et al*) do not. They have a commonly practical, if dark, world view. Williams' *Financial Astrology* (American Federation of Astrologers) is the major English-language work dedicated to market analysis and provides a good grounding in research.

Almost as an antidote to the Hamburg school (where traditional house systems and more conventional planetary correlations are happily ignored), one should study William Lilly's *Christian Astrology* (Regulus) and Barbara Watters' *Horary Astrology & Judgment of Events* (American Federation of Astrologers). Horary/event/mundane/elections provide the wordly thesaurus of astrologese. They also share a "dynamic" concept of waxing, culminating and waning events. Several of these dynamic horary premises are important in market analysis. I would also recommend the writings of Grant Lewi, which are available reprinted in paperback. He was a writer with a more mundane viewpoint who applied astrological concepts to daily (though not financial) events. Charles E. O. Carter wrote a slim volume entitled *Political Astrology* (L. N. Fowler), which is also an example of the same realistic interpretive outlook.

Judy Johns

Judy Johns is an internationally known astrologer whose field of expertise is mundane astrology—the study of this planet's people and their power structures and struggles.

She began her astrological studies in 1960 and by 1965 she had begun her career as counselor, lecturer and teacher. She is very active in a number of astrological associations, having served as VP of Aquarius Workshops, Inc., as well as director of publications for *Aspects* magazine. She is currently Los Angeles coordinator for AFAN.

A popular and respected lecturer, Judy has spoken before many prestigious organizations including SWAC, ASSC, SDAS, NCGR in San Francisco, UAC '86 and, of course, Aquarius Workshops, Inc. Judy has taught and lectured at Immaculate Heart College in Los Angeles, Cal-State, Northridge, various Los Angeles area schools and professional organizations. She also contributes her services to local drug abuse programs for young people.

An accomplished author, she contributes the Mundane column for *Aspects* and has written for Llewellyn's "Astrological Guide" series as well as their calendars. She is presently completing a book on political astrology soon to be published by ACS.

THE GANN TECHNIQUE

W. D. GANN: 1878-1955

W. D. Gann was born June 6, 1878, on a ranch located in Lufkin, Texas. He was brought up in a very strict Methodist family, was said to have memorized significant portions of the Bible and was mathematically gifted.

Lufkin, in east Texas, is cotton-growing country. Being raised there adds even more to the amazing story of this man. Somewhere along the line, a teen-age cotton warehouse clerk became a young stockbroker and then transformed himself into a Wall Street giant. In 1910 he offered an advisory service which cost $3,000 to $4,000 dollars a year. This was during the time when an average wage was just $15 per week. During his 50-year career, Gann pulled over $50,000,000 from the stock and commodity markets by knowing well ahead of time just what the markets would do. "I figure things by mathematics," Mr. Gann explained. "There is nothing mysterious about any of my predictions. If I have the data, I can use algebra and geometry and tell exactly by the theory of cycles when a certain thing is going to occur again."

Gann made his first trade in commodities on August 15, 1902, to inaugurate a spectacular trading career. On May 12, 1908, he left Oklahoma City for New York City and opened a brokerage office. On August 8th of the same year, he made one of his greatest mathematical discoveries for predicting the trend of stocks and commodities. He started trading with $300 in his account and made $25,000. He opened another account with $130 and generated over $12,000 in a mere 30 days.

On October 1, 1909, Gann publicly demonstrated his skills as a trader. Before a group of reporters and numerous witnesses, he made 286 trades during a 25-day period. Of these trades, 254 were profitable. An unbelievable 92% success rate! It must be assumed that the 25-day period Gann selected was not by random choice even though the stock market of October 1909 appears not to have been in any significant trend. In September, October and November of 1909, the Dow was at 71.46, 71.32 and 71.90, respectively.

One of the famous trades made by Gann occurred during the summer of 1909 when he predicted that September wheat would sell at $1.20. This meant that it must touch that figure before the end of the month of September. At twelve o'clock Chicago time on September 30th (the last day), the option was selling below $1.08, and it looked as though his prediction would not be fulfilled. Gann said, "If it does not touch $1.20 by the close of the market, it will prove that there is something wrong with my whole method of calculation. I do not care what the price is now; it must go there." It is now legend that September wheat surprised the whole country by selling at $1.20 and no higher in the very last hour of trading, closing at that exact price.

Gann was a workaholic and a deeply religious man. All of his published works are liberally sprinkled with quotations from the Bible. He often researched prices of stocks or commodities back as far as 700 years when the date was available. He was deeply immersed in number theory and often claimed his work was based on "natural laws." "Time progresses as the Earth rotates and is measured by the progression of numbers." Gann believed the market had a *natural pace of movement* based on a time and price relationship. Therefore, a trend would remain in effect until time "had run out." This natural movement followed certain trend lines which could be calculated.

In 1914 he predicted the World War and the panic in stocks. In 1918 he predicted the end of the war and the Kaiser's abdication. In his "Annual Forecast" published in the fall of 1918, he indicated that 1919 would bring a boom in oil stocks as well as a general Bull Market in stocks, events which actually occurred. In November of 1920, his "Annual Forecast" on stocks for the coming year predicted a panic and an extreme low for stocks for August of 1921. He also predicted improvement in the overall business climate to begin in the summer of 1921.

In 1923 he wrote *Truth of the Stock Tape*. This book, pronounced by experts as the best book ever written on the stock market, was favorably reviewed by the *Wall Street Journal*, the *Financial Times* of London, and other newspapers in the United States and Canada.

In November of 1928, Gann's "Annual Forecast" predicted the end of the great Bull Market in stocks to occur on September 3, 1929. He added that he felt that the greatest panic in history would follow. Gann wrote, "September— One of the sharpest declines of the year is indicated. There will be loss of confidence by investors and the public will try to get out after it is too late. Storms will damage crops and the general business outlook will become cloudy. War news will upset the market and bring unfavorable developments in foreign countries. A 'Black Friday' is indicated and a panicky decline in stocks with only small rallies. The short side will prove the most profitable. You should sell short and pyramid on the way down."

History proved his uncanny accuracy, and his term "Black Friday" became a household word.

Gann wrote a booklet called "Wall Street Selector" which was published in June of 1930. One of the chapters titled "Investors Panic" described conditions just as they occurred during 1931-33. From pages 203-4: "The coming

investors panic will be the greatest in history because there
are at least 15 to 25 million investors in the United States
who hold stocks in the leading corporations, and when
once they get scared, which they will after years of decline,
then the selling will be so terrific that no buying power can
withstand it. Stocks are so well distributed in the hands of
the public since the 1929 panic many people think that the
market is panic-proof, but this seeming strength is really
the weakest feature of the market." In April 1930 when this
was written, the Dow Jones Industrial Averages were selling at 297.50. The DJIA declined to 40.50 on July 8, 1932—
the all-time historical low.

DEVELOPMENT OF THE GANN TECHNIQUE

Gann found it interesting that Charles Dow was one of
the first to recognize the ten-year cycle in stock market
averages. For each month in the years 1873 to 1923, 50
years of record embracing 600 months, there was a definite
ten-year cycle. Dow and others noted the appearance of the
cycle, but treated it as a mere curiosity and never tried to
apply mathematical reasoning to it. The ever-curious Gemini
must have been asking himself, "Why?"

In his astrological studies, he discovered that these
ten-year cycles were due to the varying distance between
the two planets Saturn and Jupiter. The time between conjunctions and oppositions is a little less than ten calendar
years. (There is some irregularity in this cycle due to retrograde periods, however.)

In all of his books, Gann writes:
There are two kinds of numbers, odd and even.
We add numbers together, which is increasing. We
multiply, which is a shorter way to increase. We subtract, which decreases, and we divide, which also
decreases. With the use of higher mathematics we
find a quicker and easier way to divide, subtract, add

and multiply.

Everything in nature is male and female, white and black, harmony or inharmony, right and left. The market moves only two ways, up and down. There are three dimensions which we know how to prove—width, length and height. We use three figures in geometry, the circle, the square and the triangle. We get the square and triangle points of a circle to determine points of time, price and space resistance. We use the circle of 360 degrees to measure time and price.

There are 360 degrees in a circle, no matter how large or small the circle may be. Certain numbers of these degrees and angles are of vast importance and indicate when important tops and bottoms occur on stocks, as well as denote important resistance levels.

Every movement in the market is the result of a natural law and of a cause which exists long before the effect takes place and can be determined years in advance. The future is but a repetition of the past, as the Bible plainly states: "The thing that hath been, it is that which shall be; and that which is done, is that which shall be done, and there is no new thing under the sun." (Eccl. 1:9).

Gann noted that *everything has a major and a minor cycle,* and in order to be accurate in forecasting the future, you must know when the major cycles are due to occur as the most money is made when extreme fluctuations in prices occur.

TIME CYCLES

Gann claimed that *time* is the most important factor in determining market movements because *the future is a repetition of the past* and each market is working out time in relation to some previous time cycle. He kept daily, weekly, monthly and yearly charts on stocks and commodities. Gann watched closely when he recorded an extreme high or extreme low price, counting out in time when he thought the cycle would alter.

The importance of time he no doubt ascribed to astrological causes. Cycles of time are as old as ancient history and as new as today as the Sun rises every morning and sets each night. It is interesting how he took these studies, applied geometrical logic and derived his system of un-matched predictability.

Gann teaches that the great time cycles are most important because they record the periods of extreme high or low prices which occur over a long period of time. These cycles are 90 years, 82 to 84 years, 60 years, 49 years, 45 years, 30 years and 20 years.

The minor time cycles are 15 years, 13 years, 10 years, 7 years, 5 years, 3 years, 2 years and 1 year. These minor cycles indicate somewhat smaller fluctuations in prices.

Gann's work is the methodical division of the circle into precise geometrical angles that we call *aspects*.

Table of Geometric Angles

30 years or 360 months
22½ years is ¾ of this cycle or 270 months
20 years is ⅔ or 240 months
15 years is ½ or 180 months
13 years is 156 months
10 years is ⅓ or 120 months
9 years is 108 months
7½ years is ¼ or 90 months
5 years is ⅙ or 60 months
3¾ years is ⅛ or 45 months
2½ years is ¹⁄₁₂ or 30 months
1⅞ years is ¹⁄₁₆ or 22½ months
¹⁄₃₂ is 11¼ months

The 90-Year Cycle

When we start from sunrise or the horizon and measure to noon, we get an arc of 90 degrees which is straight up and down from the bottom. Ninety months or 90 years is a very significant time period because it is two times the 45-year cycle and three times the 30-year cycle. This can be translated as a classical explanation of why the sharpest angle in astrology, the square, produces the most action. This angle divides the sidereal year into quarters. Gann evidently found that this division also proves important in much larger time frames.

The 82-84-Year Cycle

This is one of the great cycles in cotton. The extreme historical high point in cotton was in 1864. In 1946, 82 years later, Gann correctly called for another high in prices between July 9th and October 5th to the 8th. The next cycle high in cotton is due in 2028. This astrologically relates to the Uranus return.

The 60-Year Cycle

The circle equals 360 degrees, and the main cotton cycle is 360 months, or 30 years. Gann said one should always use this cycle of 30 years and proportionate parts of it on all charts. The 60-year cycle is double the 30-year cycle. For example, a high on cotton prices occurred in 1864; a low in 1894; and another high during 1923-1924, 30 years from the bottom, completing the 60-year cycle. Gann carried these time cycles forward on all his charts. He liked to trade during the periods of extreme pricing, when the moves are sharp, quick and the most profitable.

The 49-Year Cycle

The 49-year period ends a major cycle for wheat, and extreme high or low prices occur 49 to 50 years apart. A period of "jubilee" years of extreme high or low prices, lasting from five to seven years, occurs at the end of the 50-year cycle. He explains that "seven" is a fatal number, referred to many times in the Bible, which brings about contraction, depression and panics. Seven times seven equals 49, which is known as the fatal evil year, causing extreme fluctuations in prices. Gann also applied this major cycle to mundane events, predicting rises and falls of governments and indicating possibilities of wars and periods of particularly poor harvests.

The 45-Year Cycle

When added together, the digits 1 through 9 total 45. Gann claimed that 45 degrees is the most important angle. Therefore, 45 years in time is a very important cycle. One half of 45 is 22½ years, or 270 months. One fourth of 45 is 11¼ years, or 135 months, which is three times 45. One eighth of 45 is 5⅝ or 67½ months. One sixteenth of 45 is 33¾ months.

The 30-Year Cycle

This is one of the main Gann cycles, and minor cycles are proportionate parts of the 30-year cycle or circle. Thirty degrees encompasses a whole astrological sign, and 12 signs complete the entire zodiac. Gann took this theory even further with his geometry, taking the natural astrological division of the year and projecting it onto a larger time framework. A 30-year cycle is roughly the Saturn return; at 15 years we experience the Saturn opposition. At 7½ years, or 90 months, we experience the first Saturn square. The second Saturn square occurs at about 22½ years of age.

The 20-Year Cycle

It is ⅓ of the 60-year cycle. Twenty years equal 240 months, which is ⅔ of the circle of 360 degrees. The 20-year cycle in business points to the repeating Jupiter/Saturn conjunctions.

The 15-Year Cycle

It is half of the 30-year cycle, 180 degrees, the first Saturn opposition. Gann used the hard-series angles in astrology.

The 13-Year Cycle

Wheat is quite sensitive to a 13-year cycle and often works out this cycle from extreme high to extreme low and back again. Extremely large crops or small crops frequently recur 13 years, or 156 months, apart. Important tops or bottoms are often found 13 years, 26 years, 39 years, then 49 to 52 years apart.

The 10-Year Cycle

This is ⅓ of the 30-year cycle, ½ of the 20-year cycle, and relates to the regular opposition of the business planets Jupiter and Saturn.

Futures trading on the Japanese yen began on May 16, 1972, in Chicago. There was a ceremony at 9 A.M. and the first contract traded five to ten minutes later. The yen opened at about .320 in 1972; ten years later in 1982, it made a cycle low at .340.

The 7-Year Cycle

You should check seven years from any important top or bottom. Also watch 14 years, 21 years, 28 years and all other multiples of seven. Tops and bottoms often come out 7½ years apart or on the 90th month. It is important to watch 90 months for a minor as well as major bottom. This Gann cycle relates, of course, to our square aspect again.

The 5-Year Cycle

This period of 60 months is important because it is ¼ of the 20-year cycle, ½ of the ten-year cycle and ⅙ of the 360-degree or 30-year period. This is one of the finest explanations of the five-year business cycle I know. The fact that this cycle also reflects proportions of other major cycles increases its significance.

The 3-Year Cycle

Culminations of major and minor moves often occur in the 34th to 36th month from major and minor tops and bottoms. Watch three years from any important top or bottom as a change in trend is likely to occur.

The 1-Year Cycle

This is the smallest cycle, but in view of the fact that there is a grain harvest in the United States every year and a spring and winter crop of wheat, important changes in trend often occur one year from previous tops and bottoms. There may not be a change in the main trend, but a reaction can run one to three months at the end of a one-year period. Whenever you begin to look for a place to make a trade, always check back and see if the market is running out a major cycle or a minor one, especially if the market is nearing extreme high or low prices.

Gann used traditional seasonal time periods for charting his commodities work, beginning his year at the Vernal Equinox.

Each March 21st, he divided the year into 22½-degree sections. March 21st to September 23rd divides the year in half. June 21st to December 21st further divides the year into quarters. We now have the division of the circle by traditional cardinal signs that Gann called "The Cardinal Cross." He further divided in half each of these sections— May 5th to November 9th and February 4th to August 5th. These divisions he called "The Fixed Cross." His next divisions of the year were halfway between the dates of these two crosses. These dates divided the year into six-teenths, each 22½ degrees apart—April 12th to October 16th, May 27th to November 30th, July 14th to January 13th, and August 31st to February 26th.

Gann Yearly Breakdown Table

May 5 ends ⅛ or 6½ weeks, 1½ months, or 45 days from March 21

June 21 ends ¼ or 13 weeks, 3 months, or 90 days from March 21

July 23 ends ⅓ or 17 weeks, 4 months from March 21

August 5 ends ⅜ or 19½ weeks from March 21

September 22 ends ½ or 26 weeks from March 21

November 8 ends ⅝ or 32½ weeks from March 21

November 22 ends ⅔ or 35 weeks from March 21

December 21 ends ¾ or 39 weeks from March 21

February 4 ends ⅞ or 45½ weeks from March 21

March 20 ends 1 year or 52 weeks from March 21

These dates mark periods when important changes in trend of a contract or commodity occur. The seventh week from March 21 (or any other important top or bottom) falls on the 45-degree angle in time and signals a change in direction. The division of the year by 16 produces a period of 22½ days, or approximately three weeks, and accounts for market movements that run three weeks up or down, then reverse trend. *As a general rule, when a commodity closes higher the fourth consecutive week, it will continue higher.* Gann said the fifth week of a contract was also very important for a change in trend with fast moves in price up or down in relation to the major cycle it is in.

Gann was an advocate of the old Chinese proverb, "One good picture is worth 10,000 words." He was an avid chartist, keeping yearly, monthly, weekly and daily charts on stocks and commodities. He tried to accumulate as much price history as possible in order to run his cycle dates as far back as he could to look for significant major moves.

He used eight spaces to the inch graph paper, marking high and low movements of prices. He drew geometrical angles from significant tops or bottoms. *The 45-degree angle was used to define a major change in trend.* The 22½-degree angle also helped him to define changes. Gann said the drawing of his lines on graph paper reduced the possibility of error. Figures might be added wrong, but the visuality of geometry permitted one to correct any mistakes.

The closing price was more important to him than inter-day highs and lows. He counted days, weeks or months across the bottom of his charts from important tops or bottoms.

Gann taught that a yearly high/low chart should run as far back as five, 10 or 20 years. The monthly high/low chart should run back at least 10 years, and the weekly high/low chart should run back two or three years. Keeping the yearly chart will show the major cycles in force; the monthly chart will show major changes in trend; and the daily charts, the minor price fluctuations.

BUYING & SELLING POWER

When any market advances, it advances on buying and increased demand. When buying power is greater than selling power, the market makes higher tops and higher bottoms and continues to move up until selling power becomes greater than buying power. Then the trend reverses.

When the supply exceeds the demand and selling power is greater than buying power, prices decline to a level where support or buying power comes in and overbalances selling power. Then a rally takes place.

In order for stocks or commodities to show an up trend and continue to advance, they must make higher bottoms and higher tops. When the trend is down, they must make lower tops and lower bottoms and continue down to lower levels. However, prices can move in a narrow trading range for weeks, months, or even years and not make a new high or low. Prices often need time to allow for consolidation. After a long period of time when commodities break into new lows, they indicate lower prices. Similarly, when commodities advance above old highs or old tops after a considerable time frame, they are in a stronger position and indicate higher prices. This is why Gann felt you must have considerable chart history in order to see just what price position a commodity is in and at what stage it is between the extreme high and extreme low.

FOLLOWING THE TREND

You will always make money by following the main trend as stocks or commodities go up or down. Commodities are never too high to buy as long as the trend is up, and they are never too low to sell as long as the trend is down. Never sell short just because the commodity is high or because you think it is too high. Never sell out and take profits just because the price is high. *Buy and sell according to definite rules and not on hope, fear or guesswork.* Never buy a commodity just because the price is low. There is usually a good reason why it is low, and it could go lower.

When making a trade, remember that you could be wrong or the market could change its trend and a "stop" will protect you and limit your losses.

Place stops below the lows of swings and not just below the lows on a daily chart. Stops must be above old tops or below old bottoms on a weekly or monthly chart. Stops placed below closing prices on the daily or weekly chart are much safer and less likely to be caught because you are moving your stops according to the trend. The swings or reversals in a market are the prices on which to place stops one way or the other.

Get out of the market quickly as soon as you see that you have made a mistake. If your position trade closes two consecutive days against you, get out of the trade. Traders who consistently keep their losses to a minimum and let their profits run are the most successful.

Never get a fixed idea of just how high any price is going to go or just how low prices are going. You cannot make the market go your way—you must go the market's way and follow the trend.

Gann said, "Most people want to get rich too quick. That is why they lose their money. They start investing or speculating without first preparing themselves or getting a commodity education. They do not have the knowledge to start with, and the result is they make serious mistakes which cost them money."

Do not try to lead the market or make the market. Follow the trend which is made by big men who make big money and you will make money. Buy when the market makers are ready for prices to move up fast, sell when they are ready for prices to move down fast, and you will make large profits in a short amount of time.

Gann advised to stay out of slow markets that are trading in a narrow range. Trade only when the market shows a definite trend, and trade according to definite rules. Gann was a patient man and a disciplined trader. He waited to trade when the markets were poised for a quick advance or a serious decline. The most money is made watching stocks or commodities in periods of accumulation or distribution, trading the breakouts of these price levels.

The longer the time period in days, weeks, months or years when prices exceed old highs or break new lows, the greater the importance of the change in trend. Remember, when prices advance to new highs, they generally react back to the old tops, which is a safe place to buy, and when they decline to new levels, as a rule they rally back to the old lows, which is a safe place to sell.

When prices decline 50% of the highest selling level, you can buy with a stop just below the low prices. The next strongest buying point is 50% between the extreme low and the extreme high.

When prices advance after being far below the 50% point and reach it for the first time, it is a selling level or place to sell short.

One of Gann's rules was to take the extreme high and low prices for a stock, subtracting the low from the high. Take this number and divide by two to get the mid-range. Add this number to the low price to determine if a stock is a buy or a sell. For example:

High - 125; Low - 50.
The low of 50 subtracted from the high of 125 equals 75. If we divide 75 by 2, the mid-range is 37.50. The low of 50 plus 37.50 produces 87.50. If a stock was trading below 87.50, it would indicate a buy. If it were trading above this price, it would indicate a sell.

The weekly high and low chart is a very important trend indicator. When prices get above a series of weekly highs or lows or decline below a series of weekly lows, it is of greater importance and indicates a greater change in trend which may last for many weeks. A minor change in trend occurs every 7, 10, 14, 20, 28, and 30 days.

When prices advance above or decline below prices which have occurred for many months past, it means a greater change in trend which can last for several months. Changes in trend occur every 30, 60, 90, 120, 135, 225, 270, 300, 315, and 360 days.

When prices advance above or decline below the prices made several years in the past, it is nearly always a sure sign of big moves which will last for a long period of time, or at least have a greater advance or decline in a short period of time. When these old highs are crossed, always watch for a reaction to come back to around the old highs, or slightly lower. After lows are broken, expect the rally to advance back to around the old highs or slightly lower. Remember, the longer the time period when price is exceeded, the greater the breakout move up or down.

THE COMMODITY MARKET

History proves that wars break out every 20 to 25 years. It also proves that there is a great wave of speculation and a boom of some kind in nearly every country every 20 to 25 years. Why do these war periods and boom times come at such regular cycles or intervals? Human nature never changes. Every 20 years, a new generation comes along. They are full of hope, optimistic and inexperienced.

It is the same with the commodity market. The young generations want to take a chance. It is the nature of youth to gamble, to take chances and to be fearless of danger. When they get into a runaway Bull Market, they have no more sense than to keep on buying. They throw caution to the wind. This increases buying power because commodities go to heights unwarranted by supply and demand. The result is when the boom is over the young generations suffer severe losses, get some valuable experience and are not so anxious to try it again.

Just as young generations come along from time to time, we will continue to have booms in business, booms in the stock market and commodities, and land booms and other waves of speculation. History repeats because human nature does not change and each coming generation has to go through the same experience as the former generation.

The human mind works in the same way most of the time. People get used to particular numbers, and they trade at these prices more than others. The average man or woman thinks in multiples of 5 and 10. The public likes to buy or sell at 25, 50, 60, 75, 100, etc. For example, traders will have selling orders at 275 contract for wheat, but the market will very often advance to 274¾ or 274⅞, not 275. The traders fail to execute their sell order at 275, and the market declines away from them. A study of the extreme high and low prices in the past will show how commodities often miss these popular trading prices in these even figures.

The Master Time and Price Calculator

The layout of this calculator consists of a series of numbers sequentially placed on a square grid with "1" occupying the center square. The numbers increase as they form ever larger perfect squares. The grid is superimposed with circles and divided by lines defining geometrical angles along with corresponding dates and times of the year. This was one of Gann's greatest discoveries and remains a mystery to many even today.

The time and price angles in order of strength and importance are defined as follows:

The 90-degree angle is the strongest angle because it is vertical or straight up and down. This angle is the astrological square. Next in strength is the 180-degree angle as it is square to the 90-degree angle, or 90 degrees from the 90-degree angle. It equates to the astrological opposition. Next in power is the 270-degree angle; it is in opposition or 180 degrees from the 90-degree angle, which divides the circle, the strongest point. 270 months equals 22½ years or one-half of 45. 360 degrees ends the circle, returning to the beginning point opposite the 180-degree or halfway point, the other angle that equals one-half of the circle.

120 and 240 degrees are ⅓ and ⅔ of the circle. 120 degrees (the trine) is 90 degrees plus 30 degrees, which is ⅓ of 90 degrees. 240 is 180 plus ⅓ or 60 degrees (sextile).

Thus, these are strong angles for the measurement of time.
Other significant angles are as follows:

45° angle	is ½ of 90 degrees
135° angle	is 90 degrees plus 45
225° angle	is 45 degrees plus 180 degrees or 180 from 45
315° angle	45 degrees from 270 degrees or 180 from 135
Cardinal	The angles of 90°, 180°, 270° and 360° form the first important cross known as "The Cardinal Cross."
Fixed	The angles of 45°, 135°, 225°, and 315° are known as "the Fixed Cross."

Another example of Gann's mathematical genius was his comparison of money to the division of the circle—his discovery that **price and time can be equal**.

The division of a circle by eight equals 45 degrees. Based on $1.00, the division of the whole unit by eighths gives us the half dollar, the quarter, and years ago we had 12½ cent pieces. Stock fluctuations are based on ⅛, ¼, ⅜, ½, ⅝, ¾, ⅞, and the whole dollar.

Figuring $1.00, or par, as a basis for stock prices and changing these prices to degrees, 12½ cents equals the 45-degree angle (semi-square), 25 cents equals the 90-degree angle (square), 37½ cents equals the 135-degree angle (sesquiquadrate), 50 cents equals the 180-degree angle (opposition), 62½ cents equals the 225-degree angle, 75 cents equals the 270-degree angle, 82½ cents equals the 315-degree angle, and $1.00 equals 360 degrees.

The squaring of price and time means an equal number of points up or down balancing an equal number of time periods, either days, weeks or months. Market corrections or reactions are simply the squaring out of minor time periods, and later the big declines or big advances are the squaring out of major time periods.

HOW TO USE THE GANN INFORMATION

When a stock sells at 50 on the 180th day, week or month, it is on the degree of its time angle.

If the bottom of a stock is 25, at the end of 25 days, weeks or months, time and price are equal. Watch for a change in trend as based on its bottom or lowest selling price. As long as a stock continues to hold one bottom and keeps advancing, you can always use this time period running across and continuing the time period.

If the top of the stock is 50, when it has moved over 50 days, weeks or months, it has reached its square in time and an important change in trend is indicated.

Both major and minor tops and bottoms on all time periods must be watched as they square out right along. Most important of all is the extreme high point on the monthly high and low chart. This may be very high and work out a long time period before it squares the top, in which case you have to divide the price into eight equal time periods and watch the most important points like $\frac{1}{4}$, $\frac{1}{3}$, $\frac{1}{2}$, $\frac{3}{4}$, but *most important of all is when time equals price.*

The life of a commodity can never be more than 12 months. Therefore, the important changes in trend occur in the 3rd, 6th, and 9th months, especially the 6th and the 9th because they are one half and three fourths the life of the contract. Traders often start trading the March contract in December, the June contract in March, the September contract in June, and the December contract in September. The 4th or last quarter, or last three months, nearly always marks a reversal in trend and a rapid move one way or the other.

The most important point on the monthly high and low chart to carry the time periods from is the extreme low of the life of the stock in addition to the date of incorporation or the date trading began on the stock exchange.

U.S. Steel was incorporated on Feb. 25, 1901. Trading

began on the NY Stock Exchange on March 28, 1901, when it opened at 42¾. February 1931 was 360 months, or 30 years, from incorporation. It then began a new cycle as it had completed 360 degrees in time. (1961 was the start of the second cycle, and in 1991 a third cycle will begin.)

The range that a stock makes between extreme high and extreme low can be squared so long as it remains in the same price range. If the range is 25 points, it squares with 25 periods of time—days, weeks, or months.

The next important price to square with time is the lowest price or bottom of any important decline. If the bottom of a stock is 25, then at the end of 25 days, weeks or months, time and price are equal. Then watch for a change in trend as based on its bottom or lowest selling price.

Another important point to square is the extreme high price of a stock. If the top of a stock is 50, then watch for a change in trend 50 days, weeks or months from this time period.

The Dow Jones made a monthly high of 1067 in January 1973; the next high occurred in September of 1976 at 1026. Forty-four months separated the two tops. 1067 - 44 = 1023. The 1976 top exceeded that number by three points. The next top occurred in September of 1980 at 978. September 1976 to September of 1980 spanned four years or 48 months. 1026 - 48 months equals 978. The September 1980 top was at 980.

W. D. Gann died in New York on June 14, 1955, ending a 75-year life filled with Gemini curiosity and Taurus perspicacity. Students of his work are always in awe of his brilliant mathematical discoveries. Those who take the time to learn astrology have a distinct advantage in understanding his magnificent work.

We haven't many clues as to what the exact spark was

that set Gann off in the pursuit of ancient wisdom, but there is little doubt that he wholeheartedly delved into ancient mathematical teachings, especially those of Euclid, Pythagoras, Aristotle; ancient numerical teaching, Far Eastern thought manifested in the areas of metaphysical consciousness, astronomy and astrology, universal laws and truths; the proportionality and the mathematics of the world's greatest and most perfect structure—the Great Pyramid of Giza; and much more. His great success was in his ability to transform this knowledge into reading the inner action of stock and commodity markets with an accuracy unmatched today.

Carol S. Mull

Carol S. Mull's lifelong interest in astrology has focused into the business and financial areas. She is owner/editor of Mull Publishing, which produces a newsletter, "The Wall Street Astrologer," and a mail-order correspondence course in financial astrology. She is the author of two books, *The Standard and Poor's "500"* and *750 Over-the-Counter Stocks*, both published by AFA. She has lectured at several conferences, been interviewed on radio and television, and has written for various astrological publications.

In 1988, Carol, in partnership with Grace Morris, founded the World Conferences of Astro-Economics which are held in Chicago each November.

She is a member of both AFA and NCGR.

Carol's résumé includes being a corporate accountant and comptroller, an accountant for a bank trust department, and teacher in a business college. Her B.A. degree from Indiana University is in Cultural Philosophy, supplemented with graduate work in Psychology and Sociology.

She also operates an obsolete pattern silver-matching service.

PREDICTING THE DOW

Most financial astrologers rely on half a dozen major aspects or cycles to predict the DJIA, but in my Virgoan complexity, I blend 30 or so factors. Another way that I differ from all but two other financial astrologers is that in my newsletter, "The Wall Street Astrologer," I make a definite daily prediction rather than a generalized weekly or monthly trend. To do this, I use cycles, planetary aspects, eclipses, the Galactic Center, the Elliott Wave, equinox and solstice charts, the charts of the New York Stock Exchange, the United States, the U.S. Treasury, the U.S. Federal Reserve, U.S. Currency, the Chicago Board of Trade, the Chicago Mercantile Exchange, and Comex, N.Y., and various stock index charts. It is also important to listen carefully to what the politicians are saying so that you will know what they plan or want to do to our economy.

ECONOMIC CYCLES
Economic cycles, as well as equinox and solstice charts, indicate the general background condition or trend of the market, but precise predictions can only be made from the planetary aspects. *Thus, the use of cycles is to provide the correct environment for your planetary aspects.* I recommend that you become a member of The Foundation for the Study of Cycles, 3333 Michelson Drive, Suite 210, Irvine, California 92715, phone 714-261-7261. *Cycles,* their monthly periodical, is very worthwhile. You might also want to contact

Nova Sun Watch of Boulder, Colorado for free sunspot information.

About ten cycles and sub-cycles affect the U.S. stock market, and there are at least seven commodity cycles. They exist because mankind moves through periods of optimism, expansion, anxiety, depression, and panic as dictated by the magnetic winds that govern our Universe. These cycles are not exact, but their study can yield results that have a high degree of probability, and the best results of all can be obtained when two or three cycles show the same trend. The three most reliable stock market cycles are **McWhirter's Moon Node Cycle**, the **28-day lunar cycle**, and the **four-year cycle** that is an overlap of the **Kitchin, Mars/ Vesta**, and **Mars/Jupiter** cycles.

The Lunar Cycle

The lunar cycle was first studied and presented to the faculty of the Graduate School of Pace University by Frank J. Guarino, in partial fulfillment of the requirements for his Master of Business Administration degree. Later, his thesis was published by the American Federation of Astrologers. Modern cyclists have carried Guarino's work much farther. Today, it is possible to predict the market with 70% accuracy using only the lunar cycle.

The Sun and the Moon are in square aspect (90°) during the first and last quarters, in opposition (180°) at the Full Moon, and in conjunction (0°) at the New Moon. They are in sextile (60°) between the New Moon and the first quarter and between the last quarter and the New Moon. See Figure 1.

For precise work, compute a *heliocentric* chart for the times that the Moon, Earth, and Sun are in exact aspect. Unless there are other overshadowing influences, trines and conjunctions will be up, squares will be down, oppositions will be somewhat up, and sextiles can be either direction.

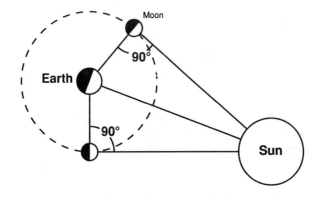

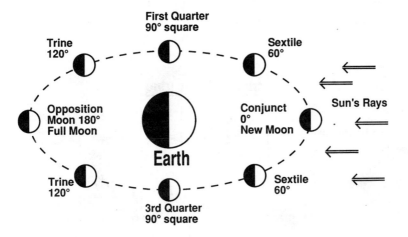

Figure 1

Most financial astrologers will tell you that oppositions (Full Moons) will send the market down, but my experience does not verify this. Apparently, the momentum of being between two trines will carry the opposition along. If the next aspect following a sextile is a conjunction, the sextile is likely to correlate with an upward movement. But if the aspect following a sextile is a square, the sextile is likely to be accompanied by a downward-moving market. See Figure 2.

Conjunction, New Moon	Up	Bull
Sextile	Downward	Bearish
Square, First Quarter	Down	Bear
Trine	Up	Bull
Opposition, Full Moon	Somewhat Up	Bullish
Trine	Up	Bull
Square, Last Quarter	Down	Bear
Sextile	Upward	Bullish
Conjunction, New Moon	Up	Bull

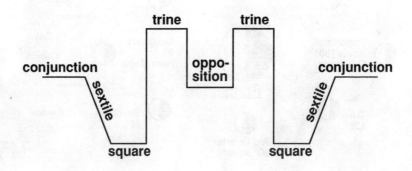

Figure 2

Another lunar cycle concerns the *elements.* The market tends to move up whenever the Moon is in an Air or Fire sign and to move downward whenever the Moon is in an Earth or Water sign.

Other recent experiments have attempted to tie the Moon's velocity and the angular rates of positive acceleration or negative acceleration to the market. These have been inconclusive.

The 3⅓-Year Kitchin Cycle

Within the average 11.094-year sunspot cycle, there are shorter periods of solar prominence which occur every 40 or 42 months. These were first recognized in 1923 by the American economist Joseph Kitchin. They account for trade fluctuations and have a marked effect on terrestrial weather, alternating between hot and dry to cold and wet.

Articles in *Cycles* magazine proclaim a 40.68-month cycle, an example of which follows:

Trough	January 1979
Crest	October 1980
Trough	June 1982
Crest	February 1984
Trough	November 1985
Crest	June 1987

The Mars/Vesta Cycle (4.17 years)

The planet Mars and the asteroid Vesta have a synodic cycle period of 4.17 years. (Mars often serves as a trigger planet to aspects of the heavier business planets (Saturn, Uranus, and Jupiter); Vesta has consistently been found in a prominent position in the natal horoscopes of stock traders.) The Dow is likely to peak at the first square (90-degree angle from the conjunction) between Mars and Vesta and to bottom at the second trine aspect (240-degree angle from the conjunction).

Based on this, you should have bought May 28, 1985, and sold on December 7, 1987. (*Ed. Note:* October 19, 1987 was Black Monday. December would have been too late in this case.)

The 4½-Year Martian Cycle

According to Lt. Comdr. David Williams, author of *Financial Astrology* (American Federation of Astrologers), the Mars/Jupiter 4½-year cycle is one of the most dependable market indicators. Mars and Jupiter are in conjunction or opposition every 2.2353 years. Thus, every other conjunction is 4.4706 years, or approximately 234 weeks.

Thomas Rieder, author of *Astrological Warnings & the Stock Market* (Pagurian Press), ties the 4½-year cycle to the synodic period of Mars. The synodic period of a planet is the length of time elapsing between two successive conjunctions of that planet with the Sun as seen from Earth. Mars conjoins the Sun at intervals of about two years and three months, so this cycle is just twice the synodic period of Mars.

The 4-Year Presidential Cycle

The 3⅓-, 4.17-, and 4½-year cycles overlap and become what is sometimes referred to as the 4-year presidential cycle. It is theorized that the government stimulates the economy at election time to provide the illusion of prosperity and to insure the re-election of the President. However, closer analysis reveals that the cycle also exists in countries where elections are held every six or eight years or not at all.

The 9.225-Year Cycle

Juglar first noticed a cycle averaging nine years, but varying from seven to ten years, which correlated with Mars/Jupiter oppositions. Later studies by the French economist Clement established the average length as 9.225

years. This particular cycle has proven to be 86% correct (as the June 1974 crest proves!). Recent predicted crests and troughs are as follows:

Crest	April 1965
Trough	January 1970
Crest	June 1974
Trough	March 1979
Crest	August 1983
Trough	May 1988

Ideally, the cycle should continue:

Crest	October 1992
Trough	July 1997
Crest	January 2002

The 11.094-Year Sunspot Cycle

The 11.094-year sunspot cycle varies from eight to 16 years, producing alterations in depression, activity, excitement, and collapse.

The variance in the heat emitted by the Sun increases and decreases in such a way that the interval from one maximum of warmth to the next is, on the average, $3\frac{1}{3}$-years, producing the Kitchin cycle. Every third fluctuation is emphasized so that there is a major variation occurring every 11.094 (average) years.

Sunspots are magnetized and these 11.094-year cycles normally occur in pairs. In one 11-year wave of the cycle, positive spots will lead in the Sun's southern hemisphere. On the next wave, this situation is reversed, so that negative spots lead in the southern hemisphere and positive spots lead in the northern hemisphere. Thus, there is a master or double sunspot cycle.

The sunspot cycle was first propounded in 1801 by the famous English astronomer Sir William Herschel and then in 1875 by the eminent English economist Professor William Stanley Jevons. High temperatures are associated with abundant sunspots and low temperatures with low sunspots. All plant life is more abundant in times of heavy sunspot activity, and this greatly affects the commodity market.

Periods of heavy sunspot activity pour forth energy and all Earth activity is increased—including the stock market.

Jupiter's orbital period is 11.86 years, and it exercises the most effect upon the sunspot cycle, with Mercury, Venus, and Mars also contributing, especially when these planets are on the same side of the Sun as the Earth. The greatest influence of all on this tidal-like force happens when Jupiter and Venus are in a heliocentric line-up with the Earth at 0°, 45°, and 90°, which happens at 11.192654-year intervals.

The well-known Dow cycles of 89, 124, and 208 weeks can be tied to the periodic pull of Jupiter, Venus, Mercury, and Mars to the Sun. To predict major market turning points (up and down), construct *heliocentric* charts for the times these planets aspect the Sun in line with the Earth.

The McWhirter Moon's North Node Cycle (18.6 Years)

Louise McWhirter describes in her book, *Astrology & Stock Market Forecasting* (ASI Pubs., Inc.), a 19-year cycle (actually 18.6) of economic fluctuation which correlates with the movement of the Moon's North Node through the zodiac.

The node effect is due to the fact that the Moon's orbit is inclined 5 degrees and 8 minutes to the plane of the Earth's orbit (the ecliptic). The point where the Moon crosses the ecliptic from south to north is called the ascending or North Node, and where the Moon crosses the ecliptic from north to south is called the descending or South Node.

The high point of business volume is reached when

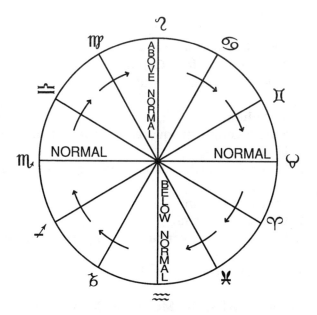

Figure 3

the North Node transits **Leo**. Taurus is the transition point, or normal point, as the curve goes from normal to below normal in business volume. When the North Node enters Aquarius, the low point of business activity has been reached. As the node transits Capricorn and Sagittarius, the normal position of the business curve is below normal going to normal. See Figure 3.

McWhirter also listed some secondary factors which will distort the North Node cycle:

Raise the Volume:
1. Jupiter conjunct the North Node
2. Saturn trine, sextile, or semi-sextile Uranus
3. Jupiter in Gemini or Cancer
4. Jupiter conjunct, sextile, or trine Saturn and Uranus when in aspect to each other
5. The North Node in Gemini
6. Favorable aspects to Pluto

Lower the Volume:
1. Saturn conjunct, square, or opposing the North Node
2. Saturn conjunct, square, opposing or semi-square Uranus
3. Saturn in Gemini
4. Uranus in Gemini
5. Uranus square, conjunct or opposing the North Node
6. Unfavorable aspects to Pluto

Of these cycles, the McWhirter Moon North Node cycle, the 4-year cycle that is an overlap of the Kitchin, Mars/Vesta, and Mars synodic cycle, and the lunar cycle are considered to be the three most reliable cycles for stock market prediction.

Kondratieff Wave of 56 Years (varies 34 to 65 years)

Nikolai D. Kondratieff, a Russian, discovered the 56-year cycle in American business affairs. Unfortunately, he was exiled to Siberia, where he presumably died, as the Kondratieff Wave theory is contrary to the Marxist theory that capitalism will self-destruct.

Regardless of Marx, wars, rebellions, population changes, industrialization, and technological and money changes, American business has been dominated by this 56-year rhythm. In each 56-year period, three major panic periods occur at 20-, 20-, and 16-year intervals. While other panic periods intervene, no discernible pattern is in evidence.

The planetary pattern for this 56-year period is believed to be the aspects of Jupiter/Uranus, Jupiter/Saturn, and Saturn/Uranus, whose time intervals between successive conjunctions are 13.81 years, 19.86 years, and 45.36 years, respectively. These so-called business planets have always been in conjunction, opposition, square, trine, or sextile during major boom and bust periods of American business.

I have done some experimenting with a heliocentric ephemeris for these conjunctions and believe it to be superior for exact timing.

Panic	1761	1817	1873	1929	1985
20-year interval					
Panic	1781	1837	1893	1949	
20-year interval					
Panic	1801	1857	1913	1969	
16-year interval					

Although the time interval indicates that the cycle was due in 1985, *the actual conjunction of Uranus and Saturn did not occur until 1988*. We are now due to see the results of this important cycle.

The Maxwell Energy Cycle and the Wheeler Culture Cycle (100 years)

The one-hundred-year Selby Maxwell weather-energy cycle and the Dr. Raymond Wheeler cultural curve combine to provide a remarkable predictor of the business cycles of *all nations*. This is because business cycles are integrated into the entire cultural pattern.

Selby Maxwell's weather cycle moves successively from warm-wet through warm-dry and cold-wet to cold-dry. The entire cycle lasts about 100 years, and our weather has now moved to cold-dry. Until around 2000 A.D., we may expect bitter cold and a lowered rate of rainfall. At the beginning of the twenty-first century, we should again experience warm-wet weather, which will bring more comfort to the world.

It is of interest that *The Indianapolis Star* reported 22° below zero on January 21, 1985, the coldest since January 5, 1884, 101 years ago. But this was topped in 1986, when Indianapolis temperatures reached 25° below.

If you place the Maxwell weather curve over the Wheeler cultural curve, you will see that they match. And according to Dr. Raymond Wheeler, the cycles of time repeat themselves with astonishing accuracy—right down to the length of hemlines, the styling of hair, and the curse of famine.

Human energies increase during cool weather trends. Business booms come at the end of a cold cycle and the beginning of the warm-wet cycle which follows. All the waves of rapid advancement throughout history have come in the cool cycles, or as a result of the cool cycles.

Human energies decrease during the warm cycle and bring decadence to human affairs. In contrast, increased production resulting from improved growing conditions occurs during the warm-wet cycles. Birthrates, however, decrease in warm times, and as the warm period advances, human energies are depleted even more. The effect of the lowered energy gradually produces an economic depression.

It is also of interest that throughout history, dictators, tyrannies, and the major wars between strong nations have come during each and every warm cycle. On the other hand, civil wars and rebellions, as well as swings to democratic forms of government, have repeatedly come on each cold cycle. Wheeler found that two kinds of wars alternated with one another. That is, there would be a time in history when international wars prevailed, then another when civil wars dominated.

Since we are now in the cold part of the cycle, we may expect civil wars and minor confrontations.

The 500-Year Civilization Cycle Used by Nostradamus

Dr. Raymond Wheeler has also charted 500-year climatic cycles throughout history. He found that every fifth cold phase is an unusually severe one and that these periods have always coincided with great waves of migration and the rise and fall of nations. Old civilizations collapse and new ones are born. The main divisions of history—ancient, medieval, and modern—coincide with these phases.

This process of rising and falling nations moves steadily around the Earth from east to west. We find the remnants of ancient civilizations in Asia, then in the Middle East, then in Europe, and finally in North America.

Now in the 1980s, the 500-year era that has belonged to Europe and her offspring, North America, is coming to an end. If the cycles repeat, the next 500 years of history may belong to Asia. Very recently, Japan is rising and the U.S. is a debtor nation.

It is also of interest to note that all major industrial nations are currently in the Northern Hemisphere and that throughout recorded history when two nations have been at war, it is the one located farthest north that triumphs.

The Elliott Wave—The Master Cycle

The Elliott Wave is a kind of master cycle—or heartbeat of the Universe—that is prevalent throughout nature. It operates both at the micro and macro.

The theory of the Elliott Wave was devised by accountant Ralph Nelson Elliott in the late 1930s. It postulates that *all market activity is a reflection of mass psychology and that for every upward move there is a downward response.*

According to the theory, all market movement occurs

in *waves,* or more specifically, three upward thrusts separated by two intervening downward corrections, then two downward strokes joined by an upward correction. Because of this pattern, it is also called the head and shoulders configuration. Each series of waves ends at a point higher than it began. Each complete cycle is just part of a larger cycle of the same pattern. See Figures 4 and 5.

With the Elliott Wave, things get better all the time. This, like the theory of evolution (both physical and spiritual), must then be working against the natural law of entropy. (One of the basic natural laws is the second law of thermodynamics, which states that energy naturally flows from a state of greater organization to a state of lesser organization, and from a state of higher differentiation to a state of lower differentiation. In other words, the Universe is in a process of winding down. Ultimately, according to the second law of thermodynamics, in billions and billions of years, the Universe will completely wind down until it reaches the lowest point as an amorphous, totally disorganized, totally undifferentiated "blob" in which nothing happens anymore. This state of total disorganization and undifferentiation is termed *entropy* or *the force of entropy.*) Both religious theologians and physicists speculate as to what force is pulling us against this natural law.

Each wave varies in length and intensity. Determining those variances is done with a mathematical sequence known as the Fibonacci numbers. This progression of numbers is achieved by adding the preceding two numbers to get the next number: 1, 1, 2, 3, 5, 8, 13, 21, etc. The sequence so intrigued the 17th-century physicist Isaac Newton that he carved a geometric version of it on the headboard of his bed. Fibonacci numbers and ratios are also found in the design of many natural phenomena, such as the swirl at the tail of Halley's comet and the spiral found in seashells, as well as in man-made objects such as the dimensions of the

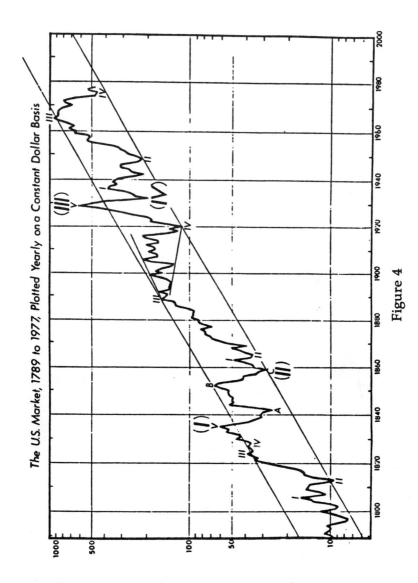

The U.S. Market, 1789 to 1977, Plotted Yearly on a Constant Dollar Basis

Figure 4

Elliott Waves in Descending Magnitude

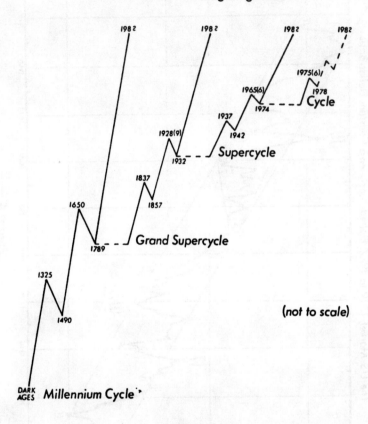

Figure 5

Chart courtesy of Robert R. Prechter, Jr. and A.J. Frost (*Elliott Wave Principle*) and New Classics Library, Inc.

Great Pyramid of Giza.

The mathematics involved in computing the exact expected length of the separate strokes is complex, but investors can become adept at foreseeing its ups and downs. The technique is to chart the Dow on a graph until the Elliott Wave is discernible, or use the graphs published in many newspapers. Then with the help of the Lunar Cycle, the time of an expected rise or fall can be forecast.

The Elliott Wave operates at both the micro and the macro. Computer technology now makes the Dow available from minute to minute, and even these graphs show the unmistakable pattern of the Elliott Wave. Gertrude Shirk of The Foundation for the Study of Cycles moved back in market history to the days of canal companies, horse-drawn barges, and meager statistics to 1000 A.D. for *Cycles* magazine and, surprisingly, found a clear Elliott pattern.

Elliott Wave Principle, Key to Stock Market Profits by A. J. Frost and Robert R. Prechter, Jr. (New Classics Library) clearly explains this cycle and its use for the investor.

These are the major economic cycles affecting the Dow. Each is important, but when as many as three are all indicating the same direction, it is especially significant. These cycles provide the backdrop against which the planetary aspects may be read.

PLANETARY INDICATORS
The McWhirter Lunation Theory

A reliable method of forecasting monthly trends on the New York Stock Exchange is described by Louise McWhirter in her book *Astrology & Stock Market Forecasting*. The technique consists of placing the planets at the lunation (New Moon) around the chart of the New York Stock Exchange and analyzing the aspects to produce a 30-day

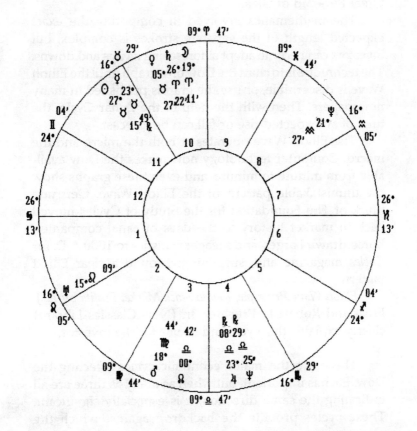

New York Stock Exchange
May 17, 1792   8:52 AM EST (rectified)
40N45   73W57
New York, New York

Chart 1 — Placidus Houses

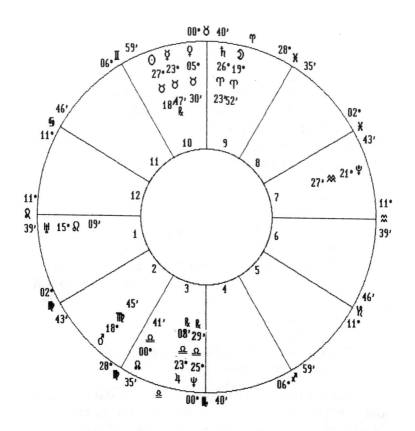

New York Stock Exchange
May 17, 1792   10:10 AM EST (rectified)
40N45   73W57
New York, New York

Chart 2 — Placidus Houses

forecast. See Charts 1 and 2. Some astrologers use 8:52 A.M. as the time for the NYSE chart; others prefer 10:10 A.M.

Pay special attention to the following:

1. Are there more trines and sextiles or squares and oppositions?
2. Does the depressing planet Saturn fall on the Exchange's Midheaven, in the 10th House or in hard aspect to its Sun and Moon?
3. Are there easy aspects forming with the Sun, Moon, Venus, or Jupiter?
4. Does the lunation Mars or Neptune make any aspects to the Exchange chart? (Mars is often the trigger to the heavier planets.)
5. Are the business planets Saturn, Jupiter, and Uranus in favorable or unfavorable aspect to one another? Favorable aspects between Saturn and Uranus always indicate an upturn in the stock market, which will last as long as the aspect is in force. All aspects between Saturn and Uranus are very significant in studying stock market trends.
6. Are there aspects to the Exchange Moon from Saturn, Mars, or Neptune?

Some financial astrologers prefer to consider this a two-week forecast. They follow the same procedure at the Full Moon for the remaining two weeks of the lunar cycle. It is also worthwhile to use this technique on a daily basis. For daily forecasting, you should always take the planetary positions at the same time each day. Eight-thirty A.M. (market opening) or noon are good choices.

The David Williams Solar Ingress Method

According to David Williams, author of *Financial Astrology*, Bull or Bear Markets can be forecast by making a chart at quarterly intervals based on the planetary patterns shown in the heavens above our national capital, Washington, D.C., at the time of the Sun's entry into the cardinal signs, Aries, Cancer, Libra, and Capricorn. (These solar ingress charts for each year are published a year in advance by the American Federation of Astrologers.)

Williams lists all the aspects in a table, circling positive aspects in green and negatives ones in red. The positive and negative aspects are then tabulated with conjunctions having a value of ten, oppositions eight, trines six, and sextiles and squares four. If the result, when added, gives a net positive aspect value, the market will be up for the next three months. If a negative value, the market will be down.

This same technique may be used on a daily basis. Simply add up the net aspect value of the major aspects (conjunction, opposition, trine, sextile, and square). If the net aspect value is positive, the world will feel optimistic and the market will rise. With a little practice,you can become quite adept at predicting daily market fluctuations.

This method of tallying what is in the heavens right now has many applications and can be used for any time frame. A chart can be run at the New Moon to predict the lunar month. I know an options trader who charts every 15 minutes when the market is open. It is a wonderful barometer of mass optimism and pessimism.

David Williams gives a partial chart of his positive and negative aspects. I have completed the chart and developed it a little farther.

Chart 3 can be used for the polarity of conjunctions when tallying aspects. For the other aspects, sextiles are positive, trines are positive, squares are negative, oppositions are negative, parallels are positive, and counterparallels are negative.

Use the following orbs: conjunction: 10°; oppositions: 8°; sextiles, squares, and trines: 5°; parallels and counterparallels: 1°.

	☽	☉	☿	♀	♂	♃	♄	♅	♆	♇
☽		+	+	+	−	+	−	+	+	−
☉			+	+	−	+	−	+	−	−
☿				+	+	+	−	+	+	+
♀					−	+	−	+	+	+
♂						+	−	+	−	−
♃							−	+	+	−
♄								+	−	−
♅									−	−
♆										−
♇										

Conjunction Values
Chart 3

Count ten points for a conjunction, ten for a trine, eight for an opposition, eight for a square, six for a sextile, and two for parallels and counterparallels. (These are my values, which differ some from those of David Williams.)

Planetary Aspects

The planet *Mars* acts as a "trigger" for certain undesirable long-term stock market movements, especially when it is square or opposing one of the other planets. *Even the conjunction is negative.* In fact, the stock market is 70% likely to develop a downward trend whenever Mars is in conjunction with one or more outer planets and simultaneously square or opposing one or more other outer planets, provided the negative pattern is not alleviated by trines and sextiles.

The following aspects are especially bad for the market: Mars conjunct Saturn, Mars square Neptune, Mars opposite Jupiter, and Mars in opposition, regardless of the planet.

All Martian retrograde stations should be regarded as "critical" to the market.

Every other conjunction of Mars and Jupiter is a market turning point, as discussed under the 4½-year Martian cycle.

Stock prices have consistently risen during the 30 days just before a conjunction of Mars with Jupiter or Mercury.

Almost any planetary aspect can affect the market, but those to the so-called business planets of Saturn, Uranus, and Jupiter, and to Mars, the Sun, and the Moon are especially powerful.

Aspects for Prosperity:

Saturn, Uranus, Jupiter in trine or sextile

Jupiter over the Midheaven of the Stock Exchange chart (Jupiter on the U.S. Midheaven, which is tenanted by the Moon (7° ♊ Ascendant), will bring wild buying.)

Jupiter in Gemini or Cancer, aspecting the U.S. Sun
or Ascendant
Uranus and Saturn in favorable aspect to each other
Conjunctions of Mars, Jupiter, and Mercury
Neptune in a Fire sign

Aspects for Economic Depression:
Saturn, Uranus, Jupiter in square or opposition (see
Kondratieff Wave)
Saturn over the Midheaven of the Stock Exchange or
U.S. chart
Saturn conjunct the North Node
Saturn in Gemini or Cancer, aspecting the U.S. Sun
or Ascendant
Saturn and Uranus in unfavorable aspect to each other
Saturn conjunct the U.S. Moon (18° Aquarius)
Jupiter/Saturn synodic conjunction every 20 years
(see Kondratieff Wave)
Neptune in an Earth sign

Aspects of the Sun and the Moon:
As discussed under the lunar cycle, aspects of the Sun
to the Moon, unless overshadowed by a heavier aspect,
give strong indications of Bull or Bear Markets. See the
Lunar Cycle table on page 214.

Aspects to the National Charts
Aspects to the charts of the United States, New York
Stock Exchange, Federal Reserve, U.S. Currency, and U.S.
Treasury will bring political or economic news that will
send the market up or down. For example, *aspects to the
Federal Reserve chart are always present whenever there is a
change in the prime rate of interest.* Both progressed aspects
and transits can have an effect. See Charts 4-6.

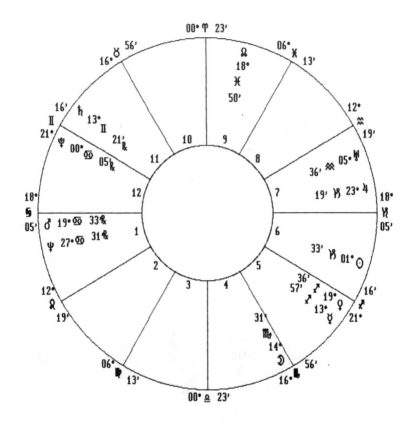

U.S. Federal Reserve
December 23, 1913 6:02 PM EST
38N53   77W00
Washington, D.C.
Source: Congressional records

Chart 4 — Koch Houses

U.S. Treasury
September 2, 1789
Time Unknown (11:59 AM EST used)
38N53   77W00
Washington, D.C.

Chart 5 — Koch Houses

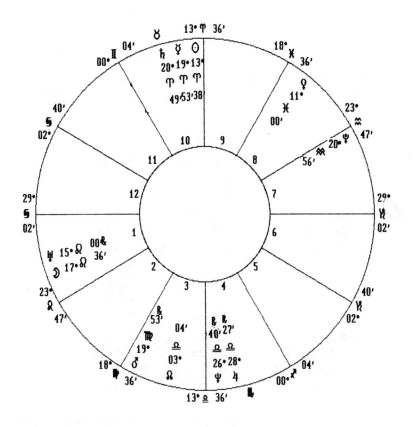

U.S. Currency
April 2, 1792
Time Unknown (11:59 AM EST used)
40N45   73W57
New York, New York

Chart 6 — Koch Houses

The Sun and the Moon through the Signs

The Sun and the Moon have great control over daily activity of the stock market. Whenever either of them transit certain planets or house cusps in the natal charts of the NYSE or of the U.S., there is a temporary effect on the market. Thus, there are certain days of the year when the market is nearly always up, and other days when the market is nearly always down.

MOON TRANSITS

Sign	Positive Degrees	Negative Degrees
Aries	7, 16	9, 20
Taurus	12, 27	2, 16
Gemini	20, 27	18, 29
Cancer	7, 25	4, 28
Leo	6, 15	9, 22
Virgo	24, 28	11, 21
Libra	14, 27	17, 29
Scorpio	12, 20	4, 15, 21
Sagittarius	4, 18	15, 26
Capricorn	19, 26	2, 5, 25
Aquarius	9, 24	5, 25
Pisces	15, 25	9, 28

The Moon moves very rapidly and can best be tracked with the aid of an ephemeris and some astrological mathematics or by the use of a computer.

The Sun moves only a degree per day. A check of the market will reveal that the market is usually up or down on the same days year after year.

Year-End Rallies

There are also certain fortunate and unfortunate periods each year, caused by the fact that the Sun's degrees normally fall on the same date each year. For example, the Sun reaches 4° Capricorn each December 26-27, which is in trine aspect to the NYSE Venus, and produces what has come to be known as the year-end rally. The same aspect exists around August 27 each year, producing a similar period of good fortune.

SUN TRANSITS

Sign	Positive Degrees	Dates	Negative Degrees	Dates
Aries	4, 11	Mar. 25, Apr. 2	18, 24	Apr. 9, 15
Taurus	12, 19	May 3, 10	6, 18	Apr. 27, May 9
Gemini	16, 18	Jun. 8, 10	5, 17	May 27, Jun. 9
Cancer	8, 16	Jun. 30, Jul. 9	13, 28	Jul. 6, 22
Leo	6, 18	Jul. 30, Aug. 11	2, 17	Jul. 26, Aug. 10
Virgo	12, 28	Sep. 5, 22	10, 13	Sep. 3, 6
Libra	21, 29	Oct. 15, 23	2, 14	Sep. 26, Oct. 8
Scorpio	11, 29	Nov. 4, 22	2, 4	Oct. 26, 28
Sagittarius	3, 24	Nov. 26, Dec. 17	16, 20	Dec. 9, 13
Capricorn	6, 11	Dec. 29, Jan. 2	16, 29	Jan. 7, 20
Aquarius	10, 14	Jan. 31, Feb. 4	17, 29	Feb. 7, 19
Pisces	13, 24	Mar. 5, 16	4, 5	Feb. 23, 24

January and September Highs

The market is usually up January 9 through 18. This is because the Sun reaches 23-25° Capricorn in mid-January, which produces a Grand Trine with Mercury at 24° Taurus, the Sun at 27° Taurus and the 7th House cusp at 26° Capricorn of the NYSE chart (Cancer rising) with Neptune at 22° Virgo and Pluto at 27° Capricorn in the chart of the United States.

A similar effect happens each September when the transiting Sun reaches 18-27° Virgo.

Transits over the Galactic Center at 26°30' Sagittarius

The Galactic Center is a pivot point in the sky around which all the other stars appear to be revolving. It is the center of our galaxy. Early astronomers placed this point in early Capricorn, but today's scientists say it is at 26°30' Sagittarius. My own observation is that it seems to be a zone from 26°30' Sagittarius to 26°43' Sagittarius.

Whenever a planet transits this point, its influence on all earthly affairs (including the stock market) is intensified. *Uranus* here will bring airline crashes and near misses as well as scientific breakthroughs and new inventions.

Saturn at this point will plunge the Earth's populace into a feeling of anxiety, causing a real economic panic. Beginning in late 1899, the Dow Jones went from 75 down to 56; Saturn was in exact conjunction on Black Friday in the 1929 crash; a 17% downward correction began in mid-1957. Saturn again crossed this point in 1988.

Jupiter and *Venus* over the Galactic Center bring optimism. Conjunctions of Mars and the Sun, Jupiter and the Sun, and superior and inferior conjunctions of Mercury and the Sun at 26°30' Sagittarius will bring higher stock prices than those 30 days previous.

Eclipses

Eclipses can "turn on" whatever planets or aspects they happen to conjunct in the charts of the NYSE or of individual companies. Their effect can be either positive or negative. They may be felt as long as two or three months later if a planet such as Mars squares the eclipse position.

At the same time an eclipse is actually in the sky, the market will be very erratic and completely unpredictable.

Retrograde Planets

A preponderance of retrograde planets can produce sluggish market conditions. Especially important are *Mercury* and *Jupiter*. Mercury rules trading, and when it is retrograde, trading is sluggish. Jupiter rules optimism, and the market never does very well when Jupiter is retrograde. It never breaks out of its trend line under a retrograde Jupiter. A retrograde Mars will also produce a slow volume of trades.

Moon perigee and apogee

Each month as it makes one round of the zodiac, the Moon reaches its perigee (closest approach to the Earth), and then about two weeks later its apogee (farthest retreat from Earth). This, the Moon's anomalistic cycle, is important in predicting stock prices.

Financial astrologers have found that stock averages like the Dow Jones Industrial and Standard & Poor's 500 tend to bottom in price halfway between the Moon's reaching its apogee from its perigee, and these averages tend to peak in price when the Moon is midway between apogee and perigee. In other words, about a week after the Moon reaches perigee, the NYSE seems to sag under the weight of a lack of buying enthusiasm. About a week after the Moon reaches apogee, there are volume upsurges and price rises.

These Moon cycles are given in *Valliere's Natural Cycles Almanac* (Astro-Graphics Services, Inc.).

Solstice and Equinox Charts

Charts run at the time of the Vernal Equinox, Summer Solstice, Autumnal Equinox, and Winter Solstice can be used to foretell conditions (including financial) during the quarters following them. To do this, follow David Williams' method of tallying positive or negative aspects.

Gann Techniques

The "patron saint" of all financial astrologers is Gann. W. D. Gann was a financier who made millions in the stock market. His trading methods were based on cosmic influences upon mass psychology. Many books have been written about Gann technology and computer programs are available. (See the chapter titled "The Gann Technique" in this book.) The method is quite involved, but to put it concisely, the process consists of averaging the angles of the six outer planets and overlaying them onto a price chart. Besides overlaying the angle itself, the angle plus or minus 30, 45, 60, 90, 120, and 180 degrees is also used.

THE PRACTICAL APPLICATION OF METHODS
October 19, 1987—Market drop of 505 points

There was an Annular Solar Eclipse on September 22, 1987, at 29°33' Virgo, just one degree away from the position of the Autumnal Equinox chart Sun. (See Chart 8.) This eclipse was conjunct the NYSE Moon's North Node.

Major aspects in the sky on October 19, 1987 (Chart 7) were:

Conjunctions: Venus conjunct Mercury, Pluto conjunct Mercury, Pluto conjunct Venus, and Uranus conjunct Saturn.

Sextiles: Uranus sextile the Sun, Pluto sextile Neptune.

Squares: the Moon square Saturn, the Moon square Uranus, Neptune square Mars, Neptune square the North Node.

Trine: Uranus trine Jupiter.

Oppositions: Jupiter opposite the Sun, Mars opposite the North Node.

Parallels: Saturn, Uranus, and Neptune, all parallel in south declination.

The transits to the NYSE chart that day were the transiting Sun conjunct NYSE Jupiter and Neptune, transiting Jupiter conjunct NYSE Saturn, and transiting Mars widely opposing the NYSE Moon.

The transits to the U.S. chart were transiting Saturn and Uranus opposite the U.S. Mars.

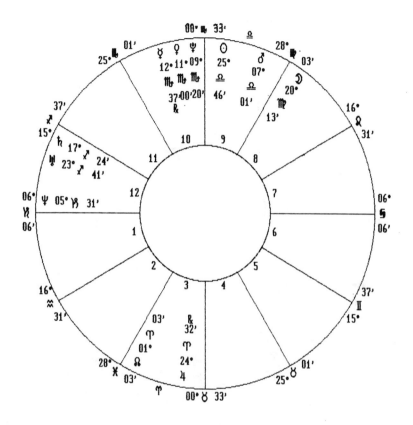

Market Drop of 505 Points
October 19, 1987   11:59 AM EDT
40N45   73W57
New York, New York

Chart 7 — Placidus Houses

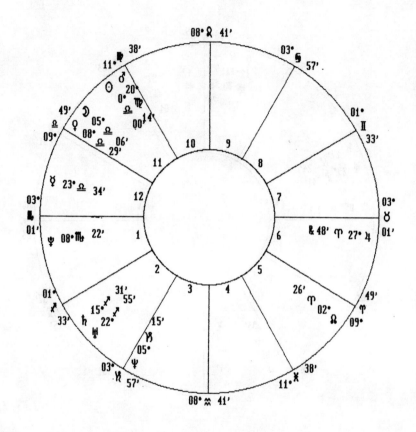

Autumnal Equinox
September 23, 1987   9:45 AM EDT
38N53   77W00
Washington, D.C.

Chart 8 — Placidus Houses

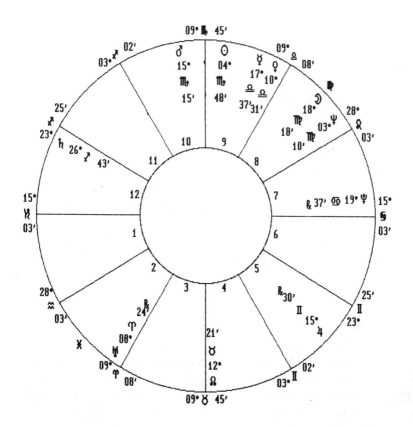

Black Friday — Market Drop of 38.33 Points, 12.8%
October 28, 1929   11:59 AM EST
40N45   73W57
New York, New York

Chart 9 — Placidus Houses

Of this long list of aspects, the most important are the eclipse on the Sun of the Fall Equinox chart, Jupiter opposite the Sun (an indication of solar flares and market turning points), transiting Jupiter conjunct the NYSE Saturn, and transiting Mars widely opposing the NYSE Moon.

An aspect tally, using David Williams' method, gives a value of 52+ and 62-. There were many very strong indications that the stock market would be severely affected on that day.

October 28, 1929—Black Friday
Chart 9 for the market crash on October 28, 1929, is another interesting example. In this chart transiting Saturn is exactly conjunct the Galactic Center. Transiting Uranus is conjunct the NYSE Midheaven (Cancer rising). Jupiter has retrograded back, but has been widely opposite Saturn most of the year. The transiting Moon is conjunct the NYSE Mars.

Conclusion
In this article, I have presented several methods for predicting the Dow. This array may be discouraging to the student, but financial astrology is not a "quick study."

Financial astrology (and all astrology) works in the same way that medicine, jurisprudence, and the ministry work. That is, there is a body of principles and laws at the core of financial astrology, but these must be in the hands of a skilled and experienced astrologer who can exercise capable judgment for good results. Like medicine, law, and theology, astrology may not always give quantifiable results, but it works nonetheless.

Computer programs have been designed using half a dozen of these factors. Or individuals, specializing in a few aspects, have gained some measure of wisdom on the subject. But the results can be disappointing.

What needs to occur can only happen through artificial intelligence. That is, *all* the specialized knowledge must be computerized so that the combination of each specialty results in a kind of wisdom. To the best of my knowledge, such a comprehensive program has yet to be designed.

Bill Meridian

Bill Meridian obtained B.S. and M.B.A. degrees in Finance from New York University. He has been studying technical analysis since the mid-sixties and has served as a fundamental and technical analyst with many Wall Street firms.

He spent seven years in training as a psychotherapist and combines his knowledge of Wall Street, psychology, and astrology to consult wth personal clients in New York City and across the country.

He and astrologer Robert Hand developed the *Astro Analyst* software program on which much of this study is based. Most recently he was Vice President of Paine-Webber's technical research department in New York City.

Bill currently publishes "Cycles Research," a newsletter covering markets on an astrological and technical basis and also following economic and political trends via long-term planetary cycles. Contact him at Cycles Research, 70A Greenwich Avenue, Suite 254, New York City, NY 10011 for a free copy, or call (212) 982-0135.

THE EFFECT OF PLANETARY STATIONS ON U.S. STOCK PRICES

Retrogradation is a well-known and powerful astrological phenomenon. Due to the practice of taking the Earth as the center of the solar system, the planets appear to slow down, stop, and go backwards during certain periods. One must remember that this is only *apparent motion* and that the planets do not actually stop and go backwards in the zodiac. However, this apparent motion is important astrologically. *As a general rule of thumb, whenever a body moves very slowly, its effect is more powerful and pronounced.* Therefore, when a planet is stationary in space, either going retrograde or direct, its effect is multiplied. One can determine these periods by looking in an ephemeris and noting when a capital R or capital D appears next to the planet in question.

The book *A Graphic Ephemeris of Sensitive Degrees* by Eleanor Bach (Planet Watch Publications) was a valuable aid in performing this analysis.

The purpose of this chapter is to demonstrate on a short-term basis the effect of these stations on the Dow Jones Industrial Averages. The *Astro Analyst* program, developed by Robert Hand and myself, is the tool used to perform the analysis and construct the graphs in this article. My intention is to give analysts and traders some idea of what to expect in terms of changes in equity prices around the times of planetary stations.

The following tables provide a picture of the frequency and duration of retrograde periods.

Expected Frequency of Retrograde Periods

Planet	Approximate Expected Frequency
Mercury	3 times per year
Venus	every 1½ years
Mars	every 2 years
Jupiter	every year
Saturn	every year
Uranus	every year
Neptune	every year
Pluto	every year

Expected Frequency of a Given Number of Planets Retrograde

# of planets retrograde	Expected frequency as % of time over the last 100 years
Zero	8%
One	19%
Two	29%
Three	27%
Four	13%
Five	4%
Six	1%
Seven	0%

Approximate Duration of Retrograde Periods by Planets

Planet	Expected Duration in # of Days
Mercury	24 days
Venus	42 days
Mars	80 days
Jupiter	120 days
Saturn	140 days
Uranus	150 days
Neptune	159 days
Pluto	160 days

Percentage of Time Each Planet
Spends in Retrograde Motion

Planet	Expected Percentage
Mercury	23%
Venus	8%
Mars	10%
Jupiter	30%
Saturn	36%
Uranus	42%
Neptune	44%
Pluto	45%

IMPORTANT FINDINGS

During the course of this analysis, some important rules were developed. They are as follows:

1. Price changes are most likely to occur when the planet goes retrograde, turns direct, or passes over the degree in the zodiac in which it went retrograde. (It will do this only after the planet has gone direct again.) Different planets rule different markets; therefore, not all stations will affect any given price series.

2. If the retrograde station affects a given price, it is likely that the direct station, and possibly even the return to the retrograde degree, will also influence the price. Examples of this will be given under the Venus and Mars sections in this chapter.

3. The probability of a trend change at a station is greatly enhanced if the planet makes aspects to other planets. In this case, aspects to the outer planets seem to carry the most weight. The closer the orb, the more powerful the effect. Thus the station of a planet within one or two degrees in the 4th Harmonic (22½ degrees, 45 degrees, 67½ degrees, 90 degrees, etc.) has the strongest effect. A similar effect will be produced if the station occurs at the midpoint of other

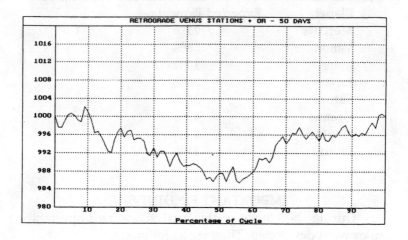

Graph 1

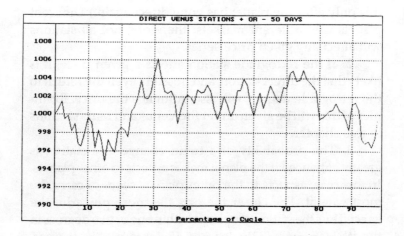

Graph 2

planets or at the midpoint of several pairs of planets (a planetary picture).

4. *Venus* and *Mars* stationary phenomena frequently yield valuable signals for short-term trades. *Uranus* stations fell closer to market bottoms with a greater frequency than did any other type of planetary station phenomena. *Neptune* stationary events frequently yield short-term drops in the DJIA. Although Jupiter, Saturn, and Pluto phenomena tended to fall near tops, they were less useful than the other planets, perhaps due to their long-term retrograde nature. These bodies were not valuable in anticipating bottoms.

READING THE GRAPHS

Each graph in this article is constructed in the same way. The **horizontal axis** represents 100 days. The left-hand side of the graph represents a period 50 days before the station of the planet, the **center point** marked 50 is the station itself, and the right-hand side of the graph represents 50 days moving away from the station. The **vertical axis** is an arbitrary index number measuring the change in the Dow. Each graph begins at 1000 and ends at 1000, thus a reading of 1010 represents an average 1% increase over the point at 1000. A reading of 990 would represent a 1% drop from the starting point of 1000. Each graph represents the average change in the Dow for all stations occurring from 1915 to the present.

Turn to Graph 1. We see the average change in the Dow from 50 days prior to a Venus station to 50 days after. The graph tells us that on an average since 1915, stocks have dropped approximately 1½% going into the retrograde station and have risen approximately 1½% in the 50 days following the Venus station.

These percentages may seem small, but one must remember that we are only analyzing a single planetary cycle in this chapter. With the addition of other valuable

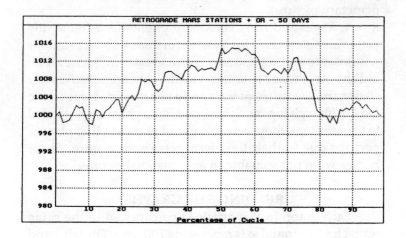

Graph 3

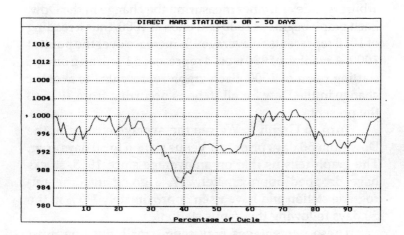

Graph 4

cycles, the percentages add up into significant movements that can be capitalized upon by the position trader.

PLANETARY RESULTS

A graph for the planet Mercury is not presented here because its effects were considered too short term for this study. *Mercury retrogradation periods result in interruption of the trend,* whether it's an up trend or a down trend, for the entire period in which the planet is retrograde. Concerning short-term moves, Mercury is most valuable when it is stationary and conjunct the Sun. Because it tends to interrupt up trends and down trends about equally, the resulting graph nets the changes out so that essentially the outcome is a flat line showing very little percentage change.

Venus

Graph 1 demonstrates how the Dow Jones Industrial Averages tend to drop 1½% from 50 days prior to the station. The market tends to bottom at the station and rise 1½% in the following 50 days. The year 1988 provided some good examples of Venus stations as turning points. Note that Venus was stationary retrograde on Sunday, May 22, and the market bottomed on the next day, May 23. (There were also other astrological indications of a bottom on this day.) The subsequent top was very close to the July 4 direct station. Note also that the market dropped on the day when Venus conjoined the original retrograde degree of May 22 on August 7.

Graph 2 demonstrates that direct Venus stations produce much less clearly defined results with the market tending to fluctuate back and forth for 25 days leading into and away from the station.

Mars

Graph 3 demonstrates that the market tends to rise

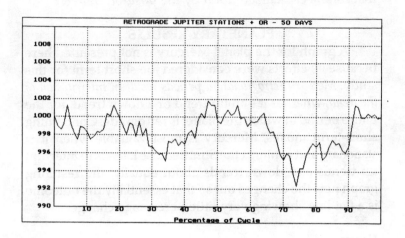

Graph 5

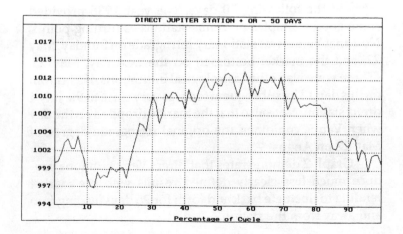

Graph 6

approximately 1½% into a Mars retrograde station and to drop 1½% 50 days later. The important point to remember is that any astrological phenomenon can signify a turning point, and as most cycle theorists know, inversions of the cycles are frequent. For example, in 1988 Mars retrograde fell near the August 26 bottom, while the direct station fell very near the October 28 top. This analysis notes that Mars retrograde tends to coincide with *tops*.

Graph 4 demonstrates that the Mars direct station tends to fall about 10 days after a bottom in the market. Again, the drop is approximately 1½% and the subsequent rise is 1½%. The rise tends to occur in the 10 days prior to the station and the 12 days leading away from it. Thus the 22-day period, on average, tends to present a good trading opportunity. When direct Mars returns to the zodiacal degree at which it previously went retrograde, we tend to get a minor bottom or a drop in the market. Over the last 20 years, the return of Mars to the station has tended to coincide with a falling market in the days around that date approximately two out of every three times.

Jupiter
Jupiter stations, perhaps due to their longer-term nature, tend to provide fewer clear opportunities for the trader. Graph 5 demonstrates that the market tends to rise approximately 1% during the 15 days prior to the retrograde station. There then tends to be a 1% drop through a period of 25 days following the station. The stations tended to fall at some distances from meaningful tops and bottoms.

Graph 6 demonstrates that the direct station of Jupiter provides more usable results. The market tends to rise approximately 2% during the 40 days going into the station and tends to drop by the same amount 50 days after the station.

Both stations and the return of Jupiter to the ret-

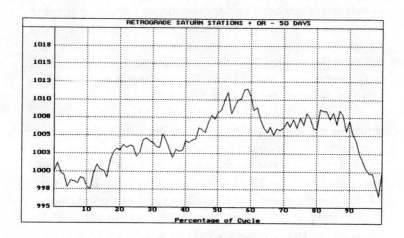

Graph 7

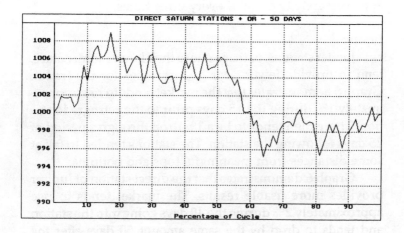

Graph 8

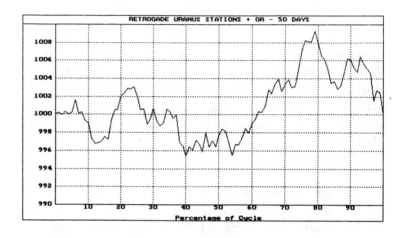

Graph 9

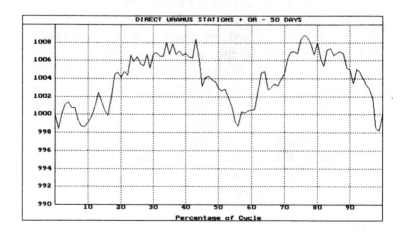

Graph 10

rograde degree tended to provide little up moves of anywhere from 10 to 25 Dow points more frequently than it provided any other type of signal. The stations of Jupiter are probably more valuable in other types of markets.

Trader and astrologer Jeanne Long of Fort Lauderdale recently pointed out to me that during the 1982-1987 Bull Market, retrograde Jupiter periods tended to coincide with corrections or with sideways movements in the averages. I have noted that these retrogradation periods seemed to coincide with the primary Elliott Wave corrections of that Bull Market.

Saturn

Graph 7 demonstrates that the market tends to rally until a period of approximately nine days after the retrograde station and tends to fall following the station.

Graph 8 demonstrates that the market chops sideways prior to a direct station and then falls sharply in the 13 days following a station.

The best example of Jupiter and Saturn stations corresponding with turning points occurred in August of 1987. The planets both changed direction on the same day. While they changed direction, they were in a hard 4th Harmonic aspect. In addition, the planets aspected the North Node of Uranus, which is a stationary point in the heavens at approximately 13 Gemini. The actual top did not come until one to two weeks later when the market topped on the closest five-planet conjunction in 396 years.

Although the results are not very significant, as in the case of Jupiter, Saturn station phenomena will most frequently fall close to *tops*.

Uranus

According to Graph 9, the market tends to rally for a period of approximately five days after a Uranus retrograde station and to peak at a point approximately 30 days after the station.

Graph 10 demonstrates that the market tends to fall from a period of about eight days prior to the direct station until approximately seven days after. Stationary Uranus phenomena tend to be more associated with *bottoms* than any other planetary station.

Neptune

In Graph 11, we can see that the market tends to drop immediately upon a retrograde Neptune and to fall for approximately 10 days afterwards. A rally then usually ensues through a period of approximately 32 days after the retrograde station.

Graph 12 gives a less clear indication as the direct Neptune station tends to occur in a period of falling prices, approximately eight days to either side of the station.

Neptune station phenomena rarely coincide with tops. A small drop of 25 to 50 Dow points frequently occurs after a Neptune station phenomenon if the market has been rising into the date in question.

Pluto

Retrograde Pluto stations tend to occur at price peaks. See Graph 13. The market tends to rally approximately 10 days into the station and to fall 10 days afterwards. A rally then usually ensues following the secondary bottom.

Direct stations (Graph 14) tend to occur in a period of declining prices and do not give as clear-cut an indication as the retrograde Pluto station does.

Pluto station phenomena is not usually useful in anticipating bottoms.

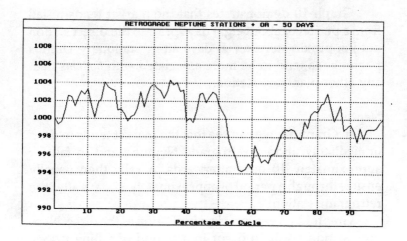

Graph 11

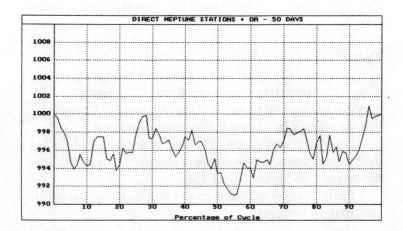

Graph 12

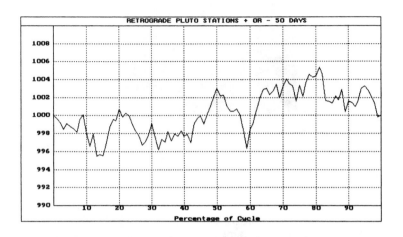

Graph 13

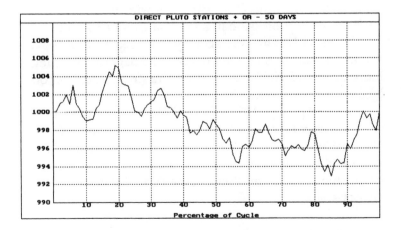

Graph 14

Georgia Stathis

Georgia Stathis received her Bachelor of Science degree from Northwestern University in 1970 where she majored in Speech and Theater. In 1978 she received her M.B.A. from Pepperdine University in Malibu, California.

After settling in California in 1971, she worked in public relations in San Francisco and handled major as well as campaign accounts. During the following years, she pursued the sales profession in advertising and real estate.

From 1971, she was actively involved in astrology. While she was pursuing her degree, she began counseling individuals and small businesses with a strong emphasis on business and investment.

Since April of 1977, she has been a full-time professional astrologer and lecturer. She is a member of The National Speakers Association. She has appeared on KSFO radio and has written for several publications as well as having her own column "Sign of the Times" in *Aquarius Rising* newspaper.

DELINEATING THE CORPORATION

If we can assign a birth chart to every living entity based on its birth date, time, and place, as well as set up birth charts for events in history, then it is appropriate that we should assign a birth chart to a corporation. There are different ways of doing this. The most commonly used birth time for a company is *noon*. Many companies are legally incorporated between the late morning and the early afternoon hours. An accurate incorporation time is very hard to come by. *The reason we usually set the time for noon is that this will place the Sun of the company at the Midheaven.*

The *Sun sign* of the company is the symbol for the chief executive officer or president of the company, so it's symbolically placed in this portion of the wheel. The 10th House or Midheaven represents what the public sees as well as the reputation of the company.

Of course, the exact moment in which the incorporation papers are submitted to the recorder's office is the most accurate. When working with a small company, it is often easier to obtain this information.

There is also a way to determine a time for a company that is not legally incorporated—when it opens its doors for business. The most commonly used time is either when the business or company takes in its first dollar or sees its first client. Calculate for noon if this other information is not available.

Many times business partners will ask the astrologer

about the planning phases of the business—when they first had the idea, when they agreed, when they met for the first time, etc. These are all important dates, but the most important is when the contract or business is SET INTO MOTION. This is considered the birth moment and the legal time that the business begins.

Incorporation dates are always changing, particularly as we enter the latter part of the 20th century when larger companies are gobbling up smaller ones in mergers; there will be frequent changes in incorporation dates and charts. The standard rule of thumb which always seems to work is the *most current incorporation date*, using the city in which it was recorded as the birth place of the company.

Several companies on the New York Stock Exchange are incorporated in either Wilmington or Dover, Delaware, so these cities are their places of birth.

Several large companies have branch offices throughout the nation and the world. The original incorporation date of the parent company is always used, but it is also important to examine the date, time and place of birth (the opening date) of the branch office, particularly if an individual is considering employment at that particular branch of the corporation or business.

A good source for incorporation dates is *Moody's Investor Services* in New York. Each quarter they publish an updated manual that lists all the companies currently offering stock on the NYSE, along with their history, their products, a value line that shows the activity of the company in recent years, and other useful information. If a company has been re-incorporated, the manual will indicate this change. Moody's Investor Services address is: 99 Church Street, New York, New York 10007.

Another way to find out the incorporation date of a company is to call the head office's librarian or reference department. Since incorporation dates are a matter of public record, they are obliged to give you that information, although it has been my experience that sometimes the data given by the librarian is incongruent with the published data.

SETTING UP A CORPORATION CHART

If a corporation has been formed, use that date, time and place for the business chart, but if you are fortunate enough to be able to plan your company chart, a few factors need to be taken into consideration. Keep in mind that probably there will always be areas that present stress or unforeseen difficulty when erecting the chart. Stress is not necessarily a bad thing to have in a company chart because squares and oppositions motivate.

As in planting, it is a good idea to set up a company between the New and Full Moon cycle, but not during a void-of-course Moon. Since the *first quarter Moon* can indicate structure and management, this phase should be considered. It is not wise to use a void-of-course Moon because the Moon rules employees and how the public sees the company. If the Moon is void of course, a vague quality may emerge and the identity of the company is never really established in the eyes of the public.

There are exceptions to this, such as a holding company (one that has no purpose but to hold other companies). See Chart A.

This is a company that was formed as a holding company for a major international cosmetic and skin care manufacturer and distributor. Sub-companies have been formed as they pass through this company's possession; then they are laid out as seen fit.

Note the Sun in Taurus ruled by Venus, the ruler of cosmetics and skin care products. The void-of-course Moon in Capricorn is in the 6th House of employees, and many different employees have moved through this company

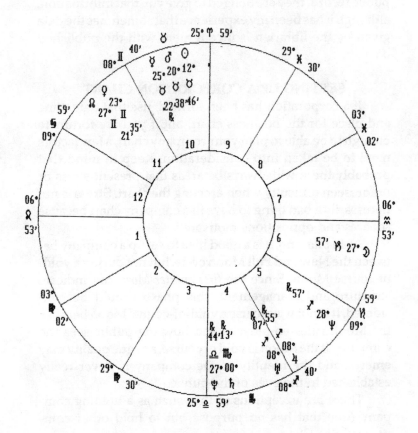

Holding Company
May 3, 1983   12:00 PM PDT
37N59   122W01
Concord, California
Source: *Moody's Handbook*

Chart A — Koch Houses

quickly. People have been hired and assigned jobs in conjunction with their varied talents.

When establishing a company, note which planets are retrograde and which are direct. There will almost always be a retrograde planet, *but Mercury, Venus and Mars should definitely not be retrograde.* Mercury retrogrades three times a year for approximately three weeks at a time. Venus retrogrades about once in 18 months for approximately 40 days and Mars retrogrades every two years for about three months.

Since Mercury rules legal contracts, communications and planning, particularly in a business chart, it is not a good idea to have a retrograde Mercury. Venus governs spending, talents, resources and monies. A retrograde Venus could indicate a company that makes inappropriate choices in partnerships or purchases or which may develop an uncomfortable working environment. Mars, the old ruler of Scorpio (banks and profit), when retrograde suggests a company that may never quite reach its projected goals because it is easily sidetracked. Mars is the planet of action and aggression, and when it is retrograde in a company chart it can indicate a lack of assertive action. Also when Mars is retrograde, it has been noted that business slows down and the market can be depressed.

A predominance of *cardinal* signs in a chart is good, suggesting a pioneering spirit that doesn't get stuck and is able to adjust to changing times. It is also important to have some *fixed* energy in the chart for follow-through and accomplishment, as well as *mutability* for a smooth flow of affairs. Too much cardinality can show a company that is very good at developing new ideas but not outstanding at completing what it starts.

The Moon in an Earth sign is positive because it suggests practicality and tangibility.

Saturn should be strongly placed. A retrograde Saturn

may actually be good. Saturn rules karma in spiritual astrology, but in a business chart it represents organization and career direction. If the business has to do with building materials and contracting, for example, then Saturn may be even more prominently placed since it rules concrete and construction. However, an angular Saturn is not necessarily suggested for most business charts.

A prominent (possibly angular) and well-aspected Jupiter is always an excellent placement since Jupiter rules sales and marketing. Jupiter placed in either the 2nd or 8th House of resources or forming a positive aspect to the rulers of the 2nd and 8th is excellent for positive financing and income.

The planets ruling the *2nd, 6th and 10th Houses* should be direct, and the signs on these Houses are indicators of the type of business represented by the chart. The planets ruling the 2nd and 8th should be well aspected for the business to be financially successful.

Chart B is an example of a planned company chart. The business had been in existence for five years prior to this date, but a new chart was set up for the opening of this individual's first office (a new venture). This chart was erected for the time the first clients were seen at the new office.

The business is a sole proprietorship and primarily consults with people about their career and business direction. The product is *information* which requires a great deal of mental preparation as well as detailed analysis. The clients are presented with alternative options as well as timing and forecasting for their businesses. Note the Scorpio Sun in the 10th House. Scorpio is the sign of psychological transformation. The consultant also speaks and presents her ideas to large groups of people. Mercury in the 10th House is an excellent placement for this type of chart. The primary source of business comes from referrals.

Uranus rules the 2nd House and is in the 11th House of

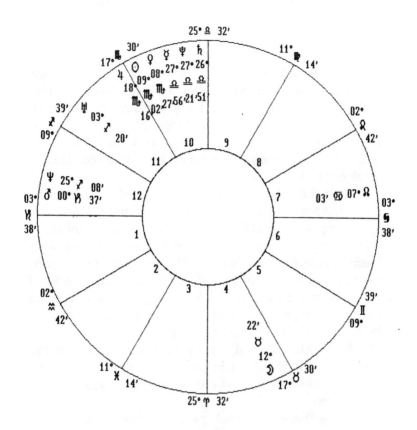

Planned Corporation
November 1, 1982   11:AM PST
37N57   122W04
Pleasant Hill, California
Source: Incorporation papers

Chart B — Koch Houses

groups, friends who can be resources for the business, and goals.

Prior to opening the office, this businesswoman worked out of her home. The Moon in Taurus in the 4th House indicates this. *The 4th House of a corporation chart signifies its roots.* A good portion of her business comes from real estate and loan agents; she was in real estate and investment prior to opening this business. The 4th House also indicates real estate and property. Since the Moon rules employees, all employees hired by this woman continue to work out of her home.

Note the balance in cardinal, fixed and mutable signs. The business continues to be very strong and balanced. As transiting Saturn and Uranus move over the Ascendant of this corporation chart into the 1st House, the company's business objectives are changing. The information researched over the last three years (transits through the 12th House of research and development) is starting to reach a larger market through writing and training workshops and is being set up to reach a more massive market.

Pluto (the ruler of mass production) conjuncts the ruler of the chart, Saturn, in the 10th House. The information presented is very new, creates controversy, and wakes people up.

Since there are a high percentage of planets in the fourth quadrant, particularly in the 10th House, the more this company matures, the more established it becomes. The chart has all the indications of hard work but of also being a late bloomer—Capricorn rising and the strong 10th House emphasis.

THE PLANETS IN A CORPORATION CHART

In order to proceed with corporate chart delineation, it is important to provide some meanings for the planets in a corporation chart. The following list is compiled from many

sources and also includes definitions for these planets as
transits through the horoscope.

Sun: The life force drive; the company itself, its founder,
chairman of the board or corporate head; the owner or top
management. The Sun can represent government and
administrators, authority figures; gold and speculation; or
theater as the primary business. If eclipsed, it can send the
company in a completely new direction.

As a transit through the chart, the Sun brings attention
and *success* through whatever part of the chart it is moving.
It can also promote recognition and success if positively
aspected.

Moon: The employees or "family" of the company and
their involvement; the public image—how the public responds
to the services or products of the company; women in the
company in general; the "home" office and its functions;
the company's ability to nurture; its products, services and
popular ideas to which the public responds; the crowds or
masses that respond to the product; harvests of crops; the
ocean or water products in general.

A stressfully aspected Moon may indicate a poor public
image; if heavily aspected by the malefics Saturn, Neptune
or Pluto, it may indicate some type of hazardous situation
around employees.

As a transit, the Moon may temporarily increase the
price of stock if it positively aspects the Sun, Venus or
Jupiter. A temporary decrease in stock price may result
from a difficult aspect to such planets as Saturn or Pluto.

Mercury: The sales, service and the communication
facilities of the company; the commercial or scientific/
analytic abilities demonstrated by management, *i.e.,* the
"brains of the company"; the work force; literature and

printing; information distributed; health and environmental concerns of the work force; company books; secretaries and clerical staff; training facilities; advertising; food product or food supply services (6th House); the media, trade and commerce; short trips; doctors; publishing and printing.

As a transit, it can bring out news or information that changes the attitudes of the employees or the public and the company investors.

Venus: The company's general assets and its appeal for partnering or merger possibilities; its popularity; public's approval or acceptance of product lines; credit. A well-placed Venus would indicate a pleasing working environment; architectural beauty; aesthetics like art, fashion, music, cosmetics; and recreation and pleasure perks. Venus retrograde is uncommon in corporate charts and should be avoided.

As a transit, Venus brings things to the attention of the public by making them popular, making them look good to investors. When Venus is well aspected, people are more content. Transiting through the 2nd or 8th House, Venus can bring a successful sale or purchase.

Mars: Indicates stock activity, new beginnings and the company's ability to act; the urge to pioneer, to be aggressive; its motivation and drive; its competitive spirit; and the desire to be the best. Negatively aspected, Mars can bring accidents, violence, epidemics, and explosions. It rules such things as the military, athletics, surgery, war, iron, steel, diamonds, explosives, machinery and equipment, munitions, and tobacco. Look at the Mars/Jupiter midpoint which can describe whether or not the company is successful.

As a transit, Mars indicates activity and volume in the markets. It can bring a general atmosphere of anxiety and action and can trigger sudden negative activities in a company. When retrograde, Mars may curtail activity.

Jupiter: Indicates the urge to grow, expand and be successful, as well as the company's moneymaking ability. Jupiter brings foreign concerns, education and philosophy, publishing possibilities and optimism. It rules bankers, brokers, courts, churches, public relations and direct mail.

As a transit, Jupiter is an excellent sell signal, increasing prices or value. It brings promise, hope. If negatively transiting, a company can overindulge, overexpand, or take a plunge.

Saturn: The administrative or management ability of a company; the corporation in general—its structure, its bones, the governing body which is usually the board of directors; the authority or policy-making branch. The part of the company in which the responsibility lies is indicated by Saturn, as well as the company's stability, conservatism and the ability to consolidate and limit in a practical way. This is where the corporation may stick to traditional expression, may retain control. Saturn represents labor or laboring places; the land as in farms, real estate, grains, mines, mountains; and the elderly and the aged.

As a transit, if well-aspected, Saturn can indicate a buy signal. It can decrease a stock price, limit or depress the market, restrict or create worry and concern within the company, or bring delays in progress.

Uranus: Indicates the innovative ability of the company and its progressive thinking and new inventions and ideas. It gives the company the urge to be unique and as a result stand out and latch on to the energy of the public. It shows future orientation. The company may be very involved in electronics, computers, high-tech developments, railways, strikes, radio energy, utilities, airlines, air carrier production or public information.

Negatively aspected, Uranus can bring sudden shocks

or changes within the company or bring acts of God such as tornadoes and hurricanes, earthquakes and explosions.

As a transit, if positively aspected, Uranus may herald news of stock splits as well as new and unique efforts. The company may depart from the conventional way of doing things through some crisis. It could indicate a breakup as in the AT&T trust bust. It could bring revolutionary breakthroughs, revolution, expansion and branching out or franchising.

Jeff Green, in his book *Uranus: Freedom from the Known* (Llewellyn Publications), states that when heavy Uranus aspects are operating sometimes there may be paralysis and then a healing. This concept can also be applied to a corporation chart.

Neptune: Represents the image of a company. It can bring a redistribution of monies and create altruism and virtue in a company, or the converse—such as drug and alcohol problems. Neptune indicates the vision held by management; illusion or dissolution; human potential; the seduction potential created by successful advertising campaigns; the potential for rumor or sabotage or behind-the-scenes problems; slander; gossip; and disappointment. It may indicate a company that deals with acting, movies, beverages, hospitals or hospital development, narcotics and pharmaceuticals, oil, shipping, photography, political idealism, or inspiration from research.

As a transit, Neptune can make a company ripe for a merger. It can be inflationary and expansive in a Bull Market, but deflationary in a Bear Market; lead to uncertainty and confusion within the company; and dissolve a portion of the business to get ready for a new way of doing things. It shows the abililty to take what is already there, reprocess it, and create something new and better. It may indicate toxic and waste management just as it can creatively inspire.

Pluto: This is the power behind the company, and every good company has a strong Pluto. It shows the potential and ability to resurrect itself from the ashes and can indicate power struggles within the company. It depicts the hidden treasure or assets of a company; its resources; and its ability to research, develop, and successfully mass produce, manufacture and distribute. It rules plumbing, sewers, rackets, plutonium, radiation, cancer research, atomic research, genetic engineering, life extension, redevelopment and urban renewal.

Negatively, it defines potential to wipe out, to go bankrupt, to sabotage; dealings with the underworld of crime and corruption; internal dictatorships; and compulsive behavior patterns like unknown gambling debts.

As a transit, Pluto can purge the company, even threaten to eliminate it, but it can also rebuild the corporation after a devastating period. It can indicate crisis and mass movements within the company that are accompanied by mass hysteria. A heavy transit of Pluto can show major change in the structure of the company. If this is positive, it is successful, particularly in large ventures. If negative, it can wipe out or bankrupt.

A strong Pluto transit can give the desire to merge with others and the need to reorganize or restructure, to eliminate and get down to basics. If a strong Pluto transit is occurring and a company has large outstanding debts, then mark time. At least be cautious. If Pluto is well aspected and the company has few debts, this usually indicates long-term growth and gain is just beginning. Pluto moves slowly and has long-term effects.

North Node: Indicates contact with the outer world and how the company is perceived by the public. Activity on the nodal points brings the company before the public.

THE HOUSES OF A CORPORATION CHART

Each house of the horoscope represents a different area. The houses of the corporation chart are similar to but different from those in a regular natal chart. For example, the 1st House of the corporation chart represents the stockholders of the company and the company's business objectives. Since the stockholders are the ones who have the say on how a company is run, it is appropriate to say that the stockholders come from the 1st House, the house of individual identity, the "me" part of the natal chart.

At the opposite end of this axis is the 7th House, representative of the "others"—the competitors—much like the 7th House of a natal chart. The 7th House of a natal chart represents how others see us and how we relate to them.

Therefore, based on the above example, the following are the assigned meanings of the houses in a corporation chart.

1st House: Personnel of the corporation, including *stockholders;* how the *stockholders* see the company; company morale; company's business objectives; general membership; place of incorporation and its relationship to the public; attitude towards competitors. (*Note the ruler of the Ascendant and its house placement.*)

2nd House: Liquid assets; revenue; activities in money-making; earnings; voluntary expenditures; ability to earn profits; disposition toward investments.

3rd House: Contacts with the public; financial and trade publications; financial and trade relations with adjacent countries and states; short-distance travel; neighboring organizations; education; library, bulletins and newsletters, magazines, publications, methods of distributing news, literary work; technical publications; rails, telephones and telegraphs; commercial radio; demand for stocks and bonds; trade volume figures; advertising; internal agreements; traffic, transportation and communication departments; interoffice communications; information dissemination within the company; relatively private public statements.

4th House: Real estate investment and holdings; tangible assets of the corporation; hazards involving property; the original home of the organization; investments in land, factory space, and office space; the people of the organization as opposed to the president; basic standards; tangible assets; direct competition; power of competitors; roots of corporation; base of operations or field of activity; location and condition of factory or office buildings. (*Virgo* in this position might signify that the organization avoids waste.)

5th House: *Executive personnel* (except for president or chairman of the board); governing body; attitudes or actions of stockholders or board of directors in opposition to the president; committees; *management teams; advertising success or failure*; income from invested capital or results of speculative ventures; motivation; speculation; the place of deposit of capital such as *safes, vaults,* and *banks*; amusement, social affairs, *conventions; educational enterprises, workshops, seminars, teaching*; examinations; banquets; dramatic or theatrical ventures.

6th House: *Workers or employees* (voluntary or paid); work and equipment; health plans and insurance; work schedules and work routines; *inventories*; lighting and heating bills; performance of workers on the job; cooperation received from employees; assistance received; health policies and attitudes of employees; corporation connection with hostelries (inns or hotels); agriculture and agricultural products; fixtures and furnishings of environment; health condition of personnel; inception of strikes and labor troubles.

7th House: Relationship to other organizations; sales appeal; how effectively a product is put across; house of adjustments; *trading volume*—how much stock is being bought; public accountings; employee income and payrolls; relationships with others (positive or hostile); political or commercial affiliates; women in the organization; trade agreements; mergers; open opposition to growth; lawsuits and legal affairs; *competitors* and their activities.

8th House: Losses or gains through death of the corporation; financial responsibilities; private conferences; *board of directors*; credit, dividends; trade secrets; *net earnings*; insurances; handling of legacies; nonprofit status; donations to nonprofit organizations; financial conditions involved in partnerships, mergers or lawsuits; financial relations with competitors; competitors' financial condition; revenue from investments or liquidation of frozen assets; loans and income from sources not under immediate control of the organization; *company treasurer*.

9th House: *Advertising department*; shipping; activities abroad; completion of merger contracts; *code of ethics and bylaws; audits*; contracts with other companies; *intercompany* communication; *philosophy of company*; publications (same as in 3rd House); any public and foreign relations; long-distance communications; results of mail-order campaigns; relations with educational institutions and publications; *professional consultants*; publicity and public relations; officials; all legal affairs.

10th House: Supreme or governing authority; *president or the chairman of the board*; figureheads; national reputation; relations with governments and associations; public image; power; general business conditions as far as its public image; *administrative department. (Look at the ruler of the 10th House and its house placement for insight into the talents or gifts of the CEO.)*

11th House: Other friendly organizations; friends; acquaintances; political connections; community connections; constitutional policies; resources available through the company head (the 2nd from the 10th); long-range goals of the organization and what it stands for; public relations through group involvement; *intangible assets;* its indebtedness; mortgages; *the treasury;* fraternal and club groups providing activities.

12th House: *Enemies and secret organizations against the organization;* sabotage; secret intelligence department; strikes and labor troubles; dissolutions and negotiations behind-the-scenes; experimentations; *research and development; trade secrets and formulas;* limitations through secret enemies that might involve inefficiency; secret assistance; organized and social units; designs for the future relating to past events; effects of litigation.

HEMISPHERIC INFLUENCES

Before any statement is made about hemispheric influence, it must be noted that any chart calculated for noon will always have several planets in either the third or fourth quadrant. If a more specific time is known, then the following may be of interest.

If there is a strong influence in the *right or western hemisphere,* much of the company experiences may be subjective. Certain choices may present themselves and the challenge may be in the choosing.

When there is a strong influence in the *left or eastern*

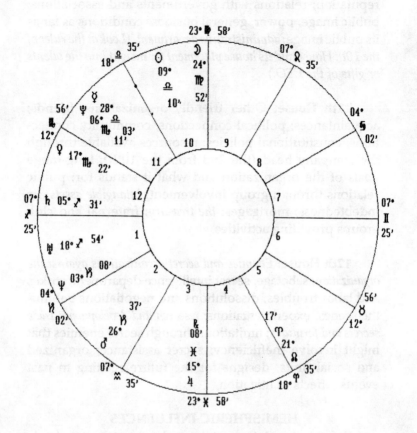

Zweig Mutual Fund
October 2, 1986   12:00 PM EDT
39N17   76W37
Baltimore, Maryland
Source: *Moody's Handbook*

Chart C — Koch Houses

hemisphere, the company has more control. Of course, in having control, it must also take responsibility for the consequences of its choices. An eastern influence may tend to make a stronger and more aggressive company, but this also depends on other factors, such as the type of company or product.

Since the Midheaven usually indicates the leadership of the company, *the ruling planet of the Midheaven and where it is placed has a lot to do with the leader's interests.* For example, in the chart for Zweig Mutual Funds (Chart C), Marty Zweig, the founder of this fund, is known for many things: his conservatism, his writing and his newsletter (Mercury rules the 10th House), and his large investments in his own company treasury (Mercury, the ruler of the 10th, in the 11th House).

The company has Sagittarius rising, and the Ascendant conjuncts natal Saturn (conservatism). Its ruling planet Jupiter is in the 3rd House of communications and newsletters— the newsletter is a moneymaker for this company. Jupiter, the chart ruler, in Pisces (intuition, perception) implies that the company operates on hunches. Just before the crash in October 1987, Zweig pulled his company out of the markets, thus saving the company's treasury (11th House).

ASPECTS IN A CORPORATION CHART

The following is an example of how aspects can be interpreted when looking at a corporate chart. The chart example (Chart D) is a graphic, photography, typesetting and layout company that was in business several years before it legally incorporated on September 24, 1987 at 11:22 A.M. in San Ramon, California. The Midheaven is Virgo ruled by Mercury, which governs advertising and graphics. At the time of this writing, the company is about to be re-incorporated as it adds a business manager and new branches.

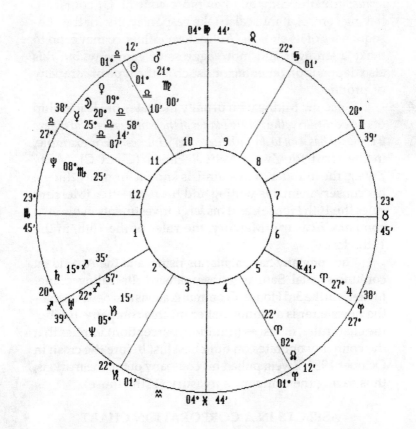

04° ♍ 44'

01° ♎ 12'
☉ 01°
♂ 21°
♍

22° ♋ 01'

♀ 09°
☽ 20° ♎
☿ 25° ♎ 58'
♎ 14'
07'

38'
27° ♎

♍ 00'
10'

20° ♊ 39'

♇ 08° ♏ 25'

23° ♏ 45'

♄ 15° ♐ 35'
57'
♅ 22° ♐ 15'
39'
♆ 05° ♑

20° ♐

22° ♑ 01'

04° ♓ 44'

10   9

11   8

12   7

1   6

2   5

3   4

23° ♉ 45'

℞ 41'
♈ 27° ♃ 38'
♈ 27°

22'
♈ 02° ☊

01° ♈ 12'

≈

Graphics Business
September 24, 1987   11:22 AM PDT
37N47   121W58
San Ramon, California
Source: Incorporation papers

Chart D — Koch Houses

The change is imminent in that this company happened to be established very close to the Solar Eclipse at 29 degrees of Virgo on September 22, 1987. A further discussion of eclipses later in this chapter demonstrates their effectiveness in corporate chart delineation.

To briefly explore aspects, we will discuss those of *Mercury* in this particular company chart as well as the actively aspected *Moon* (the ruler of employees).

Mercury is conjunct the Moon in Libra and close to Venus in Libra in the 11th House of the treasury, goals, friends and acquaintances.

Mercury generally rules the clerical staff. A high percentage of the staff in this organization is female (Mercury conjunct the Moon) as are the primary contributors to the treasury. Major clerical assistants have contributed their portion of profits to own the company as a collective. There are, however, two major company holders.

This has had a positive as well as a negative effect on how the company does business. Positively, there is a great deal of support from the community, New Age organizations they belong to, and friends, but everyone has something to say about how things should be run, which sometimes gets in the way of production. With so many opinions and with a stellium in Libra, there is a lot of vacillation or sitting on the fence about decisions.

There is, however, an incredible sense of fairness about these same decisions in the organization. Mercury conjuncting the Moon suggests that many past decisions have been emotional ones; many decisions are changed based on the latest input.

Since the Moon rules the 9th House of professional consultants, recently a consultant was called in to help the organization run more efficiently and practically.

The result of this consultation is that the company is reorganizing, taking on a business manager who will help them be more definitive about decisions and an appropriate amount of money to charge for their services. A new corporation is forming.

Mercury, the ruler of the 8th, and Jupiter, the ruler of the 2nd, oppose each other, and the struggle has always been having enough revenue and taking a stand about financial issues.

Mercury sextiles Uranus, which is an excellent aspect for a company that produces graphics from computers and for ideas that exhibit an innovative quality. Uranus rules computers as well as New Age thinking. One of their big accounts is a monthly nationally distributed publication that they design.

When transiting Jupiter enters Gemini in March of 1989, it will transit this company's 7th and 8th Houses while trining its Sun, Venus, Moon and Mercury (ruler of the 8th and 10th Houses) and sextiling natal Jupiter, the ruler of the 2nd and 4th Houses. With the new incorporation and restructuring (transiting Saturn and Uranus squared its Sun), the company should begin to realize a profit (good aspects to the planets that rule the business and Mercury, as well as the 2nd and 8th House rulers).

THE NODES AND ECLIPSES

The North and South Node, both natally placed and transiting, play an important part in delineating a corporate chart. Since the lunar nodes are created by the intersection of the orbital paths of the Earth and the Moon, they can indicate the public's response. Where the transiting **North Node** is moving is where the company is experiencing *gain*, and where the **South Node** is transiting is where the company is having to *let go*. The transiting nodes coincide with *eclipses*, and the axis on which this pattern occurs lights up a company chart, creating opportunities for major change.

The natal nodes and the last Solar Eclipse occurring

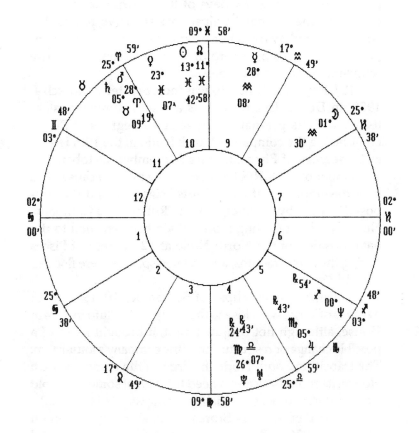

R.J. Reynolds
March 4, 1970   12:00 PM EST
39N10   75W32
Dover, Delaware
Source: *Moody's Handbook*

Chart E — Koch Houses

prior to or within a few days of the incorporation of the company (the pre-natal eclipse) are sensitive points that when aspected by transit or progression will put the company in the news or before the public in some way. The following are some examples.

R. J. Reynolds (Chart E) was incorporated on March 4, 1970, in Dover, Delaware. It is a Pisces company established with its pre-natal eclipse at 16 degrees of Pisces conjuncting the company's North Node in the 10th House at 12 degrees of Pisces. During September, October, and November of 1988, RJR has been in the news because of its new development of an "ashless" cigarette and the proposed buy out by Kohlberg, Kravis, Roberts and Company. Note that the transiting North Node had returned to the natal position of the North Node at 12 degrees of Pisces during the above months, and the newspapers were flooded with RJR's news.

Since the Solar Eclipse of September 10, 1988, at 18 degrees of Virgo was close to the company's Pluto in the 4th House, although not conjuncting it, it brought news of a possible change or restructuring of the company's foundation. The transiting South Node in Virgo in the company's 4th House, its roots, indicates a need to let go of some of the old ways and structures on which the company was founded.

Chart F of Safeway Stores' original incorporation on March 24, 1926, in Baltimore, Maryland, shows a pre-natal Solar Eclipse at 23 degrees of Capricorn in the 7th House of competitors. In July 1986, the Haft Corporation took over Safeway, creating a new incorporation chart for August 29, 1986, in Dover, Delaware (Chart G).

At the time of the takeover, the transiting North Node was in Aries exactly square the pre-natal Solar Eclipse in the original company's chart and square the original natal nodes at 21 degrees of Cancer/Capricorn in the 1st and 7th Houses. At the same time, transiting Neptune was three

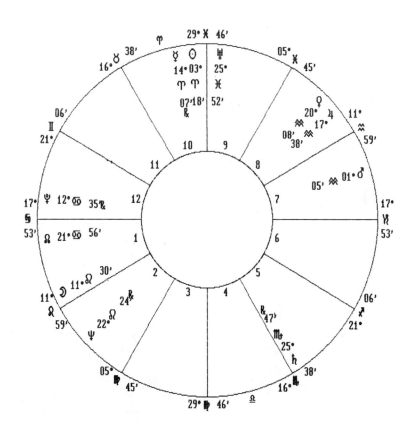

Original Safeway Stores
March 24, 1926   12:00 PM EST
39N19   76W37
Baltimore, Maryland
Source: *Moody's Handbook*

Chart F — Koch Houses

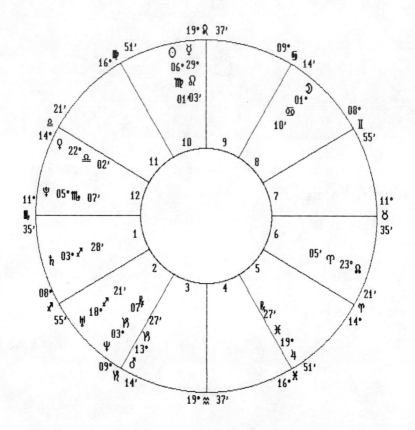

Safeway Corporation
August 29, 1986   12:00 PM EDT
39N10   75W32
Dover, Delaware
Source: *Moody's Handbook*

Chart G — Koch Houses

degrees Capricorn *exactly* square the company's natal Sun at three degrees Aries—a common indicator of takeovers and mergers.

The current Safeway chart (G) incorporated in 1986 has its pre-natal eclipse near the North Node at 19 degrees of Aries in the 6th House of labor strikes and labor troubles.

Whereas the original chart (Chart F) appeared to show a company that either led the field of competition or was very competitive (the nodes on the original 1st/7th House axis), it is now in the news mostly because of labor disputes and environmental concerns—recall the huge Safeway warehouse fire of July 11, 1988. Transiting Pluto was exactly conjunct the Pluto/Ascendant midpoint.

With the recent series of eclipses in Pisces and Virgo transiting the company's 4th/10th House axis, there have been many changes in their facilities; with the South Node transiting the 10th House during the last Virgo eclipses, many managers or figureheads were let go for various reasons. Recently information came out about improperly graded meat, reported to be of inferior quality, found in some of the stores. Resulting from this, several bosses in the company were discharged. Transiting South Node (letting go) in Virgo was in the 10th House of people in charge!

MERGER MANIA

In the last four years since transiting Neptune entered Capricorn, there have been more and more buy outs and mergers. As Pluto moves into its perigee at 15 Scorpio, there should be more buy-out and merger activity.

These two planets have a great deal to do with mergers. **Neptune** dissolves and reforms whatever it touches and, in the process, can add a great deal of confusion to the situation. **Pluto** transforms and regenerates a situation into a new more workable solution. Pluto sextiling Neptune combines this opportunity and ability for individuals as well as corporations.

Other merger indicators are the **Solar and Lunar Eclipses that take place on or near a company's Sun or angles.** As in a natal chart, an eclipse that hits the Sun will temporarily cut out the "light" so that the corporation can get in touch with its "shadow" side and make a life change.

Several examples of mergers have been mentioned: Chart D, the typesetting and graphics company; Chart E, R.J. Reynolds Company; and Charts F and G for Safeway Stores. Another chart is that of Continental Illinois Bank (Chart H), incorporated on October 15, 1932.

Continental Illinois had its Sun in late Libra. In the summer of 1984, the federal government came in and bailed out the long-failing Continental Illinois. Transiting Pluto had moved to 29 degrees of Libra and was retrograding back across its Midheaven at 28 degrees of Libra, restructuring the public's view.

Since its Ascendant was early Capricorn and since transiting Neptune was conjuncting transiting Jupiter in early degrees of Capricorn and retrograde on the Ascendant, the stockholders were asked to dissolve their investment in a protective move for the company. This bail out had profound ramifications. Continental Illinois had been one of the leading banks in the world, and this was the beginning of the many bank failures that have occurred since that time.

As mentioned earlier, the graphics company (Chart D) was incorporated after a Solar Eclipse and is currently being reincorporated as transiting Saturn, Uranus and Neptune square its Sun in early Libra. Its North and South Nodes square its 2nd House Neptune at five degrees of Capricorn.

R.J. Reynolds, Chart E, has two degrees of Capricorn on its 7th House of competition. On October 20, 1988, RJR management announced a private company buy out as

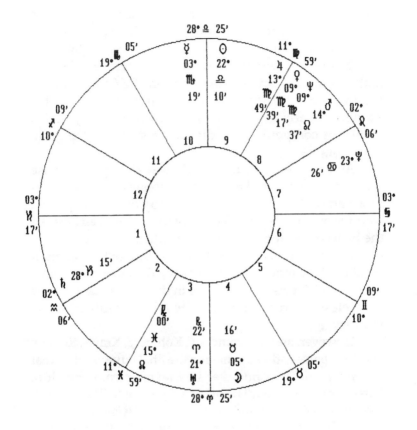

Continental Illinois Bank
October 15, 1932   12:00 PM CST
41N52   87W39
Chicago, Illinois
Source: *Moody's Handbook*

Chart H — Koch Houses

transiting Mercury turned direct at 11 degrees Libra conjunct natal Uranus in the 4th House and as transiting Mars was stationing direct at 29 degrees of Pisces in the 10th House square the 1st/7th House axis, representative of stockholders and competition. Transiting Saturn and Uranus had conjuncted for the last time on the 7th House of competition on October 18, 1988, and were now quickly heading to early degrees of Capricorn conjuncting the 7th House of competitors—indicating a sudden change in trade volume!

As it turned out, the public was outraged because Shearson Lehman had been selling bonds for RJR and was now part of the proposed in-house buy out. Many people were furious because they felt that Shearson Lehman lowered the bond prices for the purpose of RJR's buy out.

The plan was that if RJR was to buy out privately it would sell the food division and keep the tobacco division. Perhaps this decision was made in the hopes that the new smokeless cigarette "Premier" would revolutionize the industry.

However, another company, Kohlberg, Kravis, Roberts and Company ended up making the final buy-out offer that was accepted. This came after another offer from Theodore Forstmann Company. The original intent of KKR was to sell the tobacco division and keep the food division.

In the process of this entire transaction, the corporate bond markets were devastated, but the stockholders (the 1st House) benefited. Transiting Jupiter was trine the natal Moon at one degree of Aquarius, the ruler of the 1st House. It is yet to be determined what will emerge from this buy out. The last Solar Eclipse at 17 degrees of Pisces occurred on March 7, 1989, and will not return for 19 years. At this time, we may hear of a new direction for RJR.

At the time of the Safeway Stores buy out (Charts F and G), transiting Neptune was at three degrees of Capricorn squaring the original company chart's Sun at three degrees of Aries. Transiting Pluto was coming up to a square to the original chart's Moon in Leo in the 1st House. Transiting Mars, the company's ruler, was squaring the company's natal Mercury in the 10th House at 14 degrees of Aries. Mercury rules the company's natal 4th House of its origins, and its roots were being uprooted!

The last Solar Eclipse had hit that same Mercury within about five degrees at 19 degrees of Aries on April 9, 1986, shortly after the company's birthday on March 24. Again, we see an example of eclipses hitting near a company's Sun sign and how it changes its face forever—quite unexpectedly.

There are obviously many factors that create a merger, but Neptune or Pluto or a series of eclipses on the company's Sun seem to trigger some type of overt directional change and are factors that should definitely be taken into consideration.

A CORPORATION IN CRISIS

On February 10, 1986, at 3:07 P.M. in New Brunswick, New Jersey, David Clare of Johnson and Johnson Pharmaceuticals, the maker of Tylenol, received a phone call that poison had been found in Tylenol capsules and had killed several people. This was not the first time that this had happened to Johnson and Johnson. On September 29, 1982, in Chicago, Illinois there had been other Tylenol poisonings. Could it be that this nightmare was happening to them again?

On February 11, 1986, all packages of Tylenol capsules were removed from all market shelves. When the Chicago poisonings happened in 1982, J&J had removed all Tylenol packages from the shelves and revolutionized the over-the-counter drug market with the now very common safety seals. When the second poisonings occurred and all capsules were removed from the shelves, J&J revolutionized the industry again by designing caplets. But at what price?

How can we foresee a crisis or a possible area of concern happening to a corporation? There are many factors involved in doing this. First, of course, we need to look at the natal chart and the progressions to that chart, particularly the **solar arc directions**, since their slow movement can truly activate a natal chart when there is an exact hit within one degree of orb. We also can look at the **solar return** for the year of the corporation, as well as the placement of the pre-natal eclipse and the effect of the current cycles of **eclipses** on the corporate natal chart.

Johnson and Johnson was incorporated on November 10, 1887, close to noon in a former wallpaper factory in New Brunswick, New Jersey. Its first products were medicinal plasters mixed with adhesive, but it soon developed a more absorbent cotton gauze dressing that was mass produced and shipped to hospitals. In the late 1800s, they (there were three brothers) began work on the development of the now-famous Band-Aid. As the years continued, the company moved into first-aid supplies, contraceptives, shampoos, disposable diapers and over-the-counter headache remedies.

It was the famous Tylenol, the non-aspirin headache remedy, that turned the company into one of the largest and most wealthy in the world, and it was this development that brought it the most grief.

Johnson and Johnson's corporate chart (Chart I) shows 29 degrees of Capricorn on the Ascendant, ruled by Saturn and Uranus (Aquarius is intercepted in the 1st House.) This Saturn/Uranus shared rulership implies changes for this company that may come quite suddenly out of some unexpected event. The energy is similar to 1988 and the Saturn/Uranus conjunction which brought a great deal of tumultuous change, but which ultimately brought people to a new awareness. Since Capricorn is rising, however, and Saturn

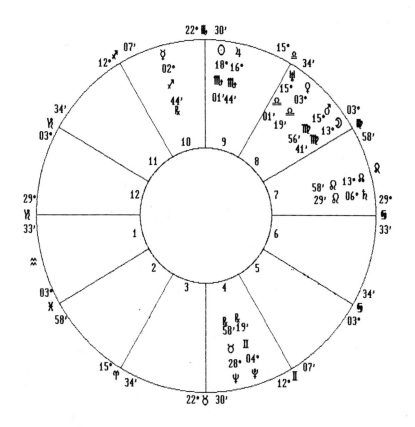

Johnson and Johnson
November 10, 1887   12:00 PM EST
40N30   74W27
New Brunswick, New Jersey
Source: *Moody's Handbook*

Chart I — Koch Houses

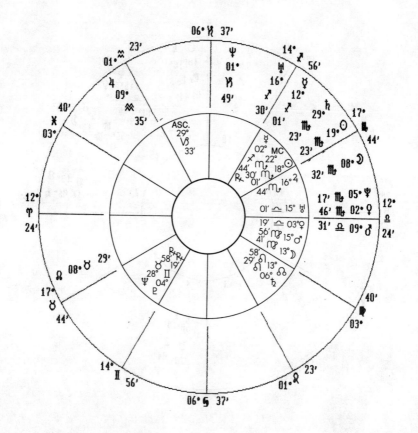

Johnson and Johnson Return Chart
November 11, 1985   3:03 PM EST
40N30   74W27
New Brunswick, New Jersey

Chart J — Koch Houses

is in the 7th House, this company will have its setbacks, but it also has the Capricornian fortitude that suggests it can do its best work when in crisis.

The company was established with the Sun in Scorpio ruled by Pluto which falls in the company's 4th House of foundations and roots. The strong Plutonian energy provides the company the extra gumption that it needs, but can also imply that, like the phoenix which burns itself into its own ashes, it re-emerges from its own tragedy, stronger each time.

The company's Moon is in Virgo, a good sign for health products, placed in the 8th House conjunct Mars in Virgo. The 8th House indicates losses or gains through death—in this case, this is particularly profound. The public and the company have experienced loss, and from this loss there has been a gain for the company. Since the Moon rules the public and is conjunct Mars, an irritant, there have been lawsuits as a result of these poisonings. Insurance claims have also been paid as a result of these losses. These are all 8th House matters.

An important aspect of this entire chart is that the pre-natal eclipse before its incorporation was in Leo at 26 degrees near the North Node at 13 degrees of Leo in the 7th House of lawsuits, legal affairs, competition, and trading volume.

In Chart J, the November 1985 solar return for J&J occurred on November 11, one day before a Solar Eclipse of 20 degrees of Scorpio on the company's Sun, squaring the pre-natal eclipse at 26 degrees Leo. As mentioned earlier, any eclipse on a company's Sun will trigger vast changes for the company, depending on the aspects at the time of the eclipse. Another rule is that one should watch exactly 87 days later or at the next New Moon that squares the eclipse point, for some change will be triggered by the square to the eclipse point. This date fell on February 10, 1986—the day David Clare received the phone call that there had been poisonings!

The solar return has Aries, ruled by Mars, on the Ascendant. At this time, transiting Mars was at nine degrees of Libra in the 6th House and was just completing a square to transiting Neptune (drugs and potential sabotage) in the 9th. It was also on the midpoint of natal Venus/Uranus, indicating an unexpected event (Uranus) that would cost money (Venus). Once an aspect hits and then releases, we frequently see results. Natal Mars at 15 degrees of Virgo was also being squared by transiting Mercury and *particularly transiting Uranus was square the natal Mars*—a sure indicator that something was up. Mars square Uranus aspects can indicate accidents and tragedy.

The Solar Eclipse of November 12, 1985, was at 20 degrees of Scorpio in the 8th House of the solar return chart and activated the midpoint between solar return Saturn at 29 Scorpio and the Sun at 19 degrees of Scorpio, again suggesting possible death and loss.

Transiting Pluto at five degrees of Scorpio activated the Venus/Moon midpoint in the 7th House of how other people viewed the company, and it also squared solar return Jupiter at nine degrees Aquarius in the 11th House of unexpected events. Pluto also squared natal Saturn at six degrees Leo, forming a T-square (natal Saturn, solar return Pluto and Jupiter). Pluto rules sabotage and death, and squaring the ruler of the company, Saturn, it almost "killed" the company in the eyes of the public.

In Chart K, we see the solar arc directions for February 1, 1986. *The solar arc is determined by directing the Sun by one arc and moving the rest of the chart by the same increment.*

This means that when a solar arc directed planet is within one to one-and-a-half degrees of aspecting the natal planets, it indicates possible significant changes.

Note how many negative aspects there were to Neptune (drugs, sabotage, dissolution and creativity) and to Pluto

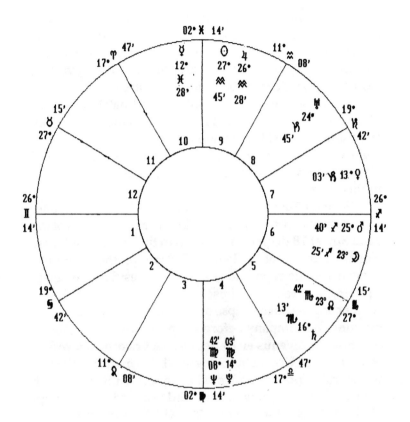

Johnson and Johnson Solar Arc Directions
February 1, 1986   12:00 PM EST
40N30   74W27
New Brunswick, New Jersey

Chart K — Koch Houses

(sabotage, wipe out, and transformation).

At the time of the crisis, the solar arc Sun at 27 Aquarius and solar arc Jupiter at 26 Aquarius were opposing the pre-natal eclipse and squaring natal Neptune at 28 Taurus in the 4th House. They also widely squared the eclipse of November 12, 1985, at 20 degrees Scorpio in the 9th.

Since the Sun rules the intercepted natal 7th House and Jupiter rules the natal 11th and 2nd Houses, Johnson and Johnson's 7th House trade volume was affected, resulting in a depletion in the 11th House treasury and the 2nd House of moneymaking activities. Neptune is also involved in this square.

Solar arc Saturn was at 16 Scorpio conjunct natal Jupiter at 16 degrees Scorpio and very close to a conjunction of the natal Sun at 18 degrees of Scorpio in the 9th. The solar arc North Node was at 23 degrees Scorpio on the natal Mid-heaven (public reputation) at 22 degrees Scorpio, again squaring the pre-natal eclipse of 26 degrees Leo and closely conjuncting the Solar Eclipse of 1985 at 20 degrees Scorpio—bringing the company before the public eye.

Solar arc Venus at 13 degrees Capricorn was widely squaring natal Uranus at 15 degrees Libra in the 8th. Venus, which rules popularity, moving through the natal 12th House of undermining activity, did not lend itself to popularity, but since it was in the 12th, which also rules research and development, the square to Uranus over that next year signified the stress which brought about a creative (Venus) solution to the tragedy—the now well-known caplets. In recent months, J&J has placed gel capsules on the market during the time that transiting Jupiter in early degrees of Gemini was trining J&J's natal Venus in the 8th at three degrees of Libra!

Solar arc Uranus was at 24 Capricorn, which may indicate an argument for an earlier incorporation time. If the incorporation Ascendant were about 24 degrees of Capricorn, then progressed Uranus on the natal Ascendant could indicate a sudden awakening by all concerned.

Chart L, the last chart in this drama, is a chart of the David Clare phone call when the poisonings were reported. This event chart can also be used as a transit chart to the natal.

Twenty-five degrees Cancer rising is almost the exact opposite of the natal chart's Ascendant at approximately 29 degrees of Capricorn, indicating a mirror image or reflection of what J&J was about to go through.

The event chart Sun (the ruler of the intercepted natal 7th) was at 21 degrees of Aquarius opposing the pre-natal eclipse in the 7th and squaring natal Jupiter at 16 degrees Scorpio, forming a very challenging T-square; the natal Sun at 18 degrees of Scorpio, natal Neptune at 28 degrees of Taurus, and the pre-natal eclipse point at 26 degrees of Leo combine with the former aspects to form a Grand Cross!

The event Moon was at 14 Pisces opposing the natal Moon in the 8th House at 13 Virgo and natal Mars at 15 Virgo. It was also squaring the solar return Mercury/Uranus conjunction in the middle degrees of Sagittarius.

Transiting Venus was at 27 degrees of Aquarius—again opposing the pre-natal eclipse—square natal Neptune (drugs/sabotage) at 28 Taurus and widely square the natal Sun at 18 Scorpio. The same squares to Neptune and the Sun and the opposition to the pre-natal eclipse at 26 degrees Leo were also activated by transiting Jupiter at 27 degrees Aquarius and transiting Mercury at 29 degrees Aquarius. Transiting Neptune was at four degrees Capricorn, just past a square to natal Venus at three degrees Libra in the 8th. Again and again and again, Neptune is disturbingly aspected.

Pluto also had some stress aspects. From the time of the company's solar return in 1985 to the February 1986 event, transiting Saturn had moved from 29 degrees Scorpio

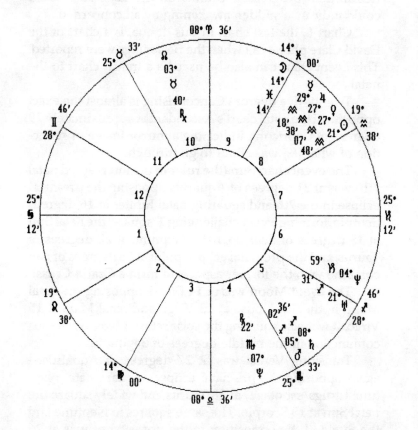

David Clare's Phone Call
February 10, 1986   3:07 PM EST
40N29   74W27
New Brunswick , New Jersey

Chart L — Koch Houses

to eight degrees Sagittarius, opposing natal Pluto at four degrees Gemini in the 4th House. This indicates a need for the company to work through the repression of all difficult events, transforming itself by careful research for the future. At this same time, transiting Pluto at seven degrees Scorpio was squaring natal Saturn at six degrees Leo in the 7th House. In fact, Pluto had just stationed retrograde at this degree on February 8, 1986!! It is the experience of this author that when Pluto retrogrades or goes direct, there are often very Plutonian events (tragedies, abandonments, deaths) prominent in the news. The transit of Pluto squaring Saturn, the natal ruler of this chart, could indicate loss or literally a killing off of the old ways.

Since Mars tends to be the trigger for most events, transiting Mars was at five degrees Sagittarius and had just opposed natal Pluto at four degrees Gemini in the 4th House. This was the very same position of transiting Mars at the time of the first Tylenol poisonings in Chicago on September 29, 1982! This is an interesting degree since five degrees of Sagittarius has as its sensitive or solstice point 25 degrees of Capricorn, the approximate degree of the company's Ascendant.

When a company chart is this activated by the solar return, the transits and the solar arcs to the natal, caution needs to be exercised. Of course, the converse is true: when all of the above is true with positive, flowing aspects, it can indicate a wonderful time for a major company expansion. The corporation chart is a breathing vehicle that can be read as accurately and specifically as a natal chart.

Robert Cole

Robert Cole's interest in astrology began in 1972 when he moved to California after receiving a degree in Traditional Metaphysics from the University of Nevada, Las Vegas. After studying with Creetus Locke and George Hurd, they opened a full-service astrology center in Santa Cruz. He took over the business in 1978 and began publishing a weekly astrology forecast in *Good Times*. The column appeared in more than 20 news weeklies. In 1980 he published *The Book of Houses* with Paul Williams.

In 1984 Cole was named one of the "Outstanding Young Men in America" by a national panel of professional business people. He moved to San Francisco that year and has maintained a personal, professional, political and business practice there.

A prolific writer, Robert has had more than 100 astrology-related articles published, has an extremely busy astrological practice and is active in AFAN, NCGR, ISAR and the National Writers' Union.

THE PREDICTABLE ECONOMY

An estimated 5000 economic forecasters work daily in every nation on Earth to predict trends in the stock and bond, the commodities, the precious metals, and the real estate markets. Most of these forecasters are highly trained technicians who believe that market directions are determined by internal factors such as inflation, unemployment, interest rates, etc. There is a small group, however, who construct their forecasts on information received from "external factors" such as the movements of the planets and the Sun and Moon. Although this article will appeal primarily to this smaller group, every economist must consider the implications of *the predictable economy*.

Until the 20th century, economic forces were as mysterious as the forces which caused earthquakes and floods and droughts. The fateful forces of nature could destroy civilizations just as easily as bestow royalty on an infant child. The poor were unlucky, the rich lucky. There was no hope of predicting the whims of fate, so praying for salvation compensated for effective management of the ecology.

In the 20th century, humanity reached the edge of its Universe. Everywhere became filled with consciousness. Earth saw herself within a vast unified field. And each person on Earth was released from class distinctions and given total economic freedom. Every man and woman began to dream about and share the future. The promise of being able to reach one's goals, to make one's dreams come true—

this was the promise of the 20th century.

Technical forecasting, once considered an occult science, is a full-fledged 20th-century profession. Economists do it. Meteorologists do it. Agribusiness does it. Even the military does it. The technology of forecasting is pushing computers to the limit as they help cast mathematical structures into the future. In all its dimensions, the future becomes more and more predictable as humanity struggles to produce its dreams.

For the last 100 years, astrologers, whose ideology naturally assumes that the future is predictable, have been employed by the rich and famous to make predictions about the economy. Most of these predictions are wildly inaccurate and intentionally designed to prop up the goals of the upper classes. Since the '60s, however, several astrologers have seriously monitored economic trends and the relationship to planetary positions in this solar system. The authors in this anthology are of the latter sort. We are diligently working on the predictable economy.

At this time in history, technical forecasters can accurately predict 90% of what's going to happen tomorrow, about 50% of what's going to happen next week, and about 20% of what's going to happen next month. Astrologers are beginning to humor themselves with the possibility of being able to stretch their system hundreds of years into the future. These pioneers are charting unknown territory, and the stars still show the way.

The transition from a *mysterious marketplace* to the predictable economy is occurring everywhere on the planet as the Global Villagers open their doors to each other in peace. But it is a gradual process.

The revision of the economic paradigm is a crucial factor in preparations for the 21st century. Remember, at one time the Universe was perceived as an empty vacuum, and it was merely a stroke of fate which bestowed wealth in mysterious measure. That's the old paradigm. In the old paradigm, work was the way to fill up an empty Universe at the risk of falling into it. One had very little control over economic status, yet self-control was believed to be the key to richness and special privilege. Fate ruled the mysterious marketplace.

Fortune rules the predictable economy. The Universe is full and it is full of fortune. It is a blissful abundance and there's so much of it, it staggers the imagination. In the new economic paradigm, each individual form of life by nature participates in great fortune which is constant and eternal. The conflict between richness and poorness which drove the old dialogue is now transformed into the fluctuations between buying and selling. The predictable economy puts ten times more emphasis on buying and selling; it ignores the rich/poor discussion altogether. In the Universe of fortune, there's no good reason for work. *In the predictable economy one doesn't work, one buys and sells.*

Over the years of gathering the research presented in this article, I have been approached by those who suggest that the concept of the predictable economy threatens cherished freedoms. For centuries, astrologers have been accused of denying freedom, free will and the rest. Astrologers never bought the idea of chaos, so a concern with personal freedoms hasn't been much of an issue in the history of astrology. Nevertheless, astrologers have developed several responses to the freedom question.

The predictable economy supports the theory that buying and selling patterns coincide with aspect relationships between the Sun and Moon and other planets in this solar system *and* each person is totally free to respond to those patterns as s/he sees fit. In ancient times, our ancestors carefully watched the migration patterns of the animals and the flooding cycles of the rivers; civilization grew as they became more astute in predicting the cycles of nature. As we approach the 21st century, we are discovering that economic cycles and patterns of buying and selling among the peoples of Earth are just as important as caribou migrations and the flooding of the Nile were to our ancestors. The consumption patterns of the human species influence the ecology of the Earth in dramatic ways. And we have only recently decided that our freedom must have some limits lest we threaten our own survival here.

I have monitored the global buying and selling patterns of the human species since 1978 and am totally convinced that such patterns are predictable. Granted that we can run our predictions by mathematical computation into the future, the real question remains: When will we begin to manage our economy freely within those parameters? The greatest challenge in the development of our civilization awaits us. As an astrologer, I have chosen to reach for the stars rather than to simply stand by watching them.

ENLIGHTENED CONSUMPTION

The concept of a *consumer*, as opposed to the concept of a trader, originated in the 14th century as the power of the landlords was replaced by the monetary authority of the merchants. Merchants relied heavily on those in the community who had earned enough money from their labor to be able to purchase the merchant's products. Economists have studied the worker/consumer relationship for centuries. Marxists point to the inherent degradation of the worker whose labor barely produces enough money to buy daily necessities. Capitalists, on the other hand, have always promoted the idea that free enterprise depends on the wealth of the consumers and not the wealth of the merchant class.

In the dictionary, *consumption* and *consumer* have very strange definitions. Basically the idea is one of gorging or overeating or wasting resources in the pursuit of one's pleasures, such as "He was *consumed* by the desire to travel."

There is a fundamental discrimination against consumption and consumers because they tend to thrive on gluttony and unconscious use of the ecology. Only at the end of the list of definitions in the dictionary do we find one which makes sense these days: "one that uses economic goods." From this definition it becomes evident that the consumer is a primary and essential factor in the economy of the modern world. Without consumers, the production of economic goods would be meaningless and wasteful.

Using the consumer as the "end-dump" for mass-produced products is oppressively demeaning. Until the 18th century, stimulation of consumption in the economy was the effort of economists who had no respect for consumers as individuals. The idea was to stimulate consumption whether the consumers needed the products or not. Merchants pushed the economy forward by driving consumers to the heights of wastefulness and overindulgence. This technique worked well in poor countries which had never witnessed the glitter of consumer goods from the industrialized world. Consumers in the poor countries were viewed merely as victims of their own desires; they were treated like garbage sacks just waiting to be filled with useless products.

But the French and American Revolutions of the 18th century totally transformed the role of the consumer in society. In the political upheaval of these revolutions, individuals won the right to vote democratically and thereby gained some direct influence on the social environment in which they lived and died. Each individual was guaranteed the right to life, liberty and the pursuit of happiness. Suddenly the merchant/monarchy no longer had total control over the people in their society; individuals had won the right to control their lives by democratic means. Political rights quickly evolved into consumer rights. In no time consumers were taking control of the economy in the same way that voters were taking control of the government.

After the democratic revolutions, merchants could no longer perceive consumers as wasteful end-dumps for their products. It became mandatory for the merchants to carefully monitor the desires of the consumers, indeed, to tend to their every desire. Consumers began to realize that their buying power could control the merchant's production process altogether. The power of the consumer to buy certain products and to reject others would soon prove to be more effective in managing the society than playing politics.

In the 20th century, the role of the consumer became truly glorified. Merchants began to develop sideline businesses just to monitor consumer trends and to poll consumer response to their products. The advent of television and mass-advertising campaigns depended clearly on the desires of the consumers in the free marketplace. The shapes of automobiles, the colors of refrigerators, the design of houses were decided by consumer demand, not by the creative authority of the merchant. Merchants, however, began to include in their prices the costs of advertising campaigns and consumer studies. So important are such procedures these days that anywhere from 25% to 45% of the cost of a product comes from the merchant's expensive campaigns to promote his or her product.

In August 1987, the planetary community on Earth experienced The Harmonic Convergence. At this point in history, all consumers became enlightened. *Choices of sizes, shapes and colors became secondary to the impact value that a product would have on the overall ecological condition of the planet.* Now enlightened consumers "vibrate" to the needs of all life on Earth, and consumption patterns have totally transcended the designs of the merchants who produce the products. As consumers consciously take up the management of Earth's resources, they will recognize the intricate relationship this planet has with other bodies in the solar system. Consumer patterns of buying and selling necessarily vibrate to the cycles of movement between the Earth, the Moon and the Sun and the other planets. Consciousness of these frequencies is the key to the predictable economy. Such profound information is available to all people on Earth through communication technology.

THE PLANETARY COMPRESSION FACTOR

In the summer of 1984, I received a phone call from Andrew Aldrich, a student of Cultural History at the University of California, Berkeley. Through a mutual friend he had heard of my research into cycles of buying and selling in the marketplace, and he told me that he had some very interesting information which he wanted to share in the hope that he could get his research published in a national publication. We met for lunch in Berkeley in one of those exquisitely bohemian vegetarian lunchettes common to the neighborhood. That afternoon we traded notes that would have a major impact on the predictability of human culture and human economics.

I explained to Andrew about my work monitoring planetary aspects and comparing them with buy and sell signals in the commercial marketplace. I was working with the theory that so-called "hard aspects" generated sell signals while "soft aspects" generated buy signals. I had been following the aspect relationships between Jupiter, Saturn, Uranus, Neptune and Pluto for several years and had actually been giving advice to some of my clients who could afford to invest in the stock and bond markets. We had not scored any fortunes, but there hadn't been any major losses either.

After about a half-hour of my explanations, Andrew pulled some papers from his briefcase and began to explain his research. He immediately explained that his interests were not specifically oriented to monitoring the consumer marketplace. In fact, his studies in Cultural History at the university were focused on the progressions of global history through liberal and conservative cycles. He had come to the conclusion that planetary relationships accurately coincide with swings toward the liberal and conservative ends of the political spectrum throughout human history. The proof of Andrew's theory was a detailed graph generated by a complex four-page computer program which he had created himself.

Andrew's computer program was designed to rate what he called "the planetary compression factor." Using Jupiter, Saturn, Uranus, Neptune, Pluto and Transpluto (a hypothetical planet for which ephemerides have been calculated but as yet which no one has scientifically observed), Andrew had been able, with his program, to observe and keep track of the *regular alignment* of planetary bodies in our solar system. When you visualize six planets in separate orbits spinning around the central Sun, you will notice that every so often there is an alignment or bunching up of planets; you can also see that there are times when the planets are evenly distributed all around the Sun. Andrew's program was capable of judging the bunching up, or the planetary compression factor; the statistics made it easy to chart the compression factor on a visual graph. Andrew's work coincided with my own speculation, and he had a computer program to prove it. We had proof that planetary aspects have a measurable impact on human activity on Earth.

Andrew showed me how he had run his program on the planetary movements through the 20th century. *He had come to the conclusion that when planets are compressed (aligned or bunched up) there are obvious trends of conservatism, nationalism and left-brain masculine chauvinism in human history.* The Russo-Japanese War, World Wars I and II, the McCarthy Era, the Nixon Administration, and the Reagan Revolution all occurred during relatively high planetary compression periods when the major planets in our solar system were in positions of exceptional alignment. On the other hand,

Teddy Roosevelt's Populist Reforms, Franklin Roosevelt's New Deal Liberalism, Lyndon Johnson's Administration, and Nixon's Resignation all occurred in periods of non-alignment when the planets were evenly spaced around the Sun with no particular alignment in effect.

I was completely enthralled with Andrew's work mainly because it coincided almost exactly with my own research. From two different directions, we had both come to the same point of revelation. We had proof that planetary relationships in the solar system actually coincide with cultural and economic patterns here on Earth. We had no rational scientific explanation for why this phenomenon occurs, but we both had proof that it does exist. We agreed to use Andrew's term "the planetary compression factor" to designate our mutual discovery.

Since that day our work has been validated by a small, knowing group of economists, historians and politicians from around the world.

BUYING IN THE NEW AGE

The planetary compression factor clearly indicates that human activity fluctuates between conservative and liberal extremes and that these fluctuations can be predicted by the movements of the major planets in the solar system. My research goes further to prove that the buying and selling patterns in the marketplaces of Earth also coincide with the planetary compression factor.

After years of monitoring the marketplaces of the world, I concluded that the planetary compression factor, or the bunching up of planets in the solar system, coincided with (or set off) *strong buying signals*. Therefore, a conjunction or an alignment between two or more planets in our heavens stimulates buying activity here on Earth. As the Earth spins, the exact moment of the conjunction of two planets overhead will occur over certain markets during the daytime when markets are open for trading; on the other side of the Earth, the same conjunction will be happening, but it will be at nighttime when the markets are closed.* It is therefore very important to watch the exact times and locations where the conjunctions and alignments occur.

In traditional astrology, there are lists of astrological aspects, *i.e.*, measured angles of relationship between two moving bodies in the heavens. Astrologers divide these aspects into "positive/soft" aspects and "negative/hard" aspects. *As previously noted, my observations indicate that positive aspects coincide with buy signals and negative aspects coincide with sell signals.*

Over the past 200 years, astrologers have carefully monitored the angular relationships between planets and have discovered that positive aspects coincide with creative and inspiring actions in individuals and groups. It made sense to me that such aspects would coincide with buying patterns because I know of nothing more exciting, relaxing and fun than to go on a buying spree. My friends agree—buying is a most positive experience. Shopping has been elevated to a form of therapy.

The positive aspects when buying and shopping are most strongly stimulated are listed as follows:

+1 = semi-sextile (30°)
+2 = decile (36°)
+3 = sextile (60°)
+4 = quintile (72°)
+5 = tri-decile (108°)
+6 = trine (120°)
+7 = bi-quintile (144°)
+8 = tri-septile (154.3°)
+9 = quadnovile (160°)
+10 = conjunction (0°)

---

* *Ed. Note:* A worldwide 24-hour market will start in 1990.

Whenever one of these aspects occurs between two bodies in our solar system, a buy signal ripples through the marketplaces on Planet Earth. In those places where the markets are open and functioning, a positive aspect brings a rush of excitement and positive energy as consumers feel a natural desire to buy products, services and merchandise of all sizes, shapes and colors. I have no rational explanation for why this happens. I cannot claim that some sort of gravitational force or influence from solar winds causes this activity in human beings as planets billions of miles away form angular relationships with each other. I can only describe to you how such coincidences regularly occur.

As you may have noticed, there are variable gradations of buying energy depending on the force of the aspect in effect. A semi-sextile seems to generate an extremely modest amount of buying power, whereas a trine seems to generate four times as much. (*Note:* I prefer to use the gradation of aspect influences found in traditional astrological research rather than adhering strictly to the planetary compression factor. While a semi-sextile may show two planets in fairly close alignment with each other, the semi-sextile has a tradition of being a weak aspect. The trine, though it may show two planets quite far apart, has a much stronger positive tradition.) Naturally a conjunction, when two planets are in exact alignment with each other, generates the most buying power.

Besides the idea that buying and shopping are positive experiences for enlightened consumers, there are several economic conditions which seem to exist when positive aspects are in effect. We can all understand the good feelings which come with shopping for our favorite things. We each approach the buying opportunity with our own style. Some are thrifty shoppers and indulge in finding the best bargains and the finest quality. Some are compulsive shoppers who get off on the urge to buy whatever strikes their fancy. Some love to shop for large items; some love to shop for lots of small items.

The trends of buying affect the monitoring systems of the marketplace, such as the Dow Jones Averages, the Standard and Poor 500 Index, the Index of Leading Economic Indicators, etc. But in this system of astrological prediction, there are several surprising impact factors which I have discovered that I want to share with you.

First, a novice who is just beginning to use this system of judging movements in the marketplace is likely to wonder why, during a buying trend, there is no compensating selling signal. In other words, if people are in the mood for buying, then shouldn't there be people who are ready to sell? I quickly came to the conclusion that the traditional relationship between buying and selling really does not exist in the New Age. The symbiotic ties between buying and selling were severed in the 19th century when our markets began to function on a surplus-maintenance system. Long gone are the days when a buyer could approach a merchant for personal goods which could be produced on the spot within a few days. Now when a consumer walks into the marketplace motivated by a buying signal, s/he is buying **surplus** which was generated during selling periods which we will discuss later. It's important to realize that when you pay for something at the supermarket by handing coins to a cashier behind an electronic register, you are far removed from a buying/selling relationship. You may be buying (accumulating wealth), but the clerk is far from selling; s/he is merely maintaining inventory control over the vast surpluses stored in the market.

Second, when a buy signal occurs among the planets, inevitably **prices on goods and services drop**, sometimes dramatically and sometimes not so dramatically, depending on the relative strength of the aspect in effect. Buy signals mean that there is going to be a big sale. Apparently, the surplus has built up to a point where it becomes necessary to offer merchandise at a cut-rate price in order to preserve economic stability. During very strong buy signals, much of the excess surplus is devoured by happy consumers responding to the sales.

Third, during a buy signal **production drops dramatically**. The surplus stifles the demand for more product, and for this reason there's usually a **drop in employment** during these times when the planets are in positive alignment with each other.

And fourth, when a strong buy signal exists **the money supply will increase proportionately**. This is to say that the flow of cash money through the economy increases to meet the needs of buying consumers. Interest rates tend to fall and savings are pushed into the marketplace for goods and services. These factors increase the cash flow overall.

Finally, I have noticed that strong buy signals are generally interpreted as **"bad times" in the stock markets;** when prices fall, production stalls and unemployment increases, economists from the Old Age react negatively. In the New Age, **there are no bosses and there are no workers** because each individual is granted full rights to free enterprise and the entrepreneurial spirit. Pure free enterprise eliminates the boss/worker relationship in society and it also destroys the passion for profit. Each individual produces services and goods without suffering from the influences of the overlord. Imagine each person being the boss of his or her own business. This is the greatest ideal of the New Age marketplace.

SELLING IN THE NEW AGE
Selling, in both the Old Age and the New Age, is a stress-producing experience. Selling requires that the individual take what s/he has accumulated through production and present it to the marketplace through commercial dis-

tribution and advertising. The process of selling is a very energetic process compared to the process of buying. For that reason, the so-called "hard/negative" astrological aspects are associated with selling trends.

The following astrological aspects represent the gradation of selling signals coinciding with planetary relationships in our solar system:

-1 = triskaidektile (27.7°)
-2 = novile (40°)
-3 = semi-square/octile (45°)
-4 = septile (51.4°)
-5 = bi-novile (80°)
-6 = square (90°)
-7 = bi-septile (102.9°)
-8 = sesquiquadrate/tri-octile (135°)
-9 = quincunx/inconjunct (150°)
-10 = opposition (180°)

According to the general theory of the planetary compression factor, when planets are separated and diffused around the solar system there are liberal trends of activity in human culture here on Earth. Liberalism is classically a type of diffusionary politics, social politics, sharing politics. And it is quite clear when the compression factor is at its lowest (when the planets are most widely distributed around the Sun) the drive to distribute goods and services throughout the human community is clearly indicated. Once again, I will be the first to admit that we have no rational explanation for why this occurs; at this time I can only tell you that the phenomenon does occur. It's for following generations to discover just exactly why this relationship is a fact.

At this point in history, the nature of selling is not only stress-producing but is also believed to be the exclusive domain of big business and complex corporations. When the consumer thinks of selling trends, s/he usually thinks of massive selling promotions for automobiles, fast food, insurance, etc. Because of the tremendous efforts put into commercial advertising programs, it seems that the arena of selling is controlled exclusively by the corporate giants such as GM, IBM, Sears, Prudential, General Foods, etc. It has become a common assumption that selling trends are influenced if not controlled by the massive corporations which compete aggressively for every spare dollar in the marketplace.

Sooner than we can presently imagine, the corporations will devour each other and the boss/worker relationship will collapse. At that moment the concept of selling will take on an entirely new meaning (a New Age meaning). I believe we can presume certain things about New Age selling patterns right now which can be of mutual benefit to all those who consider themselves enlightened consumers.

First, it is crucially important that consumers realize that they have **the power to sell**. Selling is not some weird concept which one gains through a series of selling seminars or college courses. It is a major mistake to believe that some people are born salespeople and others are not. This illusion is promoted by corporate management in order to eliminate much of the competition in the open marketplace. I believe that every single consumer is not only capable of buying products and services, but every single consumer is a natural salesperson of products and services, especially the ones made by oneself.

What most consumers sell is their *labor* and their *time*. When we use the term "working," it generally refers to a condition in which the consumer is selling his or her time to a boss to help manage the business controlled by the boss. Eighty-five percent of the jobs in the 20th century have little or no creativity inherent in the work process; these jobs are merely exercises in moving products from one place to another. The worker, in exchange for the time spent "working," receives a modest, often pitiful wage. Workers' organizations since the Industrial Revolution have attempted to teach the workers about the value of their labor time. In some nations, workers have realized the value of their labor and revolutions have taken place. When consumers realize that labor time equals the value of products consumed, then the New Age of the predictable economy will come true.

Second, consider the possibility that selling is a **form of communication** with others in your social environment. Selling is distributing the ideas, services and products which you have created with your own genius. Every person is a natural distributor of his or her own ideas and opinions. It may take extra effort, but the stimulus is as natural as breathing. Buying is inhaling; selling is exhaling.

Contrary to traditional economics, there are factors in New Age selling which must be taken into consideration if the enlightened consumer is to take full advantage of the predictable economy.

When sell signals occur in the astrological aspects, **prices increase**. The wise consumer operating in such an environment will raise the prices on his or her products and services when a sell signal is in effect. How high the price depends on the slope and intensity of the aspect. Naturally, the individual's greed is also a major factor in judging the upper limits of price increases during a sell signal.

Production and therefore employment seem to increase dramatically when a sell signal goes into effect. Because of the inherent stress in a hard astrological aspect, it's logical to assume that production will increase as a way of burning off the extra physical energy which has accumulated.

During a sell period, **the money supply dries up**, interest rates increase, and the cost of financing expansion increases depending on the intensity of the angular relationship between the planets.

Finally, as mentioned earlier, the old-fashioned symbiosis between buying and selling no longer holds true in New Age economics. In other words, when a selling signal is in play it does not necessarily mean that there must be someone who is willing to buy. Selling (the amount of it) does not depend on the amount of buying. Selling is the distribution of goods and services throughout the community; it's more of a sharing experience than anything else. Selling is the distribution of surplus. *Selling is making available what each person creates with personal genius and with respect for the ecological totality.*

LOOKING AT THE PAST RECORD

In order to study the effectiveness of the system of economic forecasting, students have the advantage of referring to econographs for any year in history. I have devised a simple visual method which indicates the intensity of the buy and sell signals coinciding with the planetary aspects in the solar system. Chart 1 shows the econograph for 1979.

In the annual econographs, only the major astrological aspects are delineated. Semi-sextiles, sextiles, trines and conjunctions are used to judge the intensity of buy signals. Semi-squares, squares, sesquiquadrates and oppositions are used to judge the intensity of sell signals. In the annual econographs, only the outermost planets in the solar system are taken into consideration, *i.e.*, Jupiter, Saturn, Uranus, Neptune and Pluto. By restricting the number of aspects and planets in this way, it is easier to get an overall pattern of economic movement between the extremes of buying and selling.

The econographs have been designed to show buy signals on the down side and sell signals on the up side because this format makes it much easier to compare the econographs with the graphs generated by the Dow Jones

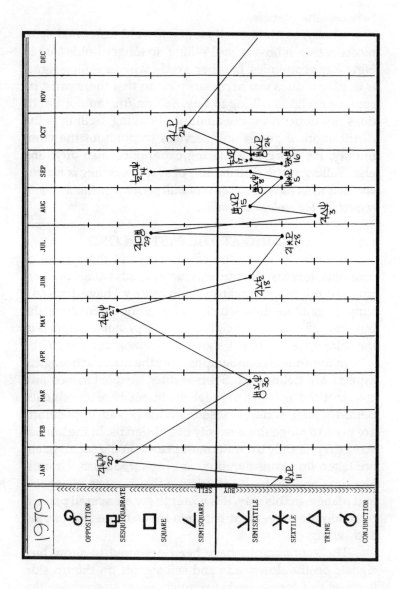

Chart 1

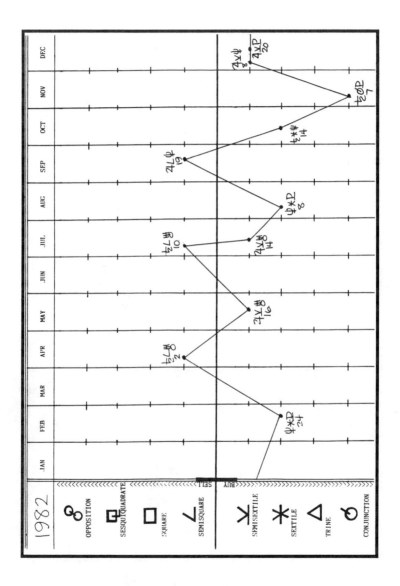

Chart 2

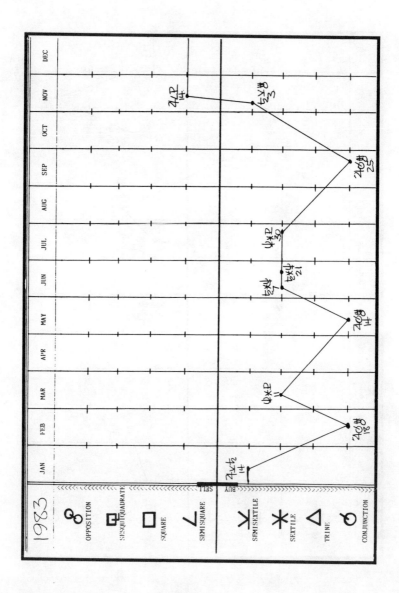

Chart 3

Industrial Averages, the S&P 500 Index and the OTC Averages. In this format the coincidences are spectacularly visible. (Daily econographs have been designed which show the hour-by-hour movements between all the planets including the Moon. The daily econographs are explained subsequently in this chapter.)

I began charting the astrological aspects on the econographs in 1978. I was always amazed at the coincidence between the movements on the econographs and the shifts in the stock market as shown on the nightly television business programs. It didn't take long for me to become solidly convinced that the global economy is predictable. And it wasn't long after that several small-time and two big-time investors became interested in my system of forecasting; we've been following the econographs for the past ten years.

The years 1982 and 1983, known as the Reagan Recession, are clearly indicated in the econographs. The drop in prices and the sluggishness of the marketplace can be easily visualized in the slope of the line on the econographs (Charts 2 and 3). It is important to realize that the impact of the Reagan economic program was not confined to the American marketplace exclusively. In fact, for the first time since World War II, there appears to be an intentional American plan to revamp the global economic structure. Checking the markets in Europe, Japan, and the equivalents of trade exchanges in the Soviet Union and China, it's obvious that American chauvinism during the first two years of the 1980s had a tremendous impact on the global economy. According to the econographs, this recession was a massive buy signal which set off a consumption of surpluses seldom before seen in modern history.

Notice the intense shifting in patterns shown in the econographs for 1986 and 1987 (Charts 4 and 5). These two years are hailed by the Reagan administration as periods of

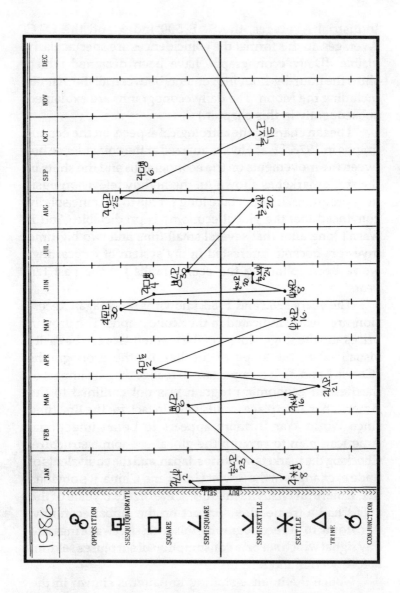

Chart 4

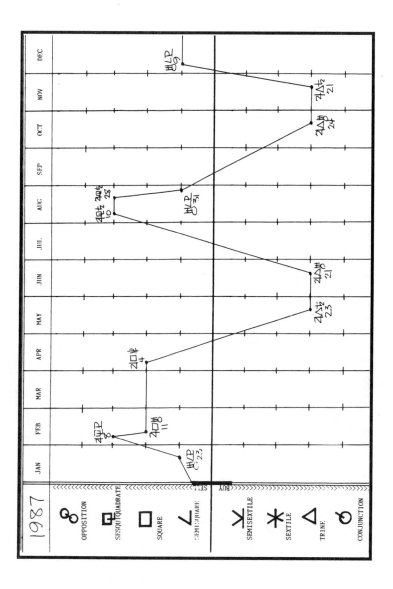

Chart 5

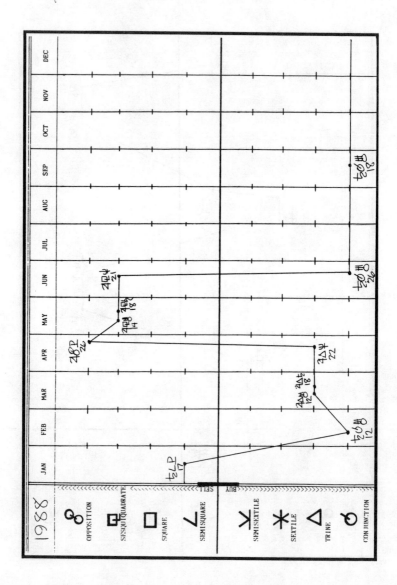

Chart 6

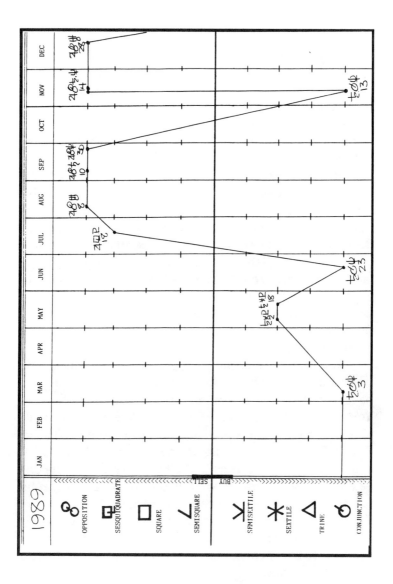

Chart 7

great recovery, the so-called Reagan Revolution. The information from the econographs indicate that this is not truly an economic recovery but more a re-establishing of the balance between buying and selling in the global marketplace. Radical shifts between buying and selling patterns will often mask the internal weakness of the marketplace. Hyperactive ups and downs in prices and other economic factors will not qualify as a substantial recovery from recession.

In the two graphs for 1988 and 1989 (Charts 6 and 7), we have obvious indicators of the ultimate results of the Reagan administration's economic policies on the global marketplace. Under the cover of statistical manipulation, the economy of the world has been forced into a compulsive consumption of all the surpluses which have been accumulated since World War II. Promoted as a period of economic expansion, it becomes more and more obvious that the world is growing at the expense of serious indebtedness. Borrowing from the world's surpluses to the point where no surplus is left is extremely dangerous.

In order to validate the econographs and the coincidence which these graphs have with the global economic changes, I have included the actual marketplace figures from the New York Stock Exchange in my *Buy'N'Sell Guide* which is available for purchase through mail order by sending $20.00 to Robert Cole, P.O. Box 884561, San Francisco, CA 94188. By studying the econographs in the *Buy'N'Sell Guide,* one can easily gain the information necessary to chart econographs for any year for which economic records are available. There are no mysterious secrets involved in this system. In fact, it's my intention to make this economic information available to every consumer. In this way we can create true economic equality.

PREDICTING THE GLOBAL ECONOMY

The early 1990s will very likely bring a true economic bonanza; my econographs will be put to the test of precision and accuracy during this period in history. As we approach the year 2000, I believe a new economic structure will be put into place. By then the global economy will be predictable and completely manageable. This opportunity for humanity to eliminate the "fate factor" in determining richness and poorness will spread the resources of the Planet Earth through all the villages with equal measure. The dreams of equal distribution of wealth will finally be realized.

Using the theory of the planetary compression factor, I have come to the conclusion that the early 1990s will be an *extremely liberal period* in the history of this century. The emphasis on private enterprise and individual creative effort will support my predictions that a great renaissance in human spirit will occur before the turn of the century. Economically speaking, this will be a period which will see the rebuilding of lost surpluses after decades of waste and consumption. Through major developments in economic management, such as the elimination of private banking, the dissolution of the boss/worker relationship, the initiation of lottery-guaranteed income and the universal guarantee of health care, each individual will be liberated to express his or her own creative genius. If a person wants to work, it will be for him- or herself rather than for a boss or corporation; if a person decides not to work, s/he will be guaranteed an income by the lottery so that everyone in the society has some income no matter what. In this atmosphere the excitement for life will be concentrated around the creation of valuable surpluses. New products and new services will replenish all the waste of the preceding 50 years. The storage of human creation will be overturned completely in preparation for the new century.

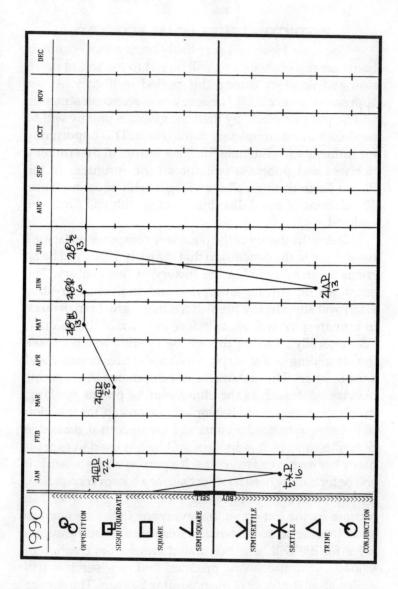

Chart 8

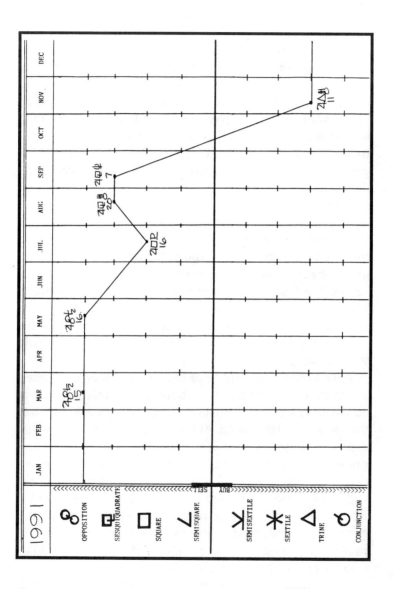

Chart 9

I must also emphasize that my astrological research has proven that the Earth is on the verge of an Ice Age, and there's little that we humans can do to stop this natural ecological transformation. From our present utopia back to the caves of our ancestors will be a journey through which very few of us will survive. But for the first time in the long history of human life on this planet, we will have the opportunity to maintain a continuous link between our present generation and the generations which will survive the Big Chill.

The econographs for 1990 and 1991 (Charts 8 and 9) clearly indicate the human spirit will be busy rebuilding a fresh new surplus of products and services in preparation for this New Age. Those who still promote the Old Age ideas of profit accumulation will become hysterical with prices soaring beyond anything previously imagined. Monopoly capitalists will drool at the possibility of consuming each other's corporations. In these two years we will see the merging of the "Big Corporations" in a truly vicious competitive atmosphere.

By 1993 the resources of the world will be controlled by no more than five corporations, all of which will be at each other's financial throats just waiting for the downfall of the weakest in the bunch. At this point the process of social democratization will rush through the masses of human population, and severe regulations will be enforced on the corporate marketplace. Economic and political pressures will force corporations into even more horrible cannibalistic policies until only one corporation exists, and then no corporations will exist. Corporate monopoly capitalism is pre-programmed to devour itself to release all individuals into a world of pure creative free enterprise.

For those who have preached the values of spiritual and social humanitarianism, the terrifying aspect of this revolution is the fact that science will become the religion of the people. Resentment of science must be overcome because eventually technology will sustain itself and the human species and it will bring us the utopia which our ancestors dreamed of for many generations. These technological and economic options will appear just as we are becoming fully aware of the great ecological crisis, the great Ice Age. Economies, money, insurance, profits and advertising become insignificant trivia in the resounding crush of ecological transformation of this scale.

The true challenge for the enlightened consumer is not to dwell on the collapse of the old civilization but to see ourselves being pushed ever onward in our evolution. This is not the end of the world, it is the beginning.

As the 20th century comes to a conclusion, the predictable economy will be a reality. The terms "buying" and "selling" will have distinctly different definitions by that time. Buying will refer to the *individual's accumulation of surplus*, or the creation of goods and services which will be used by the community in the future. Buying signals will inspire people with creative wealth, with saving for the future, with the storing of creative excesses. Selling will refer to the *distribution of surpluses throughout the community*, taking one's goods and services into the marketplace and sharing them with others. Selling signals will inspire individuals to use up their surpluses in an effort to satisfy personal and social needs.

The econographs for 1999 and 2000 (Charts 10 and 11) indicate that the global economy will once again be in "balance" and that the buying and selling signals will be in equal proportion during this time frame. Upon careful observation, a diligent student will notice that overall there are a few more selling signals during this time than there are buying signals. I believe we can look at this condition as another indicator that humanity in the year 2000 will definitely be continuing its preparations for major ecological

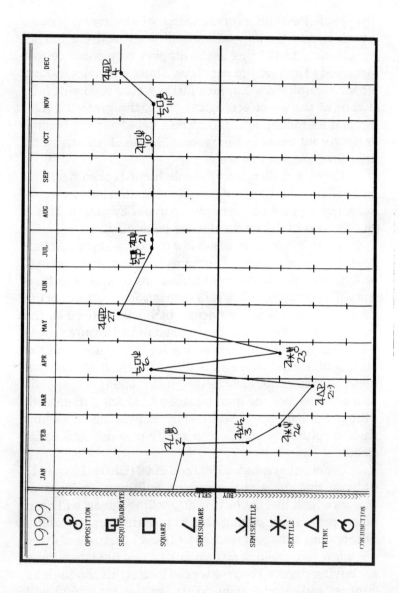

Chart 10

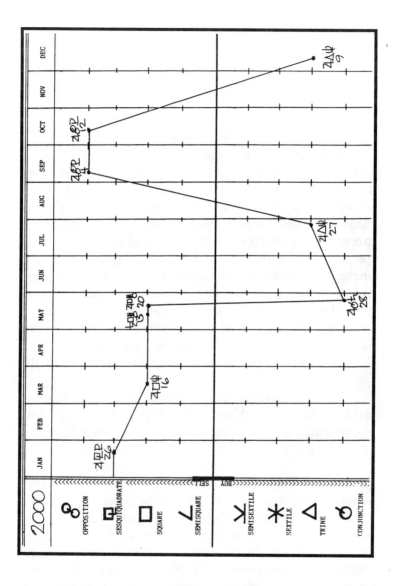

Chart 11

change. My one concern is that we do not use up all our surpluses in the panic of this change.

The function of equal distribution of wealth is exclusively dependent on the capacity of every individual in the system to be fully informed and competent in the workings of the system.

DAILY ECONOGRAPHS

Computer programming has invaded the old buy'n'sell marketplace with a vengeance. At the beginning of the 20th century, orders were placed on the market, and a few hours, sometimes days, later the order was completed. Tallies of daily sales were not available for a week, and there were no programmed buy'n'sell systems, the likes of which were responsible for the crash of 1987. Today the market is managed completely with computer technology. Walking into a brokerage firm even in the most remote communities, you discover stacks of computer hardware linked with the telephone and a well-trained broker who has memorized all the keys and codes necessary to bring uptown New York statistics into his or her little rural office with the push of a button.

The intrusion of the computer in the marketplace has actually created a backlash so that well-meaning legislators are passing laws restricting the use of computers in certain areas to protect the integrity of human choice in the management of the world's resources. However, in a few years the "human factor" will be fully eliminated as self-sustaining computers will manage the goods and services produced by human beings and will operate on incredibly efficient and easily predictable programs. Eliminating the human choice will do much to eliminate the greed, the intrigue and the mystery of wealth. Computerized management of our resources will insure an even distribution by the year 2000.

The advent of the personal computer in the early 1970s brought full-fledged marketplace activity right into the homes of those who could afford to own one. The statistics of the stock exchanges and commodities markets could easily be programmed into the home computer and searched for cycles or recurring sequences which then could be stretched into the future for forecasting purposes. This phenomenon was particularly popular among astrologers who have always believed that all nature, even the mundane marketplace, proceeds through recognizable cycles; measuring these cycles has been the work of astrologers for centuries. Now with home computers millions of bits of information could be correlated and compared for repeating series. Throughout the 1980s, astrologers worked to present their data in national publications, and by the end of the decade they had earned themselves positions of prestige in most national and international economic forecasting associations. Several top-name economists have admitted they now include astrological factors in judging the ups and downs in the market.

In 1986 I contacted a computer genius named Neil Michelsen in San Diego, California and asked if he could compute daily econographs which would include all the necessary planets and all of the traditional aspects. I wanted a print-out of the exact times when any one of the 20 aspect angles would be formed between any two of the planets in our solar system including the Earth's Moon. Michelsen programmed his mainframe computer to analyze this mass of data and came up with a mutual transit report which I named the "daily econograph."

The daily econograph shows **minute-by-minute aspects between all the planets** (including the Moon) which appear in our heavens daily. The times can be adjusted for any time zone on Earth; in the following example Pacific Daylight Time is used. Obviously, there will be certain aspects which

April 9		
☽	160 ♇	01:57
☽	45 ☉	01:59
☽	40 ☿	02:29
☽	0 ♃	02:56
☽	150 ♅	03:24
☽	45 ♀	04:03
☽	144 ♆	05:09
☿	40 ♃	05:56
☽	144 ♄	07:30
☿	102.9 ♆	07:39
☽	154.3 ♅	10:36
☽	154.3 ♇	11:33
☽	45 ☿	12:21
☽	51.4 ☉	13:37
♂	154.3 ♄	13:49
☽	150 ♆	15:17
☽	51.4 ♀	15:57
☽	150 ♄	17:42
☽	150 ♇	18:50
☉	45 ♃	19:17
☽	160 ♅	20:20
☽	154.3 ♆	22:37
☿	102.9 ♄	23:57

Chart 12

will be in effect during the hours when the markets are open in the Pacific time zone. These aspects will have a particular influence on the markets in the western United States, especially in San Francisco, Los Angeles and Seattle. But in the daily econograph there are also listings which occur very early in the morning or very late in the night when the Pacific Coast markets are closed; however, these aspects are affecting markets on other parts of the planet. For example, while aspects are occurring in the very early morning on the West Coast, the same aspects are occurring during market hours in New York. Similarly aspects which are timed for late night on the West Coast are actually occurring during open market hours in Japan.

The daily econograph includes all 20 traditional astrological aspects, and it shows the plus-buy/minus-sell factors generated during each minute of the day. See Chart 12.

Translation:

Moon quadnovile Pluto, 1:57 AM PDT=	+9	BUY
Moon semi-square Sun, 1:59 AM PDT =	-3	SELL
Moon novile Mercury, 2:29 AM PDT =	-2	SELL
Moon conjunct Jupiter, 2:56 AM PDT =	+10	BUY
Moon quincunx Uranus, 3:24 AM PDT =	-9	SELL
Moon semi-square Venus, 4:03 AM PDT =	-3	SELL
Moon bi-quintile Neptune, 5:09 AM PDT =	+7	BUY
Mercury novile Jupiter, 5:56 AM PDT =	-2	SELL
MARKETS OPEN IN CALIFORNIA		
Moon bi-quintile Saturn, 7:30 AM PDT =	+7	BUY
Mercury bi-septile Neptune, 7:39 AM PDT =	-7	SELL
Moon tri-septile Uranus, 10:36 AM PDT =	+8	BUY
Moon tri-septile Pluto, 11:33 AM PDT =	+8	BUY
Moon semi-square Mercury, 12:21 PM PDT =	-3	SELL
Moon septile Sun, 1:37 PM PDT =	-4	SELL
Mars tri-septile Saturn, 1:49 PM PDT =	+8	BUY
Moon quincunx Neptune, 3:17 PM PDT =	-9	SELL
Moon septile Venus, 3:57 PM PDT =	-4	SELL
MARKETS CLOSED IN CALIFORNIA		
Moon quincunx Saturn, 5:42 PM PDT =	-9	SELL
Moon quincunx Pluto, 6:50 PM PDT =	-9	SELL
Sun semi-square Jupiter, 7:17 PM PDT =	-3	SELL
Moon quadnovile Uranus, 8:20 PM PDT =	+9	BUY
Moon tri-septile Neptune, 10:37 PM PDT =	+8	BUY
Mercury bi-septile Saturn, 11:57 PM PDT =	-7	SELL

Considering the fact that the planetary compression factor regulates not only the movements in the marketplace but general human tensions, one can consult the daily econographs for information on stress-increasing periods and stress-decreasing periods throughout the day. Such information is valuable to parents, teachers, artists, physicians and managers in every sector of the community.

Daily econographs can be ordered directly through

Neil Michelsen at Astro Computing Services, P.O.Box 34487, San Diego, CA 92108. Request the following in your order:
   a) mutual transit report
   b) for which days
   c) in which time zone
   d) planets included: Moon, Mercury, Venus, Sun, Mars, Jupiter, Saturn, Uranus, Neptune and Pluto
   e) aspects included: opposition (180°), quincunx (150°), sesquiquadrate (135°), bi-septile (102.9°), square (90°), bi-novile (80°), septile (51.4°), semi-square (45°), novile (40°), triskaidektile (27.7°), semi-sextile (30°), decile (36°), sextile (60°), quintile (72°), tri-decile (108°), trine (120°), bi-quintile (144°), tri-septile (154.3°), quadnovile (160°), conjunction (0°).

INGRESSES

   The ancient astrologers measured the motion of the Moon and the Sun and other planets by using a primitive system of zodiacal symbols developed by the wandering tribespeople of the prehistoric world. The 12 zodiacal symbols have survived thousands of years of scientific and mathematical development and still persist in astrological conversation.

   Each one of the zodiacal signs carries with it a *quality of feeling and motion*. Under one zodiacal sign the frequencies of motion may be fast and fiery, while under another sign the frequencies may be slow and grounded.

   The following list of the signs of the zodiac describes the types of energy which each sign rules:

Aries . . . fast and fiery
Taurus . . . slow and practical
Gemini . . . moderate and theoretical
Cancer . . . fast and cooling
Leo . . . slow and fiery

Virgo . . . moderate and practical
Libra . . . fast and theoretical
Scorpio . . . slow and cooling
Sagittarius . . . moderate and fiery
Capricorn . . . fast and practical
Aquarius . . . slow and theoretical
Pisces . . . moderate and cooling

Changes in the attitude in the marketplace can be monitored by following the planetary ingresses into the different signs. Planetary ingresses are often listed on astrological calendars and in consumer almanacs. A complete listing of planetary ingresses can be found in astrological ephemerides which are generally available at all metaphysical bookstores.

For example, on April 29, 1989, at 12:54 PM PDT, the planet Mercury left Taurus and entered Gemini. This change implies that Mercury, which rules communications technology and transportation industries, shifted from a "slow and practical" frequency to a "moderate and theoretical" frequency. The change in the signs should speed up the transactions in this area of the market ruled by Mercury.

Each one of the planets in our solar system has been assigned a certain sector of the marketplace. The following list is gleaned from traditional resources and is supplemented with my own observations through the 1980s.

Moon = rules general moods of interaction. Buying and selling patterns are slowed or quickened by the Moon's movements through the signs of the zodiac.
Mercury = rules communications technologies and transportation industries.
Venus = rules entertainment and leisure industries, apparel, cosmetics and art.
Sun = rules the political and governmental influences on the market.

ASPECT TRANSLATION KEY

symbol	±	name	angle	translation
☍	-10	opposition	180°	FAST PLANET brings out the very worst in SLOW PLANET
⅄	-9	quincunx/inconjunct	150°	FAST PLANET dampens the power of SLOW PLANET
⊡	-8	sesquiquadrate/tri-octile	135°	FAST PLANET forces analysis of SLOW PLANET
2S	-7	bi-septile	102°51'	FAST PLANET increases weird coincidences with SLOW PLANET
□	-6	square	90°	FAST PLANET causes major stress in SLOW PLANET
2N	-5	bi-novile	80°	FAST PLANET activates practical activity in SLOW PLANET
S	-4	septile	51°26'	FAST PLANET enhances the occult mystery of SLOW PLANET
∠	-3	semi-square/octile	45°	FAST PLANET causes a breakdown in SLOW PLANET
N	-2	novile	40°	FAST PLANET refines spiritual understanding of SLOW PLANET
▽	-1	triskaidektile	27°41'	FAST PLANET puts a hex on SLOW PLANET
⅄	+1	semi-sextile	30°	FAST PLANET stimulates clarity in SLOW PLANET
⊤	+2	decile	36°	FAST PLANET creates sparkle in SLOW PLANET
✳	+3	sextile	60°	FAST PLANET creates charm in SLOW PLANET
Q	+4	quintile	72°	FAST PLANET exposes essence of SLOW PLANET
3D	+5	tri-decile	108°	FAST PLANET expands the aura of SLOW PLANET
△	+6	trine	120°	FAST PLANET reduces major stress in SLOW PLANET
⊞	+7	bi-quintile	144°	FAST PLANET reveals unknown aspect of SLOW PLANET
3S	+8	tri-septile	154°17'	FAST PLANET points out cosmic power of SLOW PLANET
4N	+9	quadnovile	160°	FAST PLANET increases the value of SLOW PLANET
☌	+10	conjunction	0°	FAST PLANET brings out the very best in SLOW PLANET

Copyright 1988

SELL SIGNALS BUY SIGNALS
<<<<<<<<<<<<<<<<<<<<<<<<<<<< POSITIVE NEGATIVE >>>>>>>>>>>>>>>>>>>>>>>>>>>>

Chart 13

Mars =   rules small construction industries, steel manufacturing, mining and competitive sports.
Jupiter =   rules professional services (legal, medical,
managerial), travel industries and agriculture.
Saturn =   rules large construction industries, banking
and finance, engineering and oil.
Uranus =   rules space research and travel, computer research and development.
Neptune =   rules international trade, international peace
arrangements and balance of international
payments.
Pluto =   rules general trends in the global marketplace.
Pluto changes zodiacal signs only once every
12 to 30 years on the average. This is a great
signal of major changes in global marketing
strategies.

RETROGRADES

Astrologers monitor a phenomenon known as *retrogradation* because it supposedly coincides with negative
patterns of planetary expression. A planet will appear to
turn retrograde in our skies when Earth, in her faster orbit,
is passing the slower planet; the slower planet actually
appears to be traveling backward from our perspective. It
has been a long-held astrological tradition that retrograde
periods are "bad times" and there will be negative consequences if projects are initiated or completed under their
influences.

My personal research has revealed that Mercury retrograde actually has measurable negative influences on the
markets. It seldom fails that when Mercury retrogrades
communications technologies and transportation industries spin into a confusing dither, prices fall, and long waits
in line prevail. Yet retrogrades of the other planets seem to
have little or no effect at all.

Information on the specific times of planetary retrogrades can be found in all astrological ephemerides and most astrological calendars. Although some astrologers place a great deal of emphasis on planetary retrogrades, there is still no solid statistical proof of their negative impact on the markets. However, there is always room for discovery. If you find a strong relationship between retrogrades and marketplace downs, please contact me.

LUNAR NODES

Of all the forces in the heavens, the Moon has gained the greatest respect of wizards and healers over the years. And in the field of economic forecasting, the constantly changing tidal influences of the Moon have inspired many economists to create incredibly complicated and detailed formulae.

The orbital relationship between the Moon and the Earth creates a rock'n'roll sensation which causes the tides in the oceans. This rhythm is also responsible for the moodiness which we experience in the marketplace.

Half of the time the Moon is hovering over the Northern Hemisphere of Earth; the highly populated and industrialized nations of the North are energized by the presence of the great lunar orb. The other half of the time the Moon is hovering over the Southern Hemisphere, which is less populated and much less developed. Obviously, lunar influences and waves of change are much less influential in the Northern Hemisphere when the Moon is hovering over the Southern Hemisphere and vice versa.

The minimal amount of research which I have done on the positions of the Moon relative to the hemispheres of Earth has yielded only modest, if not useless, information. It appears that when the Moon is overhead, the markets are ruled by temperament rather than logic, by emotions rather than competent management. It is much more likely that panic, depression and generally unpredictable conditions will occur.

A much more significant factor in the motion of the Moon from the Northern to the Southern Hemispheres and back again is the Moon's crossings over the Earth's equator. Traditionally known as the Nodes of the Moon, these are significant points in space and time. When the Moon crosses the equator of Earth headed for the Northern Hemisphere, this point in space and time is known as the *North Node of the Moon*. When the Moon crosses the equator headed for the Southern Hemisphere, this point is known as the *South Node of the Moon*.

In the interpretation of personal horoscopes, the Moon's Nodes are used to define opportunities to accumulate debt or to pay off debt. Although little research has been done on the Moon's Nodes' effect on the market, I feel justified in extending the basic personal definitions of debt management onto the general marketplace. In other words, the Moon at the North Node is a time when debts are best *paid*. The Moon at the South Node is the best time to *incur* debts. I would also assume that fluctuations in the interest rates may very well be associated with the Moon's Nodes, but I have no statistical information on this idea.

The Moon's Nodes change every two weeks. Exact timing of the Moon's Nodes for any length of calendar time can be obtained from Neil Michelsen at Astro Computing Services, P.O. Box 34487, San Diego, CA 92108.

STAY IN TOUCH

On the following pages you will find listed, with their current prices, some of the books and tapes now available on related subjects. Your book dealer stocks most of these, and will stock new titles in the Llewellyn series as they become available. We urge your patronage.

However, to obtain our full catalog, to keep informed of new titles as they are released and to benefit from informative articles and helpful news, you are invited to write for our bi-monthly news magazine/catalog. A sample copy is free, and it will continue coming to you at no cost as long as you are an active mail customer. Or you may keep it coming for a full year with a donation of just $2.00 in U.S.A. ($7.00 for Canada & Mexico, $20.00 overseas, first class mail). Many bookstores also have *The Llewellyn New Times* available. Ask for it. Stay in touch! In *The Llewellyn New Times'* pages you will find news and reviews of new books, tapes and services, announcements of meetings and seminars, helpful articles, news of authors, and much more.

The Llewellyn New Times
P.O. Box 64383-Dept. 382, St. Paul, MN 55164-0383, U.S.A.

• • •

TO ORDER BOOKS AND TAPES

If your book dealer does not have the books and tapes described on the following pages available, order direct from the publisher by sending full price in U.S. funds, plus $2.00 for postage and handling for orders of $10 and under. Orders over $10 will require $3.50 postage and handling. There are no postage and handling charges for orders over $100. UPS Delivery: We ship UPS whenever possible. Delivery guaranteed. Provide your street address as UPS does not deliver to P.O. Boxes. UPS to Canada requires a $50 minimum order. Allow 4-6 weeks for delivery. Orders outside the U.S.A and Canada: Airmail—add $5 per book; add $3 for each non-book item (tapes, etc.); add $1 per item for surface mail.

FOR GROUP STUDY AND PURCHASE

Because there is a great deal of interest in group discussion and study of the subject matter of this book, we offer a special quantity price to group leaders or agents. Our Special Quantity Price for a minimum order of five copies of *Financial Astrology for the 1990s* is $38.85 Cash-With-Order. This price includes postage and handling within the United States. Minnesota residents must add 6% sales tax. For additional quantities, please order in multiples of five. For Canadian and foreign orders, add postage and handling charges as above. Credit Card (VISA, Master Card, American Express) Orders are accepted. Charge Card Orders only may be phoned free ($15.00 minimum order) within the U.S.A. by dialing 1-800-THE MOON (in Canada call: 1-800-FOR-SELF). Customer Service calls dial 1-612-291-1970. Mail Orders to:

LLEWELLYN PUBLICATIONS
P.O. Box 64383-Dept. 382 / St. Paul, MN 55164-0383, U.S.A.

NEW TRENDS IN MODERN ASTROLOGY
Edited by Joan McEvers

This is the first book in a new series offered by Llewellyn called the *New World Astrology Series*. Edited by award-winning astrologer, lecturer and writer Joan McEvers, this book pulls together the latest thoughts by the best astrologers in the field of Spiritual Astrology.

She has put together this outstanding group with these informative and exciting topics.
- Gray Keen: Perspective: The Ethereal Conclusion.
- Marion D. March: Some Insights Into Esoteric Astrology.
- Kimberly McSherry: The Feminine Element of Astrology: Reframing the Darkness.
- Kathleen Burt: The Spiritual Rulers and Their Role in the Transformation.
- Shirley Lyons Meier: The Secrets Behind Carl Payne Tobey's Secondary Chart.
- Jeff Jawer: Astrodrama.
- Donna Van Toen: Alice Bailey Revisited.
- Philip Sedgwick: Galactic Studies.
- Myrna Lofthus: The Spiritual Programming Within a Natal Chart.
- Angel Thompson: Transformational Astrology.

0-87542-380-9, 288 pgs., 5¼ x 8, softcover   **$9.95**

CHIRON
by Barbara Hand Clow

This little-known planet was first sighted in 1977. It has an eccentric orbit on a 50-51-year cycle between Saturn and Uranus. It brought farsightedness into astrology because Chiron is the *bridge to the outer planets*, Neptune and Pluto, from the inner ones.

This is the most important astrological book yet about Chiron! *Chiron* presents exciting new insights on astrology. The small but influential planet of Chiron reveals *how* the New Age Initiation will affect each one of us. It is an Initiator, an Alchemist, a Healer, and a Spiritual Guide.

For those who are astrologers, *Chiron* has more information than any other book about this planet.

- Learn *why* Chiron rules Virgo and the Sixth House.
- Have the necessary information about Chiron in each house, in each sign, and how the aspects affect each person's chart.

The influences of Chiron are an important new factor in understanding capabilities and potentials which we all have. Chiron rules: Healing with the hands, Healing with crystals, Initiation and Alchemy and Alteration of the body by Mind and Spirit. Chiron also rules Cartomancy and the Tarot reader. As such it is an especially vital resource for everyone who uses the Tarot.

0-87542-094-X, 320 pgs., 6 x 9, charts, softcover   **$9.95**

ARCHETYPES OF THE ZODIAC
by Kathleen Burt

The horoscope is probably the most unique tool for personal growth you can ever have. This book is intended to help you understand how the energies within your horoscope manifest. Once you are aware of how your chart operates on an instinctual level, you can then work consciously with it to remove any obstacles to your growth.

The technique offered in this book is based upon the incorporation of the esoteric rulers of the signs and the integration of their polar opposites. This technique has been very successful in helping the client or reader modify existing negative energies in a horoscope so as to improve the quality of his or her life and the understanding of his or her psyche.

There is special focus in this huge comprehensive volume on the myths for each sign. Some signs may have as many as *four different myths* coming from all parts of the world. All are discussed by the author. There is also emphasis on the Jungian Archetypes involved with each sign.

This book has a depth often surprising to the readers of popular astrology books. It has a clarity of expression seldom found in books of the esoteric tradition. It is very easy to understand, even if you know nothing of Jungian philosophy or of mythology. It is intriguing, exciting and very helpful for all levels of astrologers.

0-87542-088-5, 592 pgs., 6 x 9, 24 illus., softcover   **$14.95**

OPTIMUM CHILD
by Gloria Star

This is a brand-new approach to the subject of astrology as applied to children. Not much has been written on developmental astrology, and this book fills a gap that has needed filling for years. There is enough basic material for the novice astrologer to easily determine the needs of his or her child (or children). All it takes is the natal chart. A brief table of where the planets were when your child was born is included in the book so that even if you don't have a chart on your child, you can find out enough to fully develop his or her potentials.

In *Optimum Child* you will find a thorough look at the planets, houses, rising signs, aspects and transits. Each section includes physical, mental and emotional activities and needs that this child would best respond to. It is the most comprehensive book yet on child astrology. This one is definitely not for children only. Every parent and professional astrologer should read it thoroughly. You should use it and help your child develop those talents and potentials inherent in what is shown within the natal chart.

0-87542-740-5, 360 pages, 6 x 9, softcover   **$9.95**

PLANETS: THE ASTROLOGICAL TOOLS
Edited by Joan McEvers
This is the second in the astrological anthology series edited by award-winning astrologer Joan McEvers, who provides a brief factual overview of the planets. Then take off through the solar system with 10 professional astrologers as they bring their insights to the symbolism and influences of the planets.

- Toni Glover: The Sun as the life force and our ego
- Joanne Wickenburg: The Moon as our emotional signal to change
- Erin Sullivan-Seale: Mercury as the multi-faceted god, with an in-depth explanation of its retrogradation
- Robert Glasscock: Venus as your inner value system and relationships
- Johanna Mitchell: Mars as your cooperative, energizing inner warrior
- Don Borkowski: Jupiter as expansion and preservation
- Gina Ceaglio: Saturn as a source of freedom through self-discipline
- Bil Tierney: Uranus as the original, growth-producing planet
- Karma Welch: Neptune as selfless giving and compassionate love
- Joan Negus: Pluto as a powerful personal force

0-87542-381-7, 380 pgs., 5¼ x 8, illus., softcover   **$12.95**

PLANETARY MAGICK
by Denning & Phillips
This book is filled with guidelines and rites for powerful magickal action. There are rites for the individual magician, rites for the magickal group. The rites herein are given *in full*, and are revealed for the first time. Planetary Magick provides a full grasp of the root system of Western Magick, a system which evolved in Babylonia and became a principal factor in the development of Qabalah.

By what means do the planetary powers produce change in people's moods, actions, circumstances? As the ancient script has it: "As above, so below." The powers which exist in the cosmos have their focal points also in you. The directing force of Mind which operates in and beyond the cosmos is the very source of your inner being. By directing the planetary powers as they exist within your psyche—in the Deep Mind—you can achieve inner harmony, happiness, prosperity, love. You can help others. You can win your heart's desire.

The rites of Planetary Magick will powerfully open up level after level of the psyche, balancing and strengthening its perceptions and powers.

1-87542-193-8, 400 pgs., 6 x 9, color plates, softcover   **$19.95**

PLUTO: The Evolutionary Journey of the Soul
by Jeff Green

If you have ever asked "Why am I here?" or "What are my lessons?," then this book will help you to objectively learn the answers from an astrological point of view. Green shows you how the planet Pluto relates to the evolutionary and karmic lessons in this life and how past lives can be understood through the position of Pluto in your chart.

Beyond presenting key principles and ideas about the nature of the evolutionary journey of the Soul, this book supplies practical, concise and specific astrological methods and techniques that pinpoint the answers to the above questions. If you are a professional counselor or astrologer, this book is indispensible to your practice. The reader who studies this material carefully and applies it to his or her own chart will discover an objective vehicle to uncover the essence of his or her own state of being. The understanding that this promotes can help you cooperate with, instead of resist, the evolutionary and karmic lessons in your life.

Green describes the position of Pluto through all of the signs and houses, explains the aspects and transits of Pluto, discusses Pluto in aspect to the Moon's Nodes, and gives sample charts and readings. It is the most complete look at this "new" planet ever.

0-87542-296-9, 6 x 9, 360 pgs., softcover $12.95

URANUS: Freedom From the Known
by Jeff Green

This book deals primarily with the archetypal correlations of the planet Uranus to human psychology and behavior to anatomy/physiology and the chakra system, and to metaphysical and cosmic laws. Uranus' relationship to Saturn, from an individual and collective point of view, is also discussed.

The text of this book comes intact in style and tone from an intensive workshop held in Toronto. You will feel as if you are a part of that workshop.

In reading *Uranus* you will discover how to naturally liberate yourself from all of your conditioning patterns, patterns that were determined by the "internal" and "external" environment. Every person has a natural way to actualize this liberation. This natural way is examined by use of the natal chart and from a developmental point of view.

The 48-year sociopolitical cycle of Uranus and Saturn is discussed extensively, as is the relationship between Uranus, Saturn and Neptune.
0-87542-297-7, 192 pgs., 5¼ x 8, softcover $7.95

TRANSITS IN REVERSE
by Edna Copeland Ryneveld

Have you wondered about whether you should take that trip or ask for that raise? Do you want to know when the best time is for a wedding? How about knowing in advance the times when you will be the most creative and dazzling?

This book is different from all others published on transits (those planets that are actually moving around in the heavens making aspects to our natal planets). It gives the subject area first—such as creativity, relationships, health, etc.—and then tells you what transits to look for. The introductory chapters are so thorough that you will be able to use this book with only an ephemeris or astrological calendar to tell you where the planets are. The author explains what transits are, how they affect your daily life, how to track them, how to base decisions on them.

With the information in each section, you can combine as many factors as you like to get positive results. If you are going on a business trip you can look at the accidents section to avoid any trouble, the travel section to find out the best date, the relationship section to see how you will get along with the other person, the business section to see if it is a good time to do business. In this way, you can choose the absolute best date for just about anything! Electional astrology as been used for centuries, but now it is being given in the most easily understood and practical format yet.

0-87542-674-3, 320 pages, 6 x 9 **$12.95**

THE ASTRO*CARTO*GRAPHY BOOK OF MAPS
by Jim Lewis & Ariel Guttman

Everyone believes there is a special person, job and *place* for him or her. This book explores those special places in the lives of 136 celebrities and famous figures.

The maps, based on the time of birth, graphically reveal lines of planetary influence at various geographic locations. A planet affecting a certain area is correlated with a person's success, failure or activities there. Astro*Carto*Graphy can also be used to bring about the stronger influence of a certain planet by showing its angular positions. Angular positions involve the Ascendant, the IC, the Descendant and the Midheaven. The maps show where planets would have been had you been born at different locations than at your birthplace.

Charts and maps of personalities in the entertainment field, such as Joan Crawford, Marilyn Monroe, James Dean, John Lennon and David Bowie, are included in this compilation. Activists like Martin Luther King, Jr. and Lech Walesa, spiritual pioneers like Freud, Jung and Yogananda and events in the lives of painters, musicians and sports figures are explored as well as the successes, problems and tendencies of such politicians as FDR, JFK, Richard Nixon, George Bush, and Margaret Thatcher.

0-87542-434-1, 300 pgs., 8½ × 11, charts, softcover **$15.95**

THE LLEWELLYN ANNUALS

Llewellyn's MOON SIGN BOOK: Approximately 400 pages of valuable information on gardening, fishing, weather, stock market forecasts, personal horoscopes, good planting dates, and general instructions for finding the best date to do just about anything! Articles by prominent forecasters and writers in the fields of gardening, astrology, politics, economics and cycles. This special almanac, different from any other, has been published annually since 1906. It's fun, informative and has been a great help to millions in their daily planning.   **State year $3.95**

Llewellyn's SUN SIGN BOOK: Your personal horoscope for the entire year! All 12 signs are included in one handy book. Also included are forecasts, special feature articles, and an action guide for each sign. Monthly horoscopes are written by Gloria Star, author of *Optimum Child*, for your personal Sun Sign. Articles on a variety of subjects written by well-known astrologers from around the country. Much more than just a horoscope guide! Entertaining and fun the year round.   **State year $3.95**

Llewellyn's DAILY PLANETARY GUIDE and ASTROLOGER'S DATE-BOOK: Includes all of the major daily aspects plus their exact times in Eastern and Pacific time zones, lunar phases, signs and voids plus their times, planetary motion, a monthly ephemeris, sunrise and sunset tables, special articles on the planets, signs, aspects, a business guide, planetary hours, rulerships, and much more. Large 5¼ × 8 format for more writing space, spiral bound to lay flat, address and phone listings, time zone conversion chart and blank horoscope chart.   **State year $6.95**

Llewellyn's MAGICKAL ALMANAC
Edited by Ray Buckland
The Magickal Almanac examines some of the many forms that Magick can take, allowing the reader a peek behind a veil of secrecy into Egyptian, Enochian, Shamanic, Wiccan and other traditions. The almanac pages for each month provide information important in the many aspects of working Magick: sunrise and sunset, phases of the Moon, and festival dates, as well as the tarot card, herb, incense, mineral, color, and name of power (god/goddess/entity) associated with the particular day.   **State year $9.95**

Llewellyn's ASTROLOGICAL CALENDAR: Large wall calendar of 52 pages. Beautiful full color cover and color inside. Includes special feature articles by famouns astrologers, introductory information on astrology. Lunar Gardening Guide, celestial phenomena for the year, a blank horoscope chart for your own chart data, and monthly date pages which include aspects, lunar information, planetary motion, ephemeris, personal forecasts, lucky dates, planting and fishing dates, and more. 10 x 13 size. Set in Central time, with conversion table for other time zones worldwide.   **State year $7.95**